SECRETS OF THE DEAD SEA SCROLLS

HUGH J. SCHONFIELD, D.S.Litt.

Secrets of the Dead Sea Scrolls

STUDIES TOWARDS THEIR SOLUTION

New York
THOMAS YOSELOFF, Inc.

Library of Congress Catalogue Card Number: 57-13387

Printed in the United States of America

TO
MILLAR BURROWS
AND THE AMERICAN SCHOOLS OF ORIENTAL RESEARCH
THIS VOLUME IS GRATEFULLY INSCRIBED

Contents

Preface

A GREAT MANY scholars having been working on the elucidation of the Dead Sea Scrolls, and as more and more of this exciting material is made known interest has steadily increased. As a result both of fresh evidence and acute investigation the field of inquiry has been considerably widened, and most of the possibilities have substantially been explored. We cannot be too grateful for the patient research devoted to a particularly difficult problem, and anyone coming in at this stage has the obvious advantage of benefiting by all that has gone before, even by the hasty but nevertheless challenging conclusions of those who first entered the field and had so much less to go upon. Someone had to make a beginning.

Practically all the documents and fragments found in Cave One at Khirbet Qumran have now been published, and a good deal from other caves and hiding places in the vicinity. The area of the settlement has also largely been explored, and excavations have been conducted of the remains of the buildings and cemetery. Consequently we are in a much better position to study the evidence, though there is still far too much room for a fundamental conflict of opinion. This is due to the fact that the People of the Scrolls did not plainly declare themselves: they wrote in riddles for the skilled to resolve. It is now usual to speak of these people as the Essenes, that mysterious Jewish sect noted for prophetic powers of which tantalising descriptions have been preserved chiefly by Philo and Josephus. But even on this point some qualification is still warranted.

I have been methodically carrying out my own investigations ever since the first find was announced, and checking my tentative conclusions with those of others as more of the material became available. I may have been over cautious in not venturing into print sooner, but I was much too doubtful of many points to commit myself, and I preferred to wait for clarification and the publication of sufficient data to enable me to see whether I had anything useful to contribute. I have not been able, even now, to satisfy myself completely, and in much of what I have written I have been feeling my way with no desire to occupy a dogmatic position. Only at the end have I stated what is my firm general conclusion.

Since, however, my studies have tended to widen still further the scope of the inquiry by the inclusion of themes and traditions which appeared to me to be relevant, and a few even novel in relation to the problem, I have decided to publish these in the hope that they will be of some service to scholars and of interest to laymen.

Even so, I have not attempted in this book to deal with numerous issues of undoubted importance, though occasionally I have furnished an indication. Neither, in what I have presented, have I aimed at comprehensiveness in listing authorities in support of any point. I have been content with sufficient quotation and references to make each matter clear to those who cannot readily look everything up. I have occasionally added supplementary references in the notes for research purposes.

The primary intention of this work is historical. Consequently I have confined myself as far as possible to information bearing on dates and events. Until we can be reasonably sure of these we have no secure foundation on which to build. Much of the evidence, literary and archaeological, places emphasis on the first century A.D., and this we thankfully accept as a guide. But it can tell us very little as yet about origins or sequels, and we have chiefly to depend on the interpretation of documents in relation to historic records of the period. Always it is essential to remember that any opinion expressed may be invalidated as more of the recovered material becomes available, and we can by no means tell what may yet come to light from further and unauthorised exploration.

The investigation has had for myself and others all the suspense and the thrills of detective work, in which the scholar has frequently to indulge. This volume, indeed, might aptly be described as a Case-Book of the Dead Sea Scrolls, and I have marshalled the evidence largely in the order in which the inquiry proceeded. As well as most gratefully using the work of scholars who have hunted up many out of the way items of information, I have quested around for additional links and leads. Nothing that might come in useful could be neglected, and odd scraps of knowledge might provide unexpected clues. The reader must be the judge of what he finds here, and I shall not quarrel with him if his conclusions differ from my own.

I have taken the liberty of dedicating these studies with deep respect to Prof. Millar Burrows, who most courteously supplied me initially with the literary means to pursue them. I am only sorry that his latest level-headed and informative work on the subject of the Scrolls reached me too late for direct employment; but having read it I do not find any of my positions affected by his careful review. Otherwise, however, I have been able to bring the material right up-to-date when correcting the proofs, to include the partial revelation of the contents of the copper scrolls and the most recently published fragments. Finally, I wish thankfully to acknowledge kindnesses from Dr. G. Lankester Harding, Prof. Paul Kahle, Prof. H. H. Rowley, and Mr. J. M. Allegro.

HUGH J. SCHONFIELD
Highgate

'I know another mystery, that books will be given to the righteous and the wise to become a cause of joy and uprightness and much wisdom. To them will the books be given, and they will believe in them and rejoice over them, and then will all the righteous be recompensed who have learnt therefrom all the paths of uprightness.'

Enoch. civ. 12-13.

THE ANCIENT ATBASH
ALPHABETICAL CIPHER.

א = ת
ב = ש
ג = ר
ד = ק
ה = צ
ו = פ
ז = ע
ח = ס
ט = נ
י = מ
כ = ל

CHAPTER ONE

The Book of the Hagu

In 1945, two years before the accidental discovery of the Dead Sea Scrolls, I included in my biography of the Apostle Paul some account of the Community of the New Covenant at Damascus, and of Paul's possible association with its members after his conversion to Nazarenism.[1] I was not the first to make this suggestion: Klausner had done so briefly in 1939 in his book *From Jesus to Paul*[2]; but I discussed the subject in some detail, and in particular offered a solution to one problem which, since the discovery of the Dead Sea Scrolls, has assumed much greater importance. So far as I am aware none of the scholars who have been studying the Scrolls has taken account of this solution, or arrived at it independently. I am therefore bringing it forward again, this time with much additional relevant material.

The existence of the Jewish Community of the New Covenant was first revealed by the chance find in the Genizah (lumber-room) of the Old Synagogue at Fostat, Egypt, of what were described by the finder Dr. Schechter as *Fragments of a Zadokite Work*,[3] but now usually called the *Damascus Document*. The fragments belong to two copies of a text, which itself represents portions of at least two original works giving some account of the history of the sect and of its organization. The sect looked back to one referred to as the Teacher of Righteousness, still unidentified, and about such a Teacher a little more has become known since the publication of one of the Dead Sea Scrolls, the *Habakkuk Commentary*. We also now know a great deal more about the tenets of the sect and its organization from another Scroll, the so-called *Manual of Discipline*, and from archaeological study of the remains of the establishments and cemetery of the Community at Khirbet Qumran, close to the caves which housed its library.

[1] See Schonfield, *The Jew of Tarsus*, p. 105 *ff*.
[2] P. 319.
[3] Published in 1910. The MSS. are now in the University Library at Cambridge. The edition employed in the present work is that of Dr. R. H. Charles, Clarendon Press, 1912, slightly revised from the translation of C. Rabin, *The Zadokite Documents*, Clarendon Press, 1954.

As a result of what has already come to light the area of inquiry has widened considerably, and it is evident that we have been brought into contact not simply with an obscure Jewish sect, but with a whole strange world of life and thought represented by the ancient Chasidim and Essenes, and having a direct bearing on the beginnings of Christianity.

What has made the task of investigation so difficult is that the people with whom we are dealing guarded their secrets as carefully as they could, using prophetic and apocalyptic language with reference to historical events, and avoiding mentioning persons by name. They had their ciphers and their signs,[1] perhaps rather childishly, and cultivated an atmosphere of mystery about matters which it would not have seemed of any great consequence if they had revealed them openly. But such has ever been the way with secret societies and eclectic groups, and to obtain illumination we have to play the game according to their rules, so far as we know them.

Let us take the problem to which I have referred, which arises in the *Damascus Document*. In three passages[2] reference is made to an authoritative work called the *Book of the Hagu*. The ten judges of each community (four of the tribe of Levi and Aaron and six of Israel) had to be 'learned in the *Book of the Hagu* and in the Ordinances of the Covenant'. The presiding priest in particular had to be expert in these works. The latter may well have corresponded to the *Manual of Discipline* which has been recovered. But what was the former? According to Father de Vaux, a fragment of the *Manual* itself contains the statement that members of the sect should be instructed from their youth in this *Book of the Hagu*.[3] The book therefore would appear to have contained venerated precepts or oracular utterances, perhaps including dicta of the Founder, the Teacher of Righteousness.

It was tempting to think that the Hebrew ספר ההגו might represent a Greek *Biblos tou Hagiou* (Book of the Holy One). This could refer to the Bible, but more likely to a work by or about the Teacher of Righteousness[4]—a kind of Gospel. This Greek interpretation of the title might have been part of the intention; but it was preferable to believe that the title had a Hebrew significance. As it stands, the word Hagu, Hago, or Hegu, whichever way it is vocalized, is meaningless, and one must suppose that it was a deliberate substitution. I therefore thought of applying to the word the ancient Hebrew form of cipher known as *Atbash*. This cipher, as the name given to it conveys,

[1] Several of the Dead Sea Scrolls, including the *Book of Isaiah*, have passages carefully marked with a number of curious symbols bearing some resemblance to Greek and Egyptian letters.

[2] *DD*, xi. 2; xv. 5; xvii. 5.

[3] See Dupont-Sommer, *The Jewish Sect of Qumran and the Essenes*, p. 60.

[4] The Messianic *Nazir*, the Holy One of God. Cp. *Mk*. i. 24, *Acts* iii. 14.

simply involved the replacement of the first letter of the Hebrew alphabet *aleph* by the last letter *tau*, the second letter *bet* by the penultimate letter *shin*, and so on, the first eleven letters being thus exchanged for the last eleven in reverse order.

Using this method the incomprehensible Hagu הגו is immediately converted into a genuine Hebrew word Tsaraph צרף meaning to refine or test, applied to the purging of precious metals from dross, and also metaphorically to proving or testing. Here we have the participle form Tsoreph used as a noun with the definite article, which can be translated 'the Refiner' or more probably in full the *Book of Proof* or *Test Book*. We still do not know exactly what this book was; but the title certainly corresponds to the consultative use to which the work was evidently put. It could be a collection of Messianic *Testimonia*, which we now know was in the possession of the sect, for a page of such a document has been found among the fragments discovered in Cave IV.[1] But this would hardly suit.

What is exciting is the recovered word with all its associations. The Teacher of Righteousness could well have been regarded as 'the Refiner', the Tsoreph or Metsareph[2] of the famous prophecy of Malachi, afterwards applied as referring to John the Baptist. It was written:

> 'Behold I will send my Messenger, and he shall prepare the way before me; and the Master (*adon*) whom you seek shall suddenly come to his Temple, even the Messenger of the Covenant whom you delight in. Behold, he shall come,' says the Lord of hosts. But who may abide the day of his coming? And who shall stand when he appears? For he is like a refiner's (*metsareph*) fire, and like fullers' soap: and he shall sit as a refiner (*metsareph*) and purifier of silver; and he shall purify the sons of Levi, and purge them as gold and silver, that they may offer to the Lord an offering in righteousness. Then shall the offering of Judah and Jerusalem be pleasant to the Lord as in the days of old, and as in former years.[3]

But the word is also significantly used in another place. At the close of the *Book of Daniel*, written about 165 B.C., the Prophet is told: 'Go your way, Daniel; for the words are closed up and sealed until the Time of the End. Many shall be purified, and made white, and tested (*yitsarephu*); but the wicked shall do wickedly; and none of the wicked shall understand; but the skilled (*maskilim*) shall understand.'[4] Here we have both a testing and an expertness in interpretation.

Further confirmation of the employment of the word Metsareph by the

[1] See Dupont-Sommer *op. cit.*, p. 174, n. 14.
[2] This word occurs in the *Manual of Discipline*, viii. 4.
[3] *Mal.* iii. 1-4.
[4] *Dan.* xii. 9-10.

Qumran sect linked with Daniel's Time of the End has now come from several recovered fragments of scrolls. A Commentary on *Ps.* ii. 1-2 speaks of 'the Elect Ones of Israel at the End of the Days, that is, the Time of Testing (עת המצרף) which is coming [upon them].' Another Commentary on *Ps.* xxxvii. 14-15, 'The wicked have drawn out the sword,' etc., explains this 'of the wicked of Ephraim and Manasseh who will endeavour to stretch forth a hand against the Priest and the men of his counsel during the Time of Testing which is coming upon them.'[1] The very same expression occurs in the New Testament, *Rev.* iii. 10: 'Because thou hast kept the word of my patience, I also will keep thee from the Time of Testing which is coming (*tes horas tou peirasmou tes mellouses*) upon all the world, to try them that dwell upon the earth.' See also *Damascus Document*, ix. 49; *Manual of Discipline*, i. 17; viii. 4.

This leads us to a consideration of the 'period of testing' which every candidate for admission into the Community of the Covenant had to undergo according to the *Manual of Discipline*. The Essenes and the Judaeo-Christian Ebionites also had probationary periods for novices and were careful to safeguard the transmission of their authoritative documents. The accepted Essene, for instance, swore 'to transmit the rules exactly as received . . . and carefully to preserve the books of the Party and the names of the angels'.[2] In the Ebionite *Epistle of Peter to James* Peter says: 'I have prayed and besought you not to communicate the books of my preaching which I have sent you to anyone, whether of our own or another nation, before trial. But if anyone, having been tested, has been found worthy, then to hand them over to him . . . in order that thus they may keep the rule of faith, and everywhere deliver the rule of truth, explaining all things after our tradition.' In the sequel James calls for the elders, and after reading the letter to them hands on Peter's charge that the books of his preachings are only to be communicated 'to one who is good and religious, who wishes to teach, and who is circumcised and faithful'. And not all at once, but by degrees during six years of proof. Then follows the solemn adjuration which the initiate has to recite.[3]

All these groups, between whom considerable likenesses have become apparent, made much therefore of 'testing' and 'proving', and perhaps this word tsaraph, yielded by *Atbash*, may additionally throw light on an obscure reference in the Talmud to a building called *Bet-Nitsarphi*, which some third-

[1] I am indebted for this information to Mr. J. M. Allegro, who courteously allowed me to see his article 'Further Light on the History of the Qumran Sect' written for the Summer 1956 issue of the *Journal of Biblical Literature*.

[2] Josephus, *Wars*, II. vii. 7. It is worth considering whether the angels were in fact Messengers of the Covenant, not heavenly beings whose names are plainly written in the pseudepigraphic literature.

[3] *Ep. Pet. ad Jac.* iii.

century Rabbis in Palestine would not visit on any account. It is mentioned in the same context as another building called *Bet-Abidan* in one of the passages relating to the Minim (Jewish sectaries) and their writings.

The particular passage with which we are concerned opens with a statement that 'the *giljonim* and books of the Minim' are to be burnt. R. Tarphon declared that not only would he burn them; he would not even excise and preserve the sacred names in the text. Further, if he was being pursued he might, if necessary, take refuge in a heathen temple, but never would he enter the places of the Minim. R. Joseph bar Chanin asked R. Abahu whether he would burn the books of the *Bet-Abidan*? He was not sure. As to going to the *Bet-Abidan*, Rab would not go, Shemuel had been, but neither on any account would go to the *Bet-Nitsarphi*. Mar bar Joseph had apparently ventured among the Minim at grave risk to his faith. Then it is stated that R. Meir called it (the book of the Minim) *Aven-giljon*, while R. Jochanan called it *Avon-giljon*. The passage winds up with an account of how Rabban Gamaliel and his sister Imma Shalom showed up a 'philosopher', evidently a Christian, who quotes from the 'law of Evangelion' a sentence reminiscent of the Sermon on the Mount in *Matthew*.[1]

Before we discuss the two buildings it is necessary to explain what is meant by 'the *giljonim*'. Travers Herford translates the word as 'margins', believing it to imply the area of a scroll not used for the text, but used possibly for annotations. This cannot possibly be correct, for in another Tosephta it is stated, 'The *giljonim* and books of the Minim do not defile the hands (i.e., are not to be regarded as sacred). The books of Ben Sira, and all books which have been written from that time onward, do not defile the hands.'[2] The word really derives from galah (to reveal) and is the Hebrew equivalent of the Greek apocalypse. This is confirmed by the Syriac title of the *Book of Revelation* in the New Testament, *Geljana deqadisha Johana* (Apocalypse of St. John). We thus learn that the Rabbis declared all the apocalyptic literature, held to be divinely inspired by the Jewish sectarians, to be uncanonical and secular. This was partly because, after the disastrous revolt of the Messianic pretender Ben Koseba (Bar Kochba), they were anxious to discourage political Messianic hopes, and denounced those who 'calculated the Time of the End'. Among those who set great store by the apocalyptic and pseudepigraphic literature were the Judaeo-Christians, and since these also had the Gospel (*Evangelion*) this easily gave rise to the puns perpetrated by Meir and Jochanan,

---

[1] *Tal. Bab. Shabb.* 116a-b. The whole passage, with parallels to the first part, is quoted and commented upon in *Christianity in Talmud and Midrash* by R. Travers Herford.

[2] *Yad.* ii. 13.

who called it respectively *Aven-giljon* (worthless revelation) and *Avon-giljon* (iniquitous revelation).

We come now to the two buildings the names of which also suggest that some word-play was involved. The *Bet-Abidan* was evidently a heathen centre of some kind. Travers Herford thinks an Odeon may be meant, where philosophical disputations were sometimes held.[1] There were several in Palestine. This may be correct. Caesar is said to have asked Joshua ben Chananiah why he did not come to the *Bet-Abidan*.[2] The name itself plays on the word *Abaddon* (Destruction), but it is to be noted that Tarphon, extreme opponent of the Minim, would take refuge in a heathen sanctuary (*Bet-Abodah Zarah*) but never in any circumstances in a building of the Minim. *Bet-Nitsarphi*, or *Nitsraphi*, will therefore almost certainly be a place used by the Minim. Shemuel, who also would never go there, once referred to 'the dates for the wine of the *Bet-Nitsarphi*, which they drink on the day of their feast'.[3] This suggests the Christian *agape*, and possibly a play on the word *Notsrim* (Nazarenes), but we cannot leave out of account that the word *Tsaraph* is also behind the name, and that it may imply a building where the sectaries offered 'proof' of some kind, and held a sacramental meal.

From all the Minim references in the Rabbinical literature it is obvious that these sectaries were of many kinds, no doubt including the remnant of the Community of the Covenant, Essenes, Baptists, etc., as well as Judaeo-Christians. Indeed, it is stated in one place that 'Israel did not go into exile until twenty-four varieties of Minim had come into existence'.[4] The Church Fathers also speak of the number of Jewish sects.

Although the Rabbinical sources of information are rather late for our purpose, they do require to be re-examined carefully, for they are of value as reflecting a period when among the Jewish sectarians a fair amount of interchange of ideas and documents had taken place, and even to an extent actual fusion. In approaching the whole intricate subject of the Community of the Covenant we have to allow for very considerable changes to have taken place in the course of centuries between the Jewish Revolt under the Maccabees and that under Bar Kochba, under the impact of altered external conditions and the rise of new movements. It may well be, as we shall discuss later, that while descriptions of the principal individuals in the literature

---

[1] *Op. cit.*, p. 167.

[2] *Tal. Bab. Shabb.* 152a. The *Habakkuk Commentary* from Cave I appears to refer to the Roman Imperial Palace as *Bet-Ashmah* (House of Idolatry), the Emperor being worshipped as a god. See Teicher, 'The Habakkuk Scroll,' *Journal of Jewish Studies*, Vol. V, No. 2. So that *Bet-Abidan* might be a temple of the Imperial cult.

[3] *Ibid.*, *Erub.* 79b–80a

[4] *Tal. Yer. Sanhed.* 29c.

remained to a degree constant, at different times these were believed to relate to different historical personages each answering to the established prophetic requirements. We can see, for instance, in the Gospels how both Jesus and John the Baptist could be held by their contemporaries to be Elijah, the Prophet like Moses, or some other Prophet reincarnated.

For the present we have a particular line of inquiry to follow up. If I have established that there are good grounds for believing that the Community of the Covenant used the *Atbash* cipher we are afforded a fresh piece of evidence and perhaps a valuable clue. If this cipher has been used in one place it could well have been used in another. It is an old cipher, employed in certain passages in the book of the Prophet Jeremiah.

CHAPTER TWO

The Prophet Jeremiah

THE *Atbash* cipher is used four times in the book of Jeremiah, twice in chapter xxv and twice in chapter li. In xxv the Prophet is told to take the wine cup of fury and make all nations drink it. The list includes the Philistines, Edom and Moab, and the children of Ammon, and in verse 25 we have, 'And all the kings of Zimri, and all the kings of Elam.' It has long been agreed that Zimri זמרי should be read as Zimchi זמכי, which by the cipher converts into Elam עילם. This is confirmed by the parallel passage in the Greek (LXX) which speaks only of Elam and omits Zimri or Zimchi altogether. At the end of the list in the following verse we read, 'And the king of Sheshach shall drink after them'. Sheshach ששך by the cipher becomes Babel בבל (Babylon). The whole clause is omitted in the LXX. Sheshach is again mentioned alongside Babel (Babylon) in chapter li. 41, where again the parallel passage in the LXX omits the Sheshach clause. In the first verse of the same chapter there is another case of *Atbash*. We read: 'Behold I will raise up against Babylon, and against them that dwell *lev-kamai*, a destroying wind'. The difficult words are converted by the cipher into *Kasdim* (Chaldeans), and the LXX parallel plainly says 'and against the Chaldeans dwelling therein'. The Septuagint translator, therefore, had knowledge of the cipher, and simply left out the clauses containing it where conversion involved a duplication of names, or, as in the last instance, converted the cipher words where no duplication was involved. What purpose was served by these cipher substitutions except what we might call fun and games is difficult to imagine. They hide no great secrets. But because of the cipher it does become important to ask, what was the date of these chapters in which it occurs?

In the Hebrew text a wide gulf separates chapter xxv from li. But in the Greek version this is not so. In the latter there is a radical difference in the arrangement of the later chapters. The group of chapters xlvi-li in the Hebrew is broken up and appears in a different order as chapters xxvi-xxxi in the Greek, and xxv. 15 to the end of the chapter in the Hebrew follows on directly in the Greek as xxxii after including what corresponds in the Hebrew to xlviii. 44. Thus in the LXX chapter xxv of the Hebrew is directly associated with xlvi-li, forming together chapters xxvi-xxxii of the Greek text, and we thus obtain a set of prophecies against the very nations listed in xxv. This is a much better arrangement and demonstrates the unity of the material. The whole section has long been held by scholarly opinion to have been written in substance about the second century B.C. Leaving aside the obvious Egypt and Babylon, the list of nations denounced is highly significant in this respect.[1] It is virtually the same list as the confederacy in *Psalm* lxxxiii, the peoples of the War of Esau against Jacob in *Jubilees* xxxvii, the peoples against whom Judas Maccabaeus fought (*I Macc.* v), and the host of the Sons of Darkness with whom the Sons of Light contended according to one of the documents among the Dead Sea Scrolls. This remarkable similarity is unlikely to be a coincidence, and points to some community of origins and a relationship to events of a specific period.

If the section of *Jeremiah*, where alone the cipher is used, belongs to the first half of the second century B.C. this may offer a rational explanation of why it was inserted, to act as a kind of trade mark of the body responsible for the composition. As *Daniel* says: 'the skilled would understand'.

During the Antiochus persecution there was wholesale destruction of the sacred books, and according to the Introduction to *II Macc.* (ii. 14) it was Judas Maccabaeus who 'gathered together for us all those writings that had been scattered by reason of the war that befell'. Much work of restoration by the scribes and pious priests must have been necessitated, and sections could well have been added to some of the Prophetic books at this time, and even to the Psalms, bearing upon the contemporary situation.[2] It was such pietists (Chasidim) who would be just the kind of people to employ the *Atbash* cipher. This would bring the employment of the cipher down to the earliest period of which the *Damascus Document* speaks.

This work opens with a statement about the origins of the Community of the Covenant. At a time of apostasy which called forth the wrath of God upon Israel there was found a remnant of priests and people who repented. This is stated to have happened 'three hundred and ninety years after He had given them into the hand of Nebuchadnezzar, king of Babylon' (i. 5). This would give a date about 196 B.C. When these penitents had been 'groping after the way for twenty years' (i.e., about 176 B.C.) God raised up for them a Teacher of Righteousness 'to lead them in the way of His heart'. Thus the

[1] It is to be noted that there is denunciation of Edom and Babylon in *Ps.* cxxxvii, which psalm is attributed to Jeremiah in the LXX.

[2] There is perhaps a hint of this in *Jubilees* xlv. 16, where it is said that Jacob bequeathed all his books and the books of his fathers to Levi his son, 'that he might preserve them and renew them for his children until this day.' *Jubilees* is believed to have been written about 140-130 B.C.

sect traced its origin to a time when, as Dr. Charles long ago noted in editing the text, they must be identical with the Chasidim. 'It is noteworthy,' he pointed out, 'that *I Enoch* xc. 6 assigns the origin of the Chasidim to the same period.'

The Chasidic Movement, about which more will be said later, was largely sponsored by members of the priesthood, and was a protest against the Hellenism which had even corrupted leading figures among the Jewish hierarchy. The life and ministry of the Prophet Jeremiah, himself a priest, would make a strong appeal to the Chasidim. It was he who had spoken of a New Covenant which God would make with His people, when He would write the Law on their hearts (xxxi. 31-34). The Community of the Covenant could not fail to have had this in mind when they determined at a certain point in their history to enter into a New Covenant in the land of Damascus, to which region they had emigrated for a time. It was Jeremiah also who gave instructions that the contracts of his purchase of a family plot of land at Anathoth should be placed in an earthenware jar, 'that they may continue many days' as a sign from the Lord that 'houses and fields and vineyards shall be possessed again in this land' (xxxii. 6-15). In connexion with this sign mention is again made of the Everlasting Covenant which God would contract with His people (xxxii. 40-41).

In his *Antiquities* Josephus says that Jeremiah 'left behind him in writing a description of that destruction of our nation which has lately happened in our days', and that he prophesied the overthrow of Babylon by the Medes and Persians and the rebuilding of the Temple and the restoration of Jerusalem (X. v. 1; vii. 3). But it is in *II Maccabees* that the Prophet is seen as a most significant figure. Reference is made to a book in which it was recorded how Jeremiah 'being warned of God, commanded that the Tabernacle and the Ark should follow with him, when he went forth into the mountain where Moses went up and beheld the heritage of God. And Jeremiah came and found a cavern in the rock, and there he brought in the Tabernacle, and the Ark, and the altar of incense; and he made fast the door. And some of those that followed with him came there that they might mark the way, and could not find it. But when Jeremiah perceived, he blamed them, saying, "Yea, and the place shall be unknown until God gather the people again together, and mercy come; and then shall the Lord disclose these things"' (ii. 1-8).[1]

[1] There is a tradition of the Samaritans that the Taheb, the expected Restorer, of the lineage of Aaron, will recover the original vessels of the old Tabernacle from their hiding place; and just before his advent the first Scroll of the Law written out by Itamar the son of Aaron will also come to light. See Gaster, *Samaritan Eschatology*, and Jos. *Antiq.* XVIII. iv. 1.

Since the Dead Sea Scrolls were preserved in earthenware jars in caves, we must surely consider in the light of what is related of Jeremiah whether the deposit was not made of set purpose, and was not simply an expedient to save the books from destruction at the hands of the Romans in the War of 67-73 A.D., as scholars have maintained. I would suggest that the documents were concealed deliberately so that, in the words of *Daniel*, they should 'be closed up and sealed until the Time of the End'. That this view is to be preferred receives further support from the *Testament of Moses* (commonly called the *Assumption of Moses*), where the Lawgiver instructs Joshua: 'Receive thou this writing that thou mayst know how to preserve the books which I shall deliver unto thee. And thou shalt set these in order and anoint them with oil of cedar, and put them away in earthen vessels in the place which God made from the beginning of the creation of the world, that His Name should be called upon until the day of repentance in the visitation wherewith the Lord shall visit them in the Consummation at the End of the Days' (ii. 16-17).

The importance of this passage as throwing light on the reason for the concealment of the books of Khirbet Qumran is obvious. But have we any indication that the Community of the Covenant anticipated the lapse of a considerable period before the Consummation took place? The answer is given in one of the Dead Sea Scrolls, the *Habakkuk Commentary*. Explaining *Habb*. ii. 1-3, the commentator writes: 'And God told Habakkuk to write what is to befall the Last Generation; but the Consummation of the Time he did not make known to him. And where he says, "that he who runs may read it," the reference is to the Righteous Teacher to whom God made known all the secrets of the words of His servants the Prophets. "For the vision is yet for an appointed time, but at the end it shall speak and not lie." The explanation is that the Last Time will be prolonged, and shall transcend (or exceed) all that the Prophets have said; for the secrets of God are wonderful. "But if it delays, wait for it; for it will surely come, and will not tarry." This refers to the Men of Truth who practise the Law, whose hands never relax from the service of the Truth, in having the Last Time extended (or delayed) for them; for all the Times of God will come in their due season, just as He decreed of them in the secrets of his prudence.'

From the comment on *Hab*. ii. 8a it is evident that the writer believed himself to be living in the Last Time. But he and his fellows now considered that the Time would be prolonged. Some of the New Testament writers took the same view, accepting the period from the calamities in Judea until the dawn of the second century A.D. as the Last Times (*II Tim*. ii; *II Pet*. iii;

I Jno. ii. 18). The passage in *II Peter* is specially interesting, because the author of the Epistle feels it necessary to explain the postponement of the Second Advent of Christ and the Consummation of the Age. Believers were disturbed by the delay, which is elsewhere alluded to in the parable of the faithful servant (*Matt.* xxiv. 48). 'Peter' argues that the delay is due to the long-suffering of God, who is not slack concerning His promises. This is the same line taken by the commentator on *Habakkuk*.

Some time after the war with Rome and the destruction of Jerusalem in 70 A.D. we still hear of the hiding away of books for the illumination of the faithful in the period of the Consummation. The evidence comes from the *Apocalypse of Ezra* (100–120 A.D.). Ezra is told to write down all the visions he has seen 'and put them in a hidden place; and teach them to the wise of thy people, (even to them) whose hearts thou knowest are able to comprehend and to keep these mysteries' (xii. 33-48). He is further instructed to take five scribes able to write quickly and dictate to them the significant works. 'And when thou shalt have finished, some of them thou shalt make public, and some thou shalt conceal, and shalt deliver them to the wise.' In forty days, it is said, ninety-four books were written down in the square Hebrew characters which Ezra is supposed to have invented. 'And it came to pass when the forty days were completed, the Most High spake to me, and said to me: "The twenty-four books that ye have written (first) make public, that both those who are worthy and those who are not worthy [from (among) the people] may read therein: but the seventy thou shalt keep and deliver them to the wise of thy people; for in them are the veins of understanding, and the fountains of wisdom and the stream of knowledge." ' (xiv. 23-26; 42-47).

But we must return to Jeremiah and *II Maccabees*. In xv. 11-16 we are told of a dream of Judas Maccabaeus in which he first saw Onias the high priest, and then 'a man of venerable age and exceeding glory, and wonderful and most majestic was the dignity around him'. Onias then declared, 'This is the lover of the brethren, he who prayeth much for the people and the holy city, Jeremiah the prophet of God.' Then Jeremiah 'stretching forth his right hand delivered to Judas a sword of gold, and in giving it addressed him thus, "Take the holy sword, a gift from God, wherewith thou shall smite down the adversaries." '

The dream was no doubt reported to inspire belief in the invincibility of Judas; but it is all of a piece with what we have brought forward regarding the importance of Jeremiah for the Chasidim that it should be he who bestows the Maccabean *Excalibur*.

Was it the Chasidim also who gave Judas the name Maccabee? According to *I Macc.* ii. 2-5 all the sons of Mattathias the priest of Modin received nicknames, some of which are difficult to explain owing to uncertainty as to how the names were written in Hebrew. In the case of Judas his descriptive nickname Maccabee is most likely to have been written מקבי. Various interpretations have been proposed, including the suggestion that his banner bore the letters מ׳כ׳ב׳י׳, representing the phrase: 'Who is like unto Thee among the gods, O Lord?' But the spelling is improbable. The most likely derivation is from *Makabah* מקבה (a hammer), making the name mean Hammerer. But even if this should be correct we have the right, in view of the use of *Atbash* in the *Damascus Document* and in the late section of *Jeremiah*, to look to that cipher for further justification of the choice of the word Maccabee. Neither are we disappointed, for מקבי is converted by *Atbash* into *Yad-Shem* יד־שם (The Hand of the Name), i.e., the Hand of God. I would not press this; but the fact that a definite meaning is obtained by *Atbash* is certainly of interest.

The Community of the Covenant was evidently familiar with what afterwards came to be called *Gematria*, the various methods, either by permutation or numerical value of letters, by which the inner truth of the sacred writings could be revealed. In the *Manual of Discipline* there is reference to the supreme sanctity of the letter N (*nun*), the value of which is 50.[1] We are therefore on safe ground in assuming that in such circles *Atbash*, one of the oldest forms of permutation, would be freely employed when necessary.[2] If this is established, it may further be held with some conviction that a definite relationship subsisted between the section of *Jeremiah* we have discussed and the development of Chasidism. We are also led to look especially to the circumstances immediately preceding and following upon the Maccabean revolt for the origins of the Community of the Covenant.

---

[1] See Dupont-Sommer, *op. cit.* pp. 115-6.

[2] Torrey, *The Chronicler's History*, p. xix, holds that Ebal in *Deut.* xxvii. 4 is an anti-Samaritan substitute for the original *Gerizim*. But perhaps Ebal is a disguise of the Samaritan centre of Shechem. Ebal, omitting the *Ayin*, (ע)יבבל converts by *Atbash* into כישך which is Shechem שכם transposed.

CHAPTER THREE

The Chasidim

THE ORIGINS of the Chasidic Party are obscure. But since it was already well established at the time of the Maccabean revolt in 167 B.C. it must have come into existence near the beginning of the second century B.C. Travers Herford dates the foundation of the Jewish senate (*gerusia*), which subsequently became the Sanhedrin, about 196 B.C., for it is mentioned in the letter of Antiochus III to Ptolemy quoted by Josephus (*Antiq.* XII. iii. 3).[1] Herford notes the coincidence in date with that furnished by the *Damascus Document*,[2] and suggests that the Chasidim were initially a group of zealots for the Law, composed of priests and laymen, within the senate.

Whether or not the Party was already organized previously, the circumstances which must chiefly have contributed towards its more formal constitution were those which immediately followed the accession of Antiochus IV in 175 B.C. At this time Jesus son of the High Priest Onias II supplanted his brother Onias III, and taking the name of Jason went over to the Greek way of life. 'And thus,' says the author of *II Macc.*, 'there was an extreme of Greek fashions, and an advance of an alien faith, by reason of the exceeding profaneness of Jason, that ungodly man and no high priest' (iv. 12). Regarding the same apostasy the writer of *I Macc.* states: 'In those days there came forth out of Israel transgressors of the Law, and persuaded many, saying, "Let us go and make a covenant with the Gentiles that are round about us; for since we were parted from them many evils have befallen us." And the saying was good in their eyes. And certain of the people were forward herein and went to the king, and he gave them licence to do after the ordinances of the Gentiles. And they built a place of exercise in Jerusalem according to the laws of the Gentiles; and they made themselves uncircumcised, and forsook the holy covenant, and joined themselves to the Gentiles, and sold themselves to do evil' (i. 11-15).

Jason was in turn supplanted as High Priest by Menelaus, as ambitious and as corrupt as Jason, and the rivalry between these two brought Jerusalem to

---

[1] *The Pharisees*, pp. 24-27.
[2] See above, p. 9.

ruin, and led directly to the persecution of the Jews by Antiochus and the attempted destruction of Jewish worship. All this took place between 172–167 B.C. 'But many in Israel were fully resolved and confirmed in themselves not to eat unclean things.[1] And they chose to die, that they might not be defiled with the meats, and that they might not profane the holy covenant: and they died. And there came exceeding great wrath upon Israel' (*I Macc.* i. 63–4).

This state of affairs is also referred to in the *Assumption of Moses*, which we have already quoted in connexion with the concealment of the sacred writings, as[2] follows. 'And there will come upon them a second visitation and wrath,[3] such as has not befallen them from the beginning until that time, in which God will stir up against them the king of the kings of the earth (i.e., Antiochus Epiphanes) and one that ruleth with great power, who will crucify those who confess to their circumcision: and those who conceal it he will torture and deliver them up to be bound and led into prison. And their wives will be given to the gods among the Gentiles, and their young sons will be operated on by the physicians in order to bring forward their foreskin. And others among them will be punished by tortures and fire and sword, and they will be forced to bear in public their idols (which are as) polluted as are the (shrines) that contain them. And they will likewise be forced by those who torture them to enter their inmost Sanctuary, and they will be forced by goads to blaspheme with insolence the Name[4]; finally after these things the laws and what they had above their altar' (viii).[5]

It is impossible to avoid the conclusion that the rise of the Chasidim and the origin of the Community of the Covenant belong to the same time and circumstances, and that in fact the Community derived from the Chasidim. This is clearly seen from the opening of the *Damascus Document*, part of a work of a testamentary character, which we must now give in full.

Now, therefore, hearken (unto me) all ye who know righteousness,
And have understanding of the works of God.
For He hath a controversy with all flesh,
And will execute judgment upon all who despise Him.
And because of the trespass of those who forsook Him,
He hid His face from Israel and from His Sanctuary,
And gave them over to the sword.
But when He remembered the covenant with the forefathers,

---

[1] This refusal to eat forbidden food is stressed in the book of *Daniel* belonging to the early Maccabean period.
[2] Above p. 11.
[3] The first visitation and wrath had been in the time of Nebuchadnezzar. This agrees with the *Damascus Document*.
[4] Cp. *Maccabee* as 'The Hand of the Name', above p. 13.
[5] The description echoes Jos. *Antiq.* XII. v. 2–3, *I Macc.* i and *II Macc.* vi.

He left a remnant to Israel,
And gave them not over to destruction.
But in the period of the Wrath He visited them,
Three hundred and ninety years after He had given them
Into the hand of Nebuchadnezzar, the King of Babylon.
And He caused to spring forth from Israel and Aaron
A root of His planting[1] to inherit the land,
And to grow fat through the goodness of His earth.
And they had understanding of their iniquity,
And they knew they were guilty men,
And they were like the blind and them that grope their way for twenty years.
And God considered their works;
For they sought Him with a perfect heart.
And He raised up for them a Teacher of Righteousness
To lead them in the way of His heart.
And He made known to succeeding generations
What He would do to the last generation, to a perfidious congregation:
Those who turn aside out of the way.
This is the time of which it was written,
'As a stubborn heifer, Israel behaved himself stubbornly,'[2]
When there arose a Scoffer,
Who distilled for Israel deceptive waters,
And caused them to stray in the trackless wilderness,
To suppress the old paths,[3]
So as to turn aside from the right ways
And remove the landmark the forefathers had set in their inheritance;
So as to make cleave to them the curses of His covenant,
So that He should deliver them to the sword that avengeth His covenant;
Because they sought after flatteries and chose deceit,
And kept watch for breaches.
They laid waste the best of the flock,[4]
And justified the wicked and condemned the righteous:
And transgressed the covenant, and violated the statute,
And attacked the soul of the righteous.
And all that walked uprightly their soul abhorred,
And they pursued them with the sword,
And rejoiced in the strife of the people.
And so the wrath of God was kindled against their congregation,
So that He laid waste all their multitude,
And their deeds were uncleanness before Him.

We are not yet ready to deal with the identity of the individuals called here the Teacher of Righteousness and the Scoffer, or Man of Mockery.

[1] Cp. *Enoch* xciii. 9-10. By contrast Antiochus Epiphanes is called 'a sinful root' (*I Macc.* i. 10).
[2] *Hos.* iv. 16.
[3] Reading נתבות for גבהות. Cp. *Jer.* vi. 16.
[4] This seems to be the best emendation.

Other material evidence requires to be presented. But the general picture is plain enough of the opposing policies, Hellenism versus Faithfulness to the Law. The italicized lines may be in the nature of comment by a later writer.[1] The testamentary work in the *Damuscus Document* is several times interrupted by a commentator, who explains the text in the light of the history of the Community, employing an extraordinary Biblical exegesis. This commentator appears to treat the earlier work as an inspired prophetic writing applicable to his sect and to later events in exactly the same way as does the author of the *Commentary on Habakkuk*. The latter part of the *Damascus Document* relates wholly to the Community and represents part of a different work. This is in narrative form and written in the third person, while approximately the first two thirds are poetic, given out by an unknown who addresses his hearers as 'my children'. In this section we have a record akin to other testamentary literature like the *Testaments of the XII Patriarchs*.

The situation, as the writings we have quoted have depicted it, was radically changed by the Maccabean revolt initiated by the example of the priest Mattathias and his five sons. 'Then were gathered together unto them a company of Chasidim, mighty men of Israel, every one that offered himself willingly for the Law. And all they that fled from the evils were added to them, and became a stay to them. And they mustered a host' (*I Macc.* ii. 42-44).

We do not hear of the Chasidim again until after the great successes of Judas Maccabaeus and the cleansing of the defiled Temple. As a body they are held not to have been concerned with the political aspects of the struggle. But at the beginning of the reign of Demetrius Soter (162 B.C.) we learn of them again in connexion with the inimical activities of Alcimus or Jacimus. 'And there came unto him (i.e., Demetrius) all the lawless and ungodly men of Israel; and Alcimus was their leader, desiring to be High Priest' (*I Macc.* vii. 6). He made accusations against Judas in these terms, according to the author of *II Macc.*: 'Those of the Jews that are called Chasidim, whose leader is Judas Maccabaeus, keep up war, and are seditious, not suffering the kingdom to find tranquillity' (xiv. 6). The same writer says that Alcimus had formerly been High Priest, 'and had wilfully polluted himself in the times when there was no mingling (i.e., with the Gentiles)'[2] (xiv. 3). Demetrius thereupon

[1] The 390 years mentioned, and another reference to 40 years (ix. 39), may have been obtained from *Ezek.* iv. 4-6.

[2] Josephus makes Alcimus succeed Menelaus as High Priest (*Antiq.* XII. ix. 7). The author of *V Macc.* (Cotton) says of the Hellenising period: 'Now there were at that time in Judea three men, the very worst of all mortals; and each of them had, as it were, a connexion in the same sort of vice. The name of one of these three was Menelaus, of the second Simeon (governor of the Temple), of the third Alcimus' (iii. 6).

decided to get rid of Judas by feigning to make peace with him, and entrusted the commission to Bacchides. 'And he sent him, and that ungodly Alcimus, and made sure to him the high priesthood, and he commanded him to take vengeance upon the children of Israel' (*I Macc.* vii. 9).

There follows a passage of great importance. 'And there were gathered together unto Alcimus and Bacchides a company of scribes to seek for justice. And the Chasidim were the first among the children of Israel that sought peace of them; for they said, "One that is a priest of the seed of Aaron is come with the forces, and he will do us no wrong." And he spake with them words of peace, and sware unto them, saying, "We will seek the hurt neither of you nor your friends." And they gave him credence: and he laid hands on three-score men of them, and slew them in one day, according to the word which he wrote, "The flesh of Thy saints (did they cast out), and their blood did they shed round about Jerusalem; and there was no man to bury them"' (vii. 12-17).

The Chasidim here take action independent of Judas and his brothers, having confidence in Alcimus as a priest, a confidence that was terribly abused. When sixty of them were murdered the writer applies to them the words of *Ps.* lxxix. 2-3. The significance of this will appear later.

Those who came to Alcimus, apparently a deputation, were scribes and associated with the priesthood. Now at this time there was a famous scribe, called in the Mishnah 'a Chasid belonging to the priesthood' (*Peah* ii. 7), who is said by tradition to have been an uncle of Jacim, or Alcimus, and who may have been the leader of the deputation. The name of this man was Joseph ben Joezer of Zeredah, perhaps a disciple of Antigonus of Socho, who in turn was a disciple of Simon the Just. The saying is attributed to him (*Aboth* i. 4), 'Let thy house be a meeting-place for the wise. Powder thyself in the dust of their feet, and drink in their words with avidity.'

According to an early Midrash, Joseph was martyred for his faith, and on his way to execution this dialogue took place between him and Alcimus. Said Alcimus, 'See the profit and honours that have fallen to my lot in consequence of what I have done, whilst thou, for thy obstinacy hast the misfortune to die as a criminal.' Joseph replied, 'If such is the lot of those who anger God, what shall be the lot of those who carry out His will?' Alcimus retorted, 'Is there anyone who has carried out His will more than thou?' To this Joseph made answer, 'If this (i.e., my martyrdom) is the end of those who carry out His will, what awaits those who anger Him?'[1] Thereupon Alcimus was smitten with remorse and died.[2]

---

[1] Cp. *Prov.* xi. 31.

[2] See *Gen. R.* lxv. 22.

Edouard Dhormé has already proposed the identification of Alcimus with the Wicked Priest of the Zadokite Chasidim, and here this High Priest is brought into direct relationship with one who could certainly be described as a Teacher of Righteousness.

The end of Alcimus is given differently in *I Maccabees*. After establishing himself as High Priest, 'in the hundred and fifty and third year (c. 160 B.C.), in the second month, Alcimus commanded to pull down the wall of the inner court of the Sanctuary: he pulled down also the works of the Prophets[1]; and he began to pull down. At that time Alcimus was stricken, and his works were hindered; and his mouth was stopped, and he was taken with a palsy, and he could no more speak anything and give orders concerning his house. And Alcimus died at that time with great torment'[2] (ix. 54-56).

After Alcimus what happened to the Chasidim? There is an account in the *Damascus Document* which suggests that not long after this there took place an emigration to 'the land of Damascus'. The passage is as follows:

> And during the period of the destruction of the land there arose those who removed the landmark and led Israel astray. And the land became desolate because they spake rebellion against the commandments of God through Moses [and also through His holy Messiah (or anointed one)],[3] and they prophesied a lie to turn away Israel from God.
> But God remembered the covenant with the forefathers:
> And He raised up from Aaron men of understanding,
> And from Israel wise men:
> And He made them to hearken,
> And they digged the well.
> 'A well the princes digged,
> The nobles of the people delved it
> By the order of the Lawgiver.'[4]
> The well is the Law, and they who digged it are the penitents of Israel who went forth out of the land of Judah and sojourned in the land of Damascus, all of whom God called princes, for they sought Him and His glory was not turned back in the mouth of one of them. And the Lawgiver is the Student of the Law, in regard to whom Isaiah said, 'He bringeth forth an instrument for His work.' And the nobles of the people are those who came to dig the well by the precepts in which the Lawgiver ordained that they should walk throughout the full period of the

[1] The Prophets Haggai and Zechariah.
[2] See also Jos. *Antiq*. XII. x. 6.
[3] These words appear to be an editorial addition.
[4] Num. xxi. 18. The Lawgiver is of course Moses.

wickedness. [And save them (i.e., the precepts) they shall acquire nothing until there arises the Teacher of Righteousness in the End of the Days.[1]][2]

This passage refers back to the first section of the testamentary document already quoted,[3] from which work, perhaps, the poetic lines are excerpted. It is quite evident that the commentator dates the emigration of the Penitents of Israel fairly early in the history of the Party. Their leader was the unnamed Student of the Law, who drew up the precepts, possibly the *Book of Testing*.

But we may be able to date this emigration exactly, thanks to Josephus. The historian tells us: 'By what means the nation of the Jews recovered their freedom when they had been brought into slavery by the Macedonians, and what struggles, and how many great battles Judas, the general of their army, ran through till he was slain as he was fighting for them, has been related in the foregoing book. But after he was dead, all the wicked, and those that transgressed the laws of their forefathers, sprang up again in Judea, and grew upon them, and distressed them on every side. A famine also assisted their wickedness, and afflicted their country, *till not a few, who by reason of their want of necessaries, and because they were not able to bear up against the miseries that both the famine and their enemies brought upon them, deserted their country, and went to the Macedonians*. And now Bacchides gathered those Jews together who had apostasised from the accustomed way of living of their forefathers, and chose to live like their neighbours, and committed the care of the country to them; who also caught the friends of Judas, and those of his party, and delivered them up to Bacchides, who, when he had in the first place tortured and tormented them at his pleasure, he by that means at length killed them. And when this calamity of the Jews was become so great, as they had never had experience of the like since their return out of Babylon, those that remained of the companions of Judas . . . came to his brother Jonathan.'[4]

This passage from Josephus is clearly in part based on *I Macc.* ix. 23-31; but the words italicised are not from this source: at least they are not in the Greek version. After the death of Judas Maccabaeus the Hellenizers temporarily gained the upper hand. There was great persecution of those who were faithful to the Covenant, whose miseries were accentuated by a severe famine. In these circumstances a number deserted their country and emigrated 'to the Macedonians' (presumably Syria, the land of Damascus). This emigration took place about 160-159 B.C., and there is certainly a strong presumption that among those who left Judea at this time and sojourned in the land of Damascus

---

[1] These words also seem to be an addition, but this is not certain.
[2] viii. 1-10.
[3] Above pp. 15-16.
[4] *Antiq.* XIII. i. 1.

were the Penitents of Israel of our document, who there formally entered into a New Covenant.[1]

Leading the Penitents was a learned Scribe 'the Student of the Law', who laid down the precepts which should govern the faithful and those who joined them throughout the full period of the wickedness. The words that follow, which we have bracketed as a possible addition, declare that the Precepts of the Student of the Law would remain the guide of the Covenanters 'until there arises the Teacher of Righteousness in the End of the Days'. Concerning this Student of the Law *Isa.* liv. 16 is quoted, and we can see how applicable to the situation is the context of this verse. 'And all thy children shall be taught of the Lord; and great shall be the peace of thy children. In righteousness shalt thou be established; thou shalt be far from oppression; for thou shalt not fear; and from terror; for it shall not come nigh thee. Behold, they (the wicked) shall surely gather together, but not by Me: whoever shall gather together against thee shall fall for thy sake . . . No weapon that is formed against thee shall prosper; and every tongue that riseth against thee in judgment thou shalt condemn. This is the heritage of the servants of the Lord, and their righteousness is of Me, saith the Lord' (*Isa.* liv. 13-17).

After the time of the emigration the Chasidim under that name disappear from the records. But there are two references in *V Macc.* to a sect called the Chasdanim, which should be noted, even though this work is late and of dubious historical value. The author distinguishes the Chasdanim from the Pharisees and Sadducees, and speaks of them as the third sect among the Jews, thus corresponding to the Essenes of Josephus. Writing of the time of Hyrcanus I (134-103 B.C.), he tells us that the Chasdanim are 'those who studied the virtues; but the author of the book (i.e., his source) did not make mention of their rule, nor do we know it except in so far as it is discovered by their name; for they applied themselves to such practices as came near the more eminent virtues; namely, to select from those other two rules (i.e., those of the Pharisees and Sadducees) whatever was most safe in belief, most sure and guarded' (xxv. 5-6). Coming down to about 71 B.C. he mentions them again in connexion with the power struggle between the other two parties in the time of Salome Alexandra, widow of Alexander Jannaeus. The queen accepts the request of the Sadducees, then out of favour, to be allowed to retire from

---

[1] I am not able to accept the view ably argued by I. Rabinowitz that the Damascus element in the *Damascus Document* refers to the spared righteous remnant carried away in the old Assyro-Babylonian captivities, and that therefore the term is only employed symbolically by the author and the sect never actually emigrated to the land of Damascus. See article, 'A Reconsideration of "Damascus" and "390 years" in the "Damascus (Zadokite) Fragments" ', *Journal of Biblical Literature*, Vol. lxxiii, Part I, 1954.

Jerusalem. 'And the Sadducees went forth of the city; and their chiefs departed with the men of war who adhered to them; and went with their cattle to those towns of Judah which they had selected, and dwelt in them; and there were joined to them those who were devoted to the virtues' (xxxii. 11-12).

The view is now widely accepted that the Chasidim merged into the Essenes, and that the Party of the New Covenant came within the framework of this classification. In that case it is difficult to see the beginnings of the Party as later than the time of the Maccabean Revolt, and therefore provisionally to assume the correctness of the *Damascus Document* in placing the coming of the Teacher of Righteousness at about 176 B.C.

CHAPTER FOUR

The Damascus Testament

THE *Damascus Document* is clearly of the utmost importance in seeking light on the history of the Party of the Covenant, especially as we are virtually without independent evidence to its fortunes. The difficulty with this work is that it is not a unity. It consists in the first place of a testament or exhortation in the first person singular, with a few editorial additions by a later writer or writers. This is followed by some further account of the Party and its problems and attitudes in the same style as the additions, forming the second half of what we may call *Testament Damascus.* As regards this second half, which possibly includes some further short excerpts from the testament itself, we have fragments of a second version (B) with distinctive variations. Finally, at the close of the primary, or (A) text, we have an epitome of the organization and laws of the Party as we find them otherwise reflected in the *Manual of Discipline* found in Cave I. The composite document lacks both commencement and conclusion, but a fragment preceding the present beginning of the document has come to light at Khirbet Qumran.

It is significant that the document has this testamentary element, because it is a characteristic product of the Maccabean era. Once the old prophetic books had become more or less fixed there developed among the Chasidim a new class of Patriarchal literature, admonitory and apocalyptic, requisitioning the personalities of the ancestors of the race. The later sections of *Enoch* are of this order. *Jubilees* contains testamentary prophecies of Isaac and Jacob. In the *XII Patriarchs* we have the testaments of the twelve sons of Jacob. The *Testament* (or *Assumption*) *of Moses* is addressed to Joshua. The Fathers are brought in to warn their descendants.[1]

The great period of this testamentary literature was roughly from 120 B.C. to 70 B.C., though there were later additions to it. By the latter part of the first century A.D. the Pseudo-Patriarchs were being quoted as if they really

[1] See especially *Enoch* xci. 1-5; *Test. Levi.* x, xiii-xvi.

were the Fathers speaking, as in the *Epistle of Jude*: 'And Enoch also, the seventh from Adam, prophesied.' The writer of the second half of our document explains in one passage: 'This means the three nets of Belial, concerning which Levi the son of Jacob spake.' This commentator was certainly acquainted with *Jubilees* and the *XII Patriarchs* and must therefore have lived at a time much later than their original composition. The new class of literature was so favoured that a testament of Mattathias the priest to his sons is given in *I Maccabees*, and in our document we have another by some venerated 'father' of the New Covenant Party. This testament may well go back to 100 B.C., since it is obviously of much higher antiquity than the comments upon it. The original Teacher of Righteousness will have been earlier still, as he is spoken of in the testamentary document itself.

We have already quoted in full what may be called section 1,[1] though this is not the actual beginning of the work, and therefore give here sections 2 and 3.

2.

And now, hearken unto me all ye who have entered the covenant,
And I will disclose to you the ways of the wicked.
God loveth knowledge; wisdom and counsel He hath set before Him:
Prudence and knowledge minister unto Him.
Longsuffering is with Him and plenteousness of forgiveness
To pardon those who repent of transgression.
But power and might and great fury with flames of fire[2]
For them who turn aside out of the way and abhor the statute,
So that there shall be no remnant, nor any to escape of them.
For God chose them not from the beginning of the world,
And before they were formed He knew their works;
And He abhorred their generations from of old,
And hid His face from their land till they were consumed.
And He knew the years of their activity,
And the number and explanation of their periods;
For all the things that belong to the ages and have been (He knoweth),
Moreover whatsoever shall come to pass in their periods for all eternity.[3]
Yet in all of them (i.e., their generations) He raised up special men,[4]
In order to leave a remnant to the earth,
And to fill the face of the earth with their seed.
And through His Messiah He shall make them know His holy Spirit;
And he is true, and in the explanation of His name are their names[5]*;*
But them He hated He made to go astray.

---

[1] Above pp. 15-16.
[2] After 'fire' is interpolated 'therein are all the angels of destruction.'
[3] The italicised lines throughout appear to be interpolations.
[4] 'Special men.' Lit. 'men called by name.'
[5] These lines break the continuity and could be a later addition.

3.

Now therefore, children, hearken unto me, and I will open your eyes
To see and to understand the works of God;
To choose what He approveth, and to reject what He hateth;
To walk uprightly in all His ways,
And not to go about in the thoughts of an evil imagination,
And with eyes full of fornication.
For many were led astray by them,
And mighty men of valour stumbled by them of old.[1]
Because they walked in the stubbornness of their heart the Watchers
[of heaven fell.
By them were they caught because they kept not the commandment of
[God.
And their children, whose height was like the loftiness of the cedars
And whose bodies were like the mountains, fell thereby.
All flesh that was on dry land perished thereby,
And they were as though they had not been;
Because they did their own will,
And kept not the commandment of their Maker,
Until His wrath was kindled against them.
By them went astray the sons of Noah and their families;
Because of them they were cut off.
Abraham did not walk in them,
And he was recorded 'friend' because he kept the commandments of God,
And chose not the will of his own spirit.
And he delivered (the commandment) to Isaac and Jacob,
And they observed (it) and were recorded as friends of God,
And members of the covenant for ever.
The sons of Jacob went astray through them,
And they were punished according to their error.
And their children in Egypt walked in the stubbornness of their heart,
So that they took counsel against the commandments of God,
And every man did what was right in his own eyes.
[2]And He cut off their males in the desert when He said to them in Kadesh:
'Go up and possess the land.' But they hardened their spirit:
And they hearkened not unto the voice of their Maker,[3]
But murmured in their tents.
And so the wrath of God was kindled against their congregation,
And their children[4] were cut off by it (i.e., the evil imagination),
And their mighty men perished by it,
And their land was made desolate by it.
By it the first that entered the covenant incurred guilt,
And they were delivered unto the sword,

[1] After 'old' is inserted 'and until now'.
[2] The text inserts: 'And they ate blood'.
[3] After 'Maker' is interpolated 'the commandments of their Teacher'.
[4] After 'children' is interpolated 'perished by it and their kings'

Because they forsook the covenant of God:
And they chose their own will,
And went about in the stubbornness of their heart,
Every man doing his own will.
But with them that held fast by the commandments of God,[1]
God confirmed the covenant of Israel for ever,
Revealing unto them the hidden things wherein all Israel had erred:
His holy sabbaths and His glorious festivals,
His righteous testimonies and His true ways;
And the desires of His will[2] He opened before them.
And they digged a well of many waters:
And he that despises them shall not live.
But they wallowed in the transgressions of man,
And in the ways of the unclean woman,
And they said, 'it is ours.'
But in His wondrous mysteries God pardoned their sins,
And forgave their transgressions.
And He built them a sure house in Israel,
The like of which ne'er arose from of old [*nor*] until this day.
They who hold fast to Him are for the life of eternity.
And all the glory of man is for them;
As God confirmed it to them by Ezekiel the prophet, saying:
'The priests and the Levites and the sons of Zadok,
That kept the charge of My Sanctuary when the children of Israel [went astray from Me,
They shall bring near unto Me fat and blood.'
The priests are the penitents of Israel who went forth out of the land of Judah;
And the Levites are they who joined them.
And the Sons of Zadok are the Elect of Israel called by name,
That arise in the End of the Days.
Behold the statement of their names according to their generations,
And the period of their activity, and the number of their afflictions,
And the years of their sojournings, and the statement of their works.[3]

For the present we will not take the document beyond this point, because in what remains there is no recurrence of the use of the first person singular. There are some further short passages which may have belonged to the testamentary work, or to comments upon it, but it will be useful first to look at the text as far as we have taken it.

The impression left by *Test. Damasc.* is of kinship with the *Testaments of the XII Patriarchs* and to certain sections of the *Book of Enoch*. It belongs clearly to the same cycle of literature, and like the *Testaments* has been subjected to later interpolation by interested editors. The theme of the author is the

[1] After 'God' is interpolated 'who were left to them'.
[2] After 'will' is interpolated 'the which if a man do, he shall live by them'.
[3] The whole of the italicized passage is a late addition.

faithful remnant, which, adhering to the covenant in times of apostasy, has again manifested itself in those of Aaron and Israel who knew they were guilty men. To them God raised up 'a Teacher of Righteousness to lead them in the way of His heart'. The Jewish sectarian commentator understands that the time at which this took place was the period of the Hellenising priesthood which brought about the terrible visitation of Antiochus Epiphanes. The author of the *Test. Damasc.* is looking back to the Teacher of Righteousness over some period of time, and therefore may himself have been writing towards the close of the second century B.C., somewhere about the time of the original writing of the *XII Patriarchs*. The Jewish sectarian editor and commentator manifestly lived very much later than this, for he speaks of what would appear to be a long series of activities and vicissitudes in his Party's history. It is likely, therefore, that he is writing at some time in the first century A.D. in 'the End of the Days'.

Taking the testamentary document without the comments and interpolations, it breathes the atmosphere of the records of the time of the Maccabean rising. 'And many in Israel . . . chose to die . . . that they might not profane the holy covenant: and they died. And there came exceeding great wrath upon Israel. In those days rose up Mattathias the son of John, the son of Simeon, a priest of the sons of Joarib, from Jerusalem, and he dwelt at Modin. And he had five sons . . . And he saw the blasphemies that were committed in Judah and Jerusalem, and he said, "Woe is me! wherefore was I born to see the destruction of my people . . . and, behold, our holy things and our beauty and our glory are laid waste, and the Gentiles have profaned them. Wherefore should we live any longer?" '[1]

We have already associated this passage in *I Macc.* with another relating to the same period in the *Assumption* (or *Testament*) *of Moses*,[2] where the persecution by Antiochus Epiphanes is described similarly as 'a second visitation and wrath'. The first visitation and wrath was associated with Nebuchadnezzar. Quite clearly *Test. Damasc.* is referring to the same 'second visitation' as 'the period of the wrath', and the editor has followed this immediately by a statement that this was three hundred and ninety years after Israel had been given into the hands of Nebuchadnezzar, king of Babylon. It is therefore as certain as anything can be that the testamentary document means us to understand that the time at which the Teacher of Righteousness arose was that of the great apostasy which brought upon Israel the 'visitation' of Antiochus Epiphanes.

[1] *I Macc.* i. 62–ii. 13.
[2] Above pp. 15–16.

We have already suggested that *Test. Damasc.* may have been written towards the end of the second century B.C. It was about this time, or a little earlier, that *I Maccabees* was written, and this work which we have seen to have some correspondence of ideas also significantly contains a testament, that of Mattathias the priest to his sons. The testament is given in *I Macc.* ii. 49-70, and begins: 'Now have pride and rebuke gotten strength, and a season of overthrow, and wrath of indignation. And now, my children, be ye zealous for the Law, and give your lives for the covenant of your fathers. And call to remembrance the deeds of your fathers which they performed in their generations, and received great glory and an everlasting name.' Mattathias then goes on to review the names of the faithful from Abraham to Daniel, somewhat as does the speaker in the testamentary document. Of course this speech of Mattathias has been composed for him by the author of *I Macc.*, who probably himself belonged to the Chasidim.

CHAPTER FIVE

The Land of Damascus

AT THE close of the testamentary section of our document we met with the following interpretation of the words of Ezekiel relating to the Priests and the Levites and the sons of Zadok: 'The *Priests* are the penitents of Israel who went forth out of the land of Judah; and the *Levites* are those who joined them. And the *Sons of Zadok* are the Elect of Israel . . . that arise in the End of the Days.' With Charles we should here understand the lapse of a considerable interval of time. The history of the Party is thus divided into three periods represented symbolically by the Priests, the Levites, the Sons of Zadok. The first period was marked by the emigration to the land of Damascus. In the second period the Community grew by the adherence of new members. Finally, very much later, we come to the time at which the commentator is writing in 'the End of the Days'. He speaks in retrospect of many generations, numbers of afflictions, and years of sojournings.

Of the second period we perhaps have an echo in the so-called *Psalms of Solomon*. 'And Jerusalem did all things according as the Gentiles did in their cities to their gods . . . and there was none amongst them that did mercy and truth in Jerusalem. They that love the assemblies of the saints fled away from them; and they flew like sparrows who fly from their nests. And they were wandering in the wilderness, in order to save their soul from evil; and precious was the sojourning with them of any soul that was saved from them (i.e., the wicked).'[1] This passage, as the context shows, relates to the decadent period of the Maccabean rulers, the years immediately prior to the capture of Jerusalem by Pompey in 63 B.C.[2]

Let us now see how the document continues after the comment on the text of Ezekiel.

---

[1] *Ps. Sol.* xvii. 16-19.
[2] The death of Pompey is mentioned in these *Psalms*.

The former saints whom God pardoned
Both justified the righteous and condemned the wicked,
And all who come after them must do according to the interpretation
In which the forefathers were instructed, [of the Law
Until the consummation of the period of these years,
In accordance with the covenant God established with the forefathers
In order to pardon their sins:
So shall God make atonement for them.
But on the consummation of the period according to the number of
[these years
They shall no more join themselves to the house of Judah;
But shall everyone stand up against his net.[1]
The wall shall have been built, the boundary far removed.[2]

This passage appears to be a continuation of the commentary and not part of the testament, since 'these years' evidently refers back to 'the years of their sojournings', and therefore relates to the intervening period between the original emigration and the particular date at which severence from the house of Judah took place.

The commentator speaks of the 'first' or 'former Saints' whom God pardoned. These *Kadoshim ha-rishonim* are the repentant remnant from Israel and Aaron of the first part of *Test. Damasc.*, who lived at the time of the 'Period of the Wrath' when Israel went astray, and by contrast with the Saints 'justified the wicked and condemned the righteous'. These Saints are doubtless to be included among those whom the rabbinical literature calls by a corresponding term, the first or former Chasidim (*Chasidim ha-rishonim*). Their rise is dated by the commentator about 196-176 B.C. Their spiritual successors obtain atonement by adhering during a protracted period of years to the Covenant and the teaching of the Law in which the forefathers were instructed. At the termination of this period, however, a separation from the Jews is made, and in this connexion the writer quotes *Micah* vii. 11. Looking at the context in *Micah* we see that he means that the Party of the Covenant would be securely established as an independent community at the time when the land of Israel would be desolate because of the evil doings of the inhabitants (*Mic.* vii. 13).[3] The true Israel, the Elect, severed itself from Judah.

The document then continues: 'And during all these years (i.e., the period prior to the separation) Belial shall be let loose against Israel, as God spake through Isaiah the prophet, the son of Amos, saying: "Fear and the pit and the snare are upon thee, O inhabitant of the land." This means the three nets

[1] Or 'Stand upon his watch tower', as Rabin reads.
[2] *D.D.* vi. 4-8.
[3] This may afford a clue to the date of the founding of the Qumran settlement. Fragments of a *Micah Commentary* were found in Cave 1.

of Belial, concerning which Levi the son of Jacob spake, by which he caught Israel and directed their faces to three kinds of wickedness. The first is fornication, the second is riches, the third is pollution of the Sanctuary. He who cometh up from this shall be caught by that, and he that escapeth from this shall be caught by that.'[1]

The situation is perfectly intelligible, for we have parallels in kindred documents. These things are written of the decadent days of the Maccabean priesthood, from the time of Alexander Jannaeus onwards. Two examples will suffice.

> In the secret places of the earth were they doing evil; the son had connexion with the mother and the father with the daughter; and all of them committed adultery with their neighbours' wives . . . They were plundering the house of God's holiness, as if there were none to inherit and to deliver. And they were treading His Sanctuary in all their pollutions . . . and they left no sins which they did not commit, and even worse than the Gentiles.[2]
>
> The offerings of the Lord ye shall rob . . . And out of covetousness ye shall teach the commandments of the Lord; wedded women shall ye pollute, and with harlots and adulteresses shall ye be joined . . . And ye shall be puffed up because of your priesthood, lifting yourselves up against men, and not only so, but also against the commands of God; for ye shall contemn the holy things with jests and laughter.[3]

The next passage in the document[4] elaborates and explains the evils, and need not detain us. The period of Belial's machinations continues.

We now come to a particularly important section by the commentator or expounder of the testamentary document, which harks back to the first period of the Party's existence when the emigration took place. We have already given this in full, and associated the emigration with that described in Josephus as having taken place about 160–159 B.C.[5] For the sake of completeness, however, we will give the passage in the *Damascus Document* again, but without notes.

> And during the period of the destruction of the land there arose those who removed the landmark and led Israel astray. And the land became desolate because they spake rebellion against the commandments of God through Moses *and also through His holy Messiah*, and they prophesied a lie to turn away Israel from God.

---

[1] vi. 9–12.
[2] *Ps. Sol.* viii. 9–14.
[3] *Test. Levi.* xiv. 5–8.
[4] vii. 1–19.
[5] Above pp. 19–20.

But God remembered the covenant with the forefathers:
And He raised up from Aaron men of understanding,
And from Israel wise men:
And He made them to hearken,
And they digged the well.
'A well the princes digged,
The nobles of the people delved it
By the order of the Lawgiver.'

The well is the Law, and they who digged it are the penitents of Israel who went forth out of the land of Judah and sojourned in the land of Damascus, all of whom God called princes, for they sought Him and His glory was not turned back in the mouth of one of them. And the Lawgiver is the Student of the Law, in regard to whom Isaiah said, 'He bringeth forth an instrument for His work.' And the nobles of the people are those who came to dig the well by the precepts in which the Lawgiver ordained that they should walk throughout the full period of the wickedness. *And save them* (i.e., the precepts) *they shall obtain nothing until there arises the Teacher of Righteousness in the End of the Days.*[1]

Passing on to the next passage in our document (viii. 11-21) we find that this outlines the religious and ethical principles of the Party. During the period which they call 'the period of the wickedness', the period in which 'Belial is let loose upon Israel', their priests are to refrain from ministering in the Sanctuary, which has been profaned by evil courses. Those who have entered into the New Covenant are to do 'according to the true meaning (or explanation) of the Law until the end of the wickedness, to sever themselves from the children of the pit, and to hold aloof from the polluted wealth of wickedness under a vow and a curse, and from the wealth of the Sanctuary'. They are to 'make a difference between the clean and the unclean, and to make men discern between the holy and the profane; to observe the Sabbath according to its true meaning, and the Feasts and the day of the Fast (i.e., the Day of Atonement) according to the utterances of them who entered into the New Covenant in the land of Damascus'. They are 'to contribute their holy things according to the true interpretation; to love everyone his brother as himself, and to strengthen the hand of the poor and the needy and the stranger, and to seek every one the peace of his brother; to hold aloof from harlots according to the Law, and that no man commit a trespass against his next-of-kin; to rebuke every one his brother according to the commandment, and not to bear a grudge from day to day; and to separate from all the pollutions according to their judgment, and no man shall make abominable his holy spirit, according as God separated these from them. As for all who

[1] viii. 1-10.

walk in these things in the perfection of holiness according to all the ordinances, the covenant of God standeth fast unto them to preserve them for a thousand generations.'

For the rest of the first work contained in the *Damascus Document* we have fragments of a second version (B) which in part supplements and in part differs from (A), the text which we have quoted so far. The section is numbered Chapter ix by Charles, and largely deals with those who turned traitor or proved unfaithful to the New Covenant. These would receive their just deserts with the wicked at the time when God would bring a further visitation upon the land (ix. 2). Peculiar to (A) is an extraordinary piece of exegesis of *Amos* v. 26–27 (ix. 4–9), in which reference is again made to the 'Student of the Law, who came to Damascus, as it is written, "There shall go forth a star out of Jacob, etc. . . ." ' But the passage adds no additional historical information. According to (B) the time of retribution will be 'when the Messiah comes from Aaron and Israel'. Except in interpolated passages in (A) there is no reference to the Messiah in that version of the first document.

The text now continues with a passage, virtually identical in both versions, which compares the future fate of those who have entered into the New Covenant, but have proved unfaithful to their undertakings, to the wrath that came upon the former Hellenizers. The latter are described in a poetic passage, which may come from the testamentary document, and which concludes:

> And they cast off restraint with a high hand
> To walk in the way of the wicked, of whom God said:
> 'Their wine is the poison of dragons
> And the cruel venom of asps.'[1]

> The dragons are the kings of the Gentiles and the wine is their ways, and the venom of asps is the head of the kings of Javan (i.e., Antiochus Epiphanes), who came to execute vengeance upon them.
> But despite all these things they who builded the wall and daubed it with untempered mortar[2] perceived not [for one who walked in the spirit of falsehood and prophesied lies prophesied unto them][3] that the wrath of God was kindled against all His congregation; nor that Moses said, 'Not for thy righteousness, nor for the uprightness of thy heart, dost thou go in to inherit these nations, but because He loved thy fathers and because He would keep the oath', as in the case of the penitents of Israel who turned aside from the (evil) way of the people. Because of the love of God for the forefathers who stirred up the people to follow Him, He loved them that came after them; for theirs is the covenant of the fathers.

[1] *Deut.* xxxii. 33.
[2] Cp. *Ezek.* xiii. 10–15; xxii. 28.
[3] The interpolated words based on *Mic.* ii. 11 are corrupt in both versions owing to the uncertainty of the copyist. (B) thought they had something to do with the wind and shower of *Ezek.* xiii. 11, which overthrew the wall.

But since He hated the builders of the wall His wrath was kindled against them. And such will be the case of all who reject the commandments of God, and forsake them and turn away in the stubbornness of their heart. (B) So are all the men who entered into the New Covenant in the land of Damascus and yet turned backward and acted treacherously and departed from the spring of living waters. They shall not be reckoned in the assembly of the people, and in its register they shall not be written, from the day when there was gathered in the Unique Teacher until there shall arise the Messiah from Aaron and Israel.[1]

So much space is devoted to denouncing those who apostasized that there must have been a considerable secession from the New Covenant Party. It is perhaps to be inferred that this took place, or at least began to take place, after the death of the Student of the Law who laid down the precepts, summarised in viii. 11-21. A number of the Covenanters deserted. It does not follow because they are castigated so unmercifully that they were bad people. We do not have their version of why they left. Our document, however, in a further passage in (B), suggests opposition to the tenets of the sect:

They have no share in the House of the Law. With a judgment like unto that of their neighbours who turned away with the scornful men they shall be judged. For they spake error against the statutes of righteousness, and rejected the covenant and the pledge of faith which they had affirmed in the land of Damascus; and this is the New Covenant. And there shall not be unto them nor unto their families a share in the House of the Law.[2]

Here we may note, by way of contrast, what is said in the *Habakkuk Commentary* of the loyal Covenanters, 'the Men of Truth who practise the Law, whose hands never relax from the service of the Truth'. These men 'God will deliver from the House of Judgment, because of their tribulation, and their faith in the Righteous Teacher'.

Those who broke away were expunged from the register of the Community. Their names were thus blotted out of the earthly counterpart of the heavenly Book of Life. The register was apparently started after the death of the Unique Teacher — the Teacher of Righteousness, who is mentioned again in the continuation of our document preserved only in (B).

And from the day when there was gathered in the Unique Teacher until all the men of war were consumed who walked with the Man of Lies about forty years (elapsed) [and during this period there shall be kindled the wrath of God against Israel, as He said: 'there is no king and no prince' and no judge, and none that rebuketh in righteousness][3] and those who

[1] ix. 10-29.   [2] ix. 35-38.

[3] This is an obvious interpolation which breaks into the sentence with a needless parenthesis.

repented of transgression in Jacob observed the covenant of God. Then they spake each man to his fellow to strengthen one another: 'Let our steps hold fast to the way of God.' And God hearkened to their words and heard, and a book of remembrance was written before Him for them that feared God and thought upon His Name [until salvation and righteousness be revealed for them that fear God. Then shall ye return and discern between the righteous and wicked, between him that serveth God and him that serveth Him not.][1] And He showeth mercy unto thousands of them that love Him and keep His commandments for a thousand generations (as He did unto those) from the house of Peleg that went forth from the Holy City. And they trusted in God throughout the period that Israel trespassed and polluted the Sanctuary and returned again to molten images.[2] The people with few words shall all be judged, each according to his spirit in the holy council. And as for all those who have broken down the landmark of the Law amongst those who have entered into the covenant, when there shall shine forth the glory of God to Israel they shall be cut off from the midst of the camp with all those of Judah who do wickedly in the days of its testing.

But all they who hold fast by these judgments in going out and coming in according to the Law, and listen to the voice of the Teacher and confess before God saying,

> We have done wickedly, we and our fathers,
> Because we have walked contrary to the statutes of the covenant,
> And true is Thy judgment against us,

and who lift not the hand against His holy statutes, His righteous judgment, and the testimony of His truth; and are chastised by the first judgments with which the children of the men of the Party were judged; and give ear to the voice of the Teacher of Righteousness, and reject not the statutes of righteousness when they hear them:

> They shall rejoice and be glad,
> And their heart shall exult,
> And they shall make themselves strong against all the [children of the world;
> And God will pardon them
> And they shall see His salvation;
> For they trust in His holy Name.[3]

Here we reach what seems to be the end of the first document. The chapters that come after this (x-xx) in (A) only, represent fragments of a second document, a book of instructions for the Community related to the *Manual of Discipline*. With this work we are not at present concerned.

We must now consider the evidence of what is contained in this last passage, together with what has been said previously about the Unique Teacher.

[1] I have doubtfully regarded these words as an interpolation. After the inserted words the quotation from *Mal.* iii. 16 is completed.

[2] Or (Rabin) 'but They returned to God'.

[3] ix. 39-54.

There has been no further reference to the Student of the Law, so that there is some uncertainty as to whether he should be indentified with the Unique Teacher of Righteousness from whom the Party drew its inspiration. If they are the same it means that the Teacher died in exile,[1] and not as a martyr prior to the migration to the land of Damascus. If they are different persons the Student of the Law will be the Teacher's successor, who carried on his work. The Party would then have had its organic beginning after the death of the Teacher (his gathering in), rather in the way the Christian Church had its organic beginning after the death of Christ. Assuming that we are correct on the basis of the passage in Josephus in dating the emigration of the Penitents of Israel about 160-159 B.C., the Teacher of Righteousness may well have appeared fifteen years earlier. There is nothing discoverable in the *Damascus Document* which would place the Teacher of Righteousness at any time later than the beginning of the Maccabean Age. We are only told that either this same Teacher would return, or more probably another final Teacher of Righteousness would arise at the End of the Days.

Reviewing our information derived from the *Damascus Document* the sequence of events is now fairly clear and straightforward. About the beginning of the second century B.C. a number of priests and laymen in Israel became conscious of their guilt in tolerating the flagrant departures from the Law for which the Hellenizers were responsible. For twenty years these repentant ones were groping after the way, until (c. 176 B.C.) God raised up for them a Teacher of Righteousness. The repentant ones listened to him and became his followers. This was during the time of wrath and tribulation in which the instrument of Divine judgment was Antiochus Epiphanes. After the death of Judas Maccabaeus the Teacher's followers under their leader emigrated from Jerusalem to the land of Damascus. This may have happened about 160 B.C. In their place of voluntary exile they became organized into a distinct community and entered into the New Covenant. This meant that they undertook to observe the Old Covenant in accordance with the statutes and precepts drawn up by the Student of the Law. A register was started of those who entered the Covenant, and all went well for a period of about forty years from the death of the Teacher of Righteousness.[2] The first emigrants, termed in exegesis 'the Priests', were later joined by others, similarly termed 'the Levites'. By this time the Teacher of Righteousness and (or) Student of the Law

---

[1] In the *Habakkuk Commentary* there is a reference to an attempt by the one called the Wicked Priest on the life of the Teacher 'in his place of exile'.

[2] The remark about the 'men of war' is a reference to *Deut.* ii. 14, the rebellious generation of the 40 years in the wilderness, and does not mean that the Man of Lies had an army. See also *Ezek.* iv. 5.

must have been dead for some years, and this fact, plus the adherence of newcomers, brought about a change. The situation is easy to imagine from the history of the early Church. There were schisms. Many left the Community, though some returned contritely to their loyalty and were received back. Hard words are said about the seceders. The traitors were expelled, excommunicated, expunged from the register: they would get their deserts with the wicked in the Judgment. All this time — 'the period of the wickedness' — Israel was being subjected to the onslaughts of Belial.

The further story of the New Covenanters speaks of wanderings, trials and vicissitudes, but also of growth and expansion and a developed organization. They held themselves to be the Elect of the Last Days, the true 'Sons of Zadok'. Of the structure of the Party of the Covenant we learn much more from the fragments of the second work contained in the *Damascus Document*, and especially in detail from the *Manual of Discipline*. Actually the Confession in our last quoted passage is taken from the *Manual*, where it has to be recited by all candidates for entrance into the Party as part of an elaborate ceremonial. Two kinds of domicile are described in our records, those who are settled in camps and those who dwell in the cities of Israel. The Party therefore had taken up its activities once more in the land of Israel, and was endeavouring to exert a widespread influence 'so that the whole nation (of Israel) may walk in them (the statutes) according to the Law always' (*Damasc. Doc.* xv. 2). During this time the priests of the Party would not participate in the Temple ritual, since the Sanctuary was for them polluted by the evil ways of the priesthood and the abominations committed by the later Maccabean priest-kings. As the 'house of Peleg', they contracted out, and separated from Judah.

The *Manual* shows us that the chief centre of the Party in the End of the Days was in the wilderness, no doubt at Khirbet Qumran, 'to prepare the way of the Lord and make straight His paths', thus linking on to the proclamation in the wilderness made by John the Baptist, whom scholars have suggested was brought up by them. The rules of the Party were very similar to those of the Essenes of the same area, and they have even been identified with those known under that name. The elaborate regulations and organization must obviously have required a considerable time to be worked out and applied, and this, taken together with the reference to many generations, numbers of afflictions, and years of sojournings, argues a fairly lengthy history, perhaps a century and a half altogether from the date of the original emigration to the land of Damascus, bringing the story down to the time called 'the End of the Days', the time when the commentator on the testamentary document was himself living and writing.

CHAPTER SIX

The End of the Days

THE OUTLINE of events presented at the close of the last chapter must be taken as no more than a rough guide. There are several uncertain elements in it. But the *Damascus Document* in conjunction with other sources of information supports the general picture we have given on the literary side. We have first of all the period of the original Teacher of Righteousness, assuming on evidence to be given later that the authorship of some works is to be credited to him. This period terminated not long after the commencement of the Maccabean revolt. The second period is represented by the testamentary document incorporated in the first work contained in the *Damascus Document*. We have seen that the production of such testamentary literature was a feature of the period extending approximately from 120-70 B.C. The third period is that of the commentator on *Test. Damasc.* His work is distinguished by a novel kind of exegesis, and is dated in the time called the End of the Days. It therefore becomes vitally important to discover when this period was believed to have commenced. Obviously it was late enough for *Test. Damasc.*, the *Book of Jubilees* and the *Test. XII Patriarchs* to have acquired an authoritative status for the commentator, and this cannot have been much before 30 B.C. The peculiar kind of exegesis seems to be without early parallel, but it is found in the *Habakkuk* and other commentaries from Qumran, and these works also must therefore have been written during the End of the Days. It would be rather late in the Time of the End, for the author of the *Habakkuk Commentary* holds the period to have been prolonged beyond what had been anticipated. We have further to note that even in the commentator's work in the *Damasc. Doc.* there are a few interpolations by some later hand. To the extent outlined we may thus hold the literary evidence to confirm the lengthy history of the New Covenant Party from an original initiative around 175 B.C. down to some time in the first century A.D.

Before we turn to the question of the time called the End of the Days it will be profitable here to glance at the archaeological evidence. According to Father de Vaux, who has played a leading part in excavating the buildings at Khirbet Qumran and investigating the contents of the neighbouring caves, the occupation of the site by its Community must have begun about or a little before 100 B.C. and lasted until about 66-70 A.D. Referring to Father de Vaux's opinion, Prof. Dupont-Sommer concludes[1] that the building, which was found to have been burnt down, was probably destroyed by the Romans during the Jewish War. Many coins have come to light, a few from the time of John Hyrcanus, about 30 of Alexander Jannaeus, some of the later Hasmoneans and of Herod the Great, and a considerable number of the Roman procurators up to 66-70 A.D. There have also been found some Roman coins bearing the inscription *Judea Capta*, and a small group of Jewish coins of the Second Revolt (132-135 A.D.). After the destruction by fire Dupont-Sommer suggests that the site may have been occupied by a Roman military post for a time, which would account for the *Judea Capta* coins. The discovery of some small buildings put up on the old site is regarded by Father de Vaux as indicating a short period of further occupation probably by guerillas of the forces of Bar Kochba, leader of the Second Revolt.

The numismatic finds, so far as they can be used to throw light on the circumstances, indicate a period of intense activity in the sixty years preceding the Jewish War. This was the period that saw the birth of Christianity, a time of great ferment and Messianic expectation, regarded as belonging to the Last Days. We can see this not only from the New Testament, but also from the *Assumption of Moses* written between 7 A.D. and 25 A.D.[2] We judge this activity to be natural in the prevailing conditions in any case, but also by the considerable number of coins of the procurators which have been recovered compared with the number from Hyrcanus to Herod the Great. As regards the end of the settlement it is by no means certain that the site was abandoned by the Community between 66-70 A.D. The forces of Vespasian reached Jericho about the end of May, 68 A.D.,[3] but were then withdrawn except for a garrison to guard that approach to Jerusalem. In 70 A.D. Titus sent the 10th Legion to advance on Jerusalem via Jericho up the Jerusalem-Jericho road.[4] At neither time is it likely that the Romans would have gone

[1] *The Jewish Sect of Qumran and the Essenes*, p.167ff.

[2] The last historical event dealt with in *Assumpt. Mos.* is the suppression of the outbreak at Jerusalem by Varus in 4 B.C., though there is an inference that Archelaus, Herod's successor, had ceased to rule Judea (6 A.D.). Immediately after the reference to Varus we read: 'And when this is done the times will be ended, in a moment . . . the four hours will come' (the four watches of the last night?), vii.1.

[3] Jos. *Wars*, IV. viii. 1.

[4] *Wars*, V. i. 6; ii. 3.

out of their way into the desert around Khirbet Qumran. It is much more probable that the settlement was destroyed when the forces under Flavius Silva were cleaning up the area west of the Dead Sea and attacking the last Jewish stronghold at Masada in the spring of 73 A.D.[1] The *Judea Capta* coins could be expected to be used in a Roman encampment around 73-74 A.D., and a camp in such a spot would only have existed to deal with the remnants of Jewish resistance. Our *terminus ad quem*, therefore, may well be 72 A.D. rather than 66-70. This would mean that books could have been written in the settlement at least as late as 69 or 70, a consideration which certainly has a bearing on the interpretation of the *Habakkuk Commentary* with its reference to the 'last priests of Jerusalem.' But it is not to be excluded that the Qumran sect resumed occupation a few years after the war.[2]

We come now to the question of the End of the Days. In this connexion we have just seen that the *Assumption of Moses* regards this time as having been reached at the very close of the first century B.C. In the New Testament the preaching of John the Baptist was in the same conviction, and *Matthew* appears to date the commencement of the Baptist's ministry in the reign of Archelaus (4 B.C.-6 A.D.).[3] When Jesus was baptised he declared, 'The time is up, and the Kingdom of God is at hand.'[4] The time of the End of the Days was therefore held to have commenced about the turn of the century from which the Christian Era is dated, and it was expected that at this time the Messiah would appear. How long the time of the End of the Days would last, and when the final Consummation would come, is the subject of the Little Apocalypse in *Matthew* xxiv and parallels. It is also dealt with in the *Apocalypse of Baruch* and that of *Ezra*, where, as in the New Testament and the *Habakkuk Commentary*, it is evident that the End had been delayed considerably beyond what had been anticipated. This consciousness of delay in works dating from the second half of the first century A.D. is itself a confirmation that the time of the End of the Days was held to have begun much earlier and by rights should already have concluded.

What gave rise to these convictions? Assuredly it was calculations based on the Book of *Daniel*, the prophet who had been told 'thou shalt rest, and stand in thy lot at the End of the Days.' It was the prophecy of the Seventy Weeks, assumed to mean 490 years (*Dan.* ix. 24-27), that influenced the calculators of the Time of the End.[5] As Josephus says, Daniel 'did not only

[1] *Wars*, VII. viii. 1.

[2] Teicher holds that both archaeological and literary evidence confirms that the Community was in occupation of the settlement in the second century A.D.

[3] *Matt.* ii. 22-iii. 2.

[4] *Mk.* i. 15.

[5] *Test. Levi*, xvi. 1-5.

prophesy of future events, as did the other prophets, but he also determined the time of their accomplishment.'[1]

While we cannot know how the New Covenant Party worked out their timetable we can see that by the usual reckoning, which dates the return from the Babylonian Exile about 536 B.C., 490 years would end at 46 B.C. If the commencement of the Exile is dated at 586 B.C. and seventy years are deducted for the Captivity, and then the 490 years, the terminal date will be 26 B.C. So that writers of the period would not have been far off the mark if they believed the Time of the End to have been reached towards the end of the first century B.C. We can thus understand why Messianic expectation should have been rife at this period, and why Herod the Great—as some think—himself had Messianic pretensions.

An interesting sidelight on the situation is afforded by a passage in the Slavonic version of Josephus's *Jewish War*. It is printed in the Appendix to Thackeray's translation in the Loeb Classical Library.[2] Part of the passage, inserted in Book I of the *Jewish War*, reads as follows:

> But Herod spent little (time) in Jerusalem, and marched against the Arabs. At that time the priests mourned and grieved one to another in secret. They durst not (do so openly for fear of) Herod and his friends.
>
> For (one Jonathan) spake: 'The law bids us have no foreigner for king. Yet we wait for the Anointed, the meek one, of David's line. But of Herod we know that he is an Arabian, uncircumcised. The Anointed will be called meek, but this (is) he who has filled our whole land with blood. Under the Anointed it was ordained for the lame to walk, and the blind to see, (and) the poor to become rich. But under this man the hale have become lame, the seeing are blinded, the rich have become beggars. What is this? or how? Have the prophets lied? The prophets have written that there shall not want a ruler from Judah, until he comes unto whom it is given up; for him do the Gentiles hope. But is this man the hope for the Gentiles? For we hate his misdeeds. Will the Gentiles perchance set their hopes on him? Woe unto us, because God has forsaken us, and we are forgotten of him! And he will give us over to desolation and to destruction. Not as under Nebuchadnezzar and Antiochus (is it). For then were the prophets teachers also of the people, and they made promises concerning the captivity and the return. And now—neither is there any whom one could ask, nor any with whom one could find comfort.'
>
> But Ananus the priest answered and spake to them: 'I know all books. When Herod fought beneath the city wall, I had never a thought that God would permit him to rule over us. But now I understand that our desolation is nigh. And bethink you of the prophecy of Daniel; for he writes that after the return the city of Jerusalem shall stand for seventy

[1] *Antiq.* X. xi. 7.
[2] Josephus, Vol. III, pp. 636–8.

weeks of years, which are 490 years, and after these shall it be desolate.' And when they had counted the years, (they) were thirty years and four. But Jonathan answered and spake: 'The numbers of the years are even as we have said. But the Holy of Holies, where is he? For this Herod he (*sc.* the prophet) cannot call the Holy one—(him) the blood-thirsty and impure.'

The historical value of this passage is very questionable. Yet it does communicate something of the atmosphere of the period, and illustrates how the Daniel prophecy was regarded in informed circles in the reign of Herod. The debate, as is pointed out in the notes on the passage, is supposed to have taken place in 32 B.C., and if the 490 years were then considered to have thirty-four years to run, the terminal date would have been 3 A.D.

At any rate we cannot be very far out if we conclude that the End of the Days was supposed to have begun about the turn of the century. This would mean that both the Commentary on *Test. Damasc.* and the *Habakkuk Commentary* were most likely written in the first century A.D.

Before the end of the term of the Daniel prophecy a Holy of Holies was to be anointed, and this expression was certainly understood later to mean the Messiah, as in the passage quoted. In the *Damascus Document* (viii. 2) similarly we find the words 'His holy anointed one' or 'holy Messiah.'

This leads us to examine the references to the Messiah in the *Damascus Document*, as these have a definite bearing on the question of date. The references in text (B) in *Test. Damasc.* differ from those in (A). In the former they are clearly part of the commentator's work, and their peculiarity is that the Messiah is expected to come 'from Aaron and Israel'. His coming is still future, and he is clearly distinguished from the Unique Teacher. There are two references which we shall now quote.

And 'they that give heed unto Him are the poor of the flock.' These shall escape during the period of the visitation, but the rest shall be handed over to the sword when the Messiah comes from Aaron and Israel (B. ix. 10).

(The apostates from the Party) shall not be reckoned in the assembly of the people, and in its register they shall not be written from the day when there was gathered in the Unique Teacher until there shall arise the Messiah from Aaron and from Israel (B. ix. 29).

We may recognise this Messianic doctrine as the true reflection of the commentator's position, for it is supported by the (A) text of the second work in the *Damascus Document*, which is related to the *Manual of Discipline*. Here also (xv. 4; xviii. 8) the Messiah is expected from Aaron and Israel. This hope is not unlike that of the *Testaments of the XII Patriarchs*,[1] where

[1] *Test.Levi*, xviii.3; *Test.Judah*,xxiv.1.

the Messiah is expected from Levi and Jacob, a priestly Messiah from Israel based on the Star prophecy of *Num.* xxiv. 17. It does not have to be assumed that the commentator thought of the Messiah as having one parent from the priests and the other from the laity. The Messiah is the anointed Holy of Holies of the Daniel prophecy, the last Messianic high-priest as Eisler suggests, and he points to the Hebrew of *I Chron.* xxiii. 13 where it is stated (literally): 'Aaron was set aside for a holy one of holies.'

In the (A) text of the Commentary, however, the references to the Messiah seem to be interpolated, and to indicate that he had already come and his name was known.

> Yet in all of them (i.e., their generations) He raised up special men, in order to leave a remnant to the earth, and to fill the face of the earth with their seed: [and through His Messiah He shall make them know His holy Spirit; and he is true, and in the explanation of his name are their names] but them He hated He made to go astray! (A. ii. 9-10).

> And the land became desolate because they spake rebellion against the commandments of God through Moses, [and also through His holy Messiah] and they prophesied a lie to turn away Israel from God (A. viii. 2).

The words within square brackets are not only unwarranted additions: they look like Judaeo-Christian additions.[1]

Evidently there was some relationship between the name borne by the Messiah, whoever he was supposed to have been, and that of his followers.

There is one other passage in (A) to which it is necessary to refer again.

> And the nobles of the people are those who came to dig the well by the precepts in which the Lawgiver ordained that they should walk throughout the full period of the wickedness. [And save them (i.e., the precepts) they shall acquire nothing until there arises the Teacher of Righteousness in the end of the Days] (A. viii. 9-10).

I have with some hesitation regarded the bracketed words as an interpolation. They may be treated as part of the commentator's text and associated with the passage quoted from (B) 'until there shall arise the Messiah from Aaron and from Israel'. In this case the coming of the final Teacher of Righteousness is still future, and he is to be identified with the expected Priestly Messiah. On the other hand the words can bear the interpretation that this final Teacher of Righteousness has already come, so far as the writer is concerned, and has given out his precepts. If this is the implication we have to think again of the teaching of Jesus as the True Prophet of the *Clementine* literature, and of the declaration of Stephen in the *Acts*: 'Which of the prophets

[1] Rabin translates, 'His anointed ones' and 'the holy anointed ones,' making these words refer to the Prophets instead of the Messiah. This change to the plural seems to me doubtful.

have not your fathers persecuted? And they have slain them which shewed before of the coming of the Just One; of whom ye have been now the betrayers and murderers' (vii. 52). However, there is no indication in any passage in the *Damascus Document* that the Messiah has been martyred, as there is in the Christian interpolations in *Test. XII Patr.* The evidence is inconclusive; but we may at least regard it as probable, first that additions were made to the (A) text after the advent of the one believed to be the Messiah, and the second that this Messiah was equated with the final Teacher of Righteousness.

It is difficult to see how any Gentile Christian interpolations could have got into this Hebrew document. But as we have pointed out, they might be Judaeo-Christian, or even Baptist. On this point we must obviously reserve judgment until we have studied other available material, especially the *Habakkuk Commentary*.

We have, nevertheless, moved forward in our investigation by looking into the question of the Time of the End. We can with reasonable certainty date the Commentary on *Test. Damasc.* in the first quarter of the first century A.D. or a little after, and the *Habakkuk Commentary*, since in this work the End is held to have been considerably delayed, as written rather later, but not much later than 70 A.D.

We have also shown that two Teachers of Righteousness have to be distinguished, the first having died not much later than the middle of the second century B.C., while the second—perhaps identified with the Messiah—was possibly held to have come already in some unspecified person when the *Habakkuk Commentary* was written and the Damascus Commentary was interpolated. It will therefore be most likely that it is this Ultimate Teacher who is the subject of the *Habakkuk Commentary*. This distinction is obviously important, because if the second Teacher is confused with the first we shall get the facts so mixed that conclusions arrived at would be bound to be wide of the mark. We may admit some likeness of the second Teacher to the first in certain features; for these would help to determine that he was the one expected. But this is not the same thing as regarding them as one and the same individual. We may also be able from what we learn of the second Teacher to deduce certain things about the first. One way in which we can look both forward and backward is to consider the subject of the Messiah as Priest. But before we do this it will be well, in confirmation of the view expressed as to the relative lateness of the Commentary material, to interject first an examination of the unusual exegesis employed in it, and next some pertinent material relating to the Men of the Caves.

CHAPTER SEVEN

Clues from Isaiah

THE STUDY of the fulfilment of prophecy only began so far as we can judge after the final redaction of the books of the Old Testament Prophets. One of the earliest references would appear to be that in *Dan.* ix. 2: 'I Daniel understood by books the number of the years, whereof the word of the Lord came to Jeremiah the prophet, that He would accomplish seventy years in the desolation of Jerusalem.' It was apparently the persecution under Antiochus Epiphanes that gave an impetus to, if it did not in fact originate such study. We have a more developed example in *I Macc.* in the reference to the slaughter of Chasidim by the High-Priest Alcimus: 'And he laid hands on three-score men of them, and slew them in one day, according to the word which he wrote (*Ps.* lxxix. 2-3), "The flesh of thy saints (did they cast out) and their blood did they shed round about Jerusalem; and there was no man to bury them."' This type of fulfilment is of the same order as that which we find subsequently in the New Testament in relation to John the Baptist (*Mk.* i. 2-4) and Jesus (*Matt.* i-ii). In its way it is quite straightforward. The same kind of interpretation is also found in the *Damascus Document*, vi. 9-10: 'And during all these years Belial shall be let loose against Israel, as God spake through Isaiah the prophet, the son of Amos, saying: "Fear and the pit and the snare are upon thee, O inhabitant of the land" (*Isa.* xxiv. 17). This means the three nets of Belial, concerning which Levi the son of Jacob spake, by which he caught Israel and directed their faces to three kinds of wickedness.'

But the *Damascus Document* and the *Habakkuk Commentary* present us with a much more intricate kind of prophetic exegesis, which must have required a considerable time to develop, and of which no written examples are extant before the first century A.D. As throwing light on this type of exegesis Dupont-Sommer quotes Philo[1] on the practice of the Essenes on the sabbath days:

[1] *Every Good Man is Free*, 82. I have quoted from Colson's translation, except the last three words, rather than from Dupont-Sommer, *The Dead Sea Scrolls*, pp. 26.

'They sit decorously as befits the occasion with attentive ears. Then one takes the books and reads aloud and another of especial proficiency comes forward and expounds what is not understood. For most of their philosophical study takes the form of allegory (*dia symbolon*), and in this they emulate an ancient method.' The last sentence is somewhat obscure; but the passage seems to relate to midrashic teaching as practised by the Scribes (*Soferim*) and is not sufficiently specific to be applied to the interpretations found in our documents.

The whole of the *Habakkuk Commentary* consists of this curious kind of prophetic exegesis, and from the fragments of comments on other Biblical books found at Qumran it is evident that the method was systematically employed. For our purposes, therefore, one example from the *Hab. Comm.* will at present suffice.

> 'For the violence inflicted on Lebanon shall return upon thee, and the oppression exercised against the cattle shall fan (the flame), because of the human blood which has been shed and the violence which has been inflicted on the country, on the city, and on all that dwell therein' (*Habb.* ii. 17). This passage refers to the Wicked Priest, to reward him for the recompense he has repaid to the Poor; for 'Lebanon' is the Party of the Community, and 'the cattle' are the simple of Judah who practice the Law. And God shall condemn him to destruction, even as he purposed to destroy the poor. And when it is said, 'because of the blood shed in the city and the violence inflicted on the country,' 'the city' refers to Jerusalem, in which the Wicked Priest has done abominable deeds and has profaned the Sanctuary. As to 'violence inflicted on the country,' (*the country* means the towns of Judah in which he robbed the Poor of their substance).

The Commentary in the *Damascus Document* contains the same kind of exegesis, of which three specimens may be quoted.

> On *Ezek.* xliv. 15. ' "The priests and the Levites and the sons of Zadok, that kept the charge of My Sanctuary when the children of Israel went astray from them, they shall bring near unto Me fat and blood." "The Priests" are the penitents of Israel who went forth out of the land of Judah, and "the Levites" are they who joined them. And "the Sons of Zadok" are the Elect of Israel called by name that arise in the End of the Days. Behold the statement of their names according to their generations, and the period of their office, and the number of their afflictions, and the years of their sojournings, and the statement of their works' (v. 7-vi. 3).

> On *Num.* xxi. 17. ' "A well the princes digged, the nobles of the people delved it, by the order of the Lawgiver." "The well" is the Law, and they who digged it are the penitents of Israel who went forth out of the land of Judah and sojourned in the land of Damascus, all of whom God called princes; for they sought Him, and His glory was not turned back in the mouth of one of them. And the "Lawgiver" is the Student of the Law, in regard to whom Isaiah said, "He bringeth forth an

instrument for His work" (*Isa.* liv. 16). And "the nobles of the people" are those who came to dig the well by the precepts in the which the Lawgiver ordained that they should walk throughout the full period of the wickedness. And save them they shall acquire nothing until there arises the Teacher of Righteousness in the End of the Days' (viii. 5-10). There shall come to pass the word which is written in the sayings of Isaiah the son of Amos the Prophet, who said, 'He will bring upon thee and upon thy people and upon thy father's house days that have (not) come from the day that Ephraim departed from Judah' (*Isa.* vii. 17). When the two houses of Israel separated, all who proved faithless were delivered to the sword, but those who held fast escaped into the land of the North, as He said, 'And I will cause to go into exile Siccuth your king and Chiun your images, (the star of your god which ye made for yourselves,[1]) beyond Damascus' (*Amos.* v. 26-27). The books of the Law are the tabernacle (*succath*) of the king, as He said, 'And I will raise up the tabernacle of David that is fallen' (*Amos* ix. 11). 'The king' is the (prince of all the)[2] congregation, and 'Chiun the images' are the books of the Prophets, whose words Israel has despised. And 'the Star' is the Student of the Law, who came to Damascus, as it is written, 'There shall go forth a star out of Jacob, and a sceptre shall rise out of Israel' (*Num.* xxiv. 17). 'The Sceptre' is the prince of all the congregation. And when he arises 'he shall destroy all the sons of Seth (or din)' (A. ix. 3-10).

There are traces of this type of exegesis in the New Testament. For instance, in the *Acts* (xv. 15-18), James the brother of Jesus gives his verdict on the conversion of Gentiles in these terms: 'With this the words of the Prophets are in agreement, as it is written, "After this I will return, and re-erect the fallen tabernacle of David, and re-erect the ruins thereof, and set it up again, that the remnant of men may seek after the Lord, and all the Gentiles upon whom My Name is called, saith the Lord who doeth this." '

The quotation from *Amos* ix. 11-12 does not here agree exactly either with the Massoretic text or the Septuagint, though the latter gives the same reading of Adam (men) for Edom in the phrase 'the remnant of men'. The variant is interesting because the Jews often spoke of Rome as Edom in later times, and in the *Habakkuk Commentary* the author identifies 'the remnant of the people' (*Hab.* ii. 8) with the Kittim, who for him are the Romans. Possibly James is making the same identification.

There is another example of such exegesis in *Galatians* iv. 22-26. Paul argues: 'It is written, that Abraham had two sons, the one by a bondmaid, the other by a freewoman . . . which things are an allegory: for these (women) are the two covenants; the one from Mount Sinai, which gendereth to bondage, which is Hagar. For this Hagar is Mount Sinai in Arabia, and

[1] These words are omitted in the manuscript.
[2] This emendation is proposed by Rabin.

answereth to Jerusalem which now is, and is in bondage with her children But Jerusalem which is above is free, which is the mother of us all.'[1]

Since there does not now on palaeographical or archaeological grounds appear to be any justification for dating any of the material relating to the New Covenant Party which has been recovered much later than 70 A.D. we shall be fairly safe in assuming that the peculiar exegesis of the Commentaries came into vogue between 30 B.C. and 70 A.D. This is the approximate date we have assigned to them for other reasons. The intense interest in the prophetic books due to the belief that the Time of the End had been reached would have encouraged a searching of the Scriptures to an unprecedented extent and produced an almost feverish exegetical activity. Whatever had been written of old under inspiration would be held to relate to contemporary persons and events of the crucial period. It is clear from the *Habakkuk Commentary* that its author is not dealing with circumstances of long ago in his application of the Prophet's message. The life of the Teacher of Righteousness of whom he speaks is as present and as vivid to him as say the life of Jesus to the writers of the first Gospels.

Some evidence of this feverish exegetical activity is provided by the host of fragments of Biblical works which has come to light, and we have to remember that these present discoveries are not the first. Teicher[2] has rightly drawn attention to a letter written in 819 A.D. by Timotheus, Metropolitan of Seleucia, in which he relates 'that Jews from Jerusalem, seeking admission to the Church, had told him that, about ten years before (i.e., at the beginning of the ninth century), a cave was discovered near Jericho containing a hoard of Hebrew manuscripts of the Bible and other writings, and that these manuscripts were taken by Jews to Jerusalem'. Among these scrolls were no less than two hundred psalms, called by Timotheus 'Psalms of David'. We also know of a similar discovery of manuscripts in this region in the third century, as reported by Origen.

However the association originated, it is now well established by the researches of scholars working on the material, that the literature of the New Covenant Community formed at least part of the heritage into which Christianity entered. The early Church was as concerned with prophetic

---

[1] A related allegorical method was employed by Philo of Alexandria to bring out what he conceived to be the inner meaning of the Biblical names. 'Let no sane man suppose that we have here in the pages of the wise legislator (Moses) an historical pedigree. What we have is a revelation through symbols of facts which may be profitable to the soul. And if we translate the names into our own tongue (i.e. Greek), we shall recognize that what is here promised is actually the case' (Philo, *The Preliminary Studies*, 44).

[2] *Journal of Jewish Studies*, Vol. II, No. 2, p. 89f. Otto Eissfeldt was the first to point out the importance of this letter in *Theologische Literaturzeitung*, Oct., 1949.

fulfilment in the Time of the End, and as relating to the Master and his enemies, as was the older Community.[1] This makes of particular importance two facts connected with the *Book of Isaiah.*

The first has to do with what we may call from its first purchaser the St. Mark's Monastery scroll of Isaiah found in Cave One. This work, as well as other scrolls,[2] was found to be marked, mainly in the margin, with a number of symbols. In the Isaiah MS. there are a dozen of these symbols, all different. Some of them look like letters of the Greek alphabet. One or two of them look like combinations of others. It is not in every case possible to determine which is the column and line of the text that is being marked, but it may well be that these symbols represent some kind of exegetical code. By way of experiment let us take first passages marked with one of the symbols, an X or Greek *chi*, and then some marked variously with other symbols.

In the first category we have the following:—

Isa. xxxii. 1, 'Behold, a king shall reign in righteousness, and princes shall rule in justice.'

xlii. 1, 'Behold, my servant, whom I uphold; my elect one, in whom my soul delighteth; I have put my spirit upon him, and he shall dispense judgment to the Gentiles.'

xlii. 6, 'I the Lord have called thee in righteousness, and will hold thine hand, and will keep thee, and give thee for a covenant of the people, for a light of the Gentiles.'

xlii. 21, 'The Lord is well-pleased for his righteousness' sake (or, for the sake of his righteous one); he will magnify the Law, and make it honourable.'

xliv. 28, 'That saith to Cyrus, thou art my shepherd, which shall perform all my pleasure: even saying to Jerusalem, Thou shalt be built; and to the Temple, Thy foundations shall be laid.'

xlix. 7, 'Thus saith the Lord God, thy redeemer O Israel, his holy one, to the despised of men, the abhorred of the nation, to the servant of rulers. Kings shall see and arise, princes also shall worship. . . .'

liv. 14, 'In righteousness shalt thou be established: thou shalt be far from oppression; for thou shalt not fear: and from terror; for it shall not come near thee.'

lv. 4, 'Behold, I have given him for a witness of the people, a leader and commander of the people.'

lvi. 1, 'Thus saith the Lord, Keep ye judgment, and do justice: for my salvation is near to come, and my righteousness to be revealed.'

---

[1] Cp. *Acts* iv. 25-28, where *Ps.* ii. 1-2 is applied to Herod, Pontius Pilate and the Gentiles, with the people of Israel, as persecutors of the Messiah Jesus.

[2] *The Manual of Discipline* 2 or 3 symbols, and the *Habakkuk Commentary* 1 symbol.

lviii. 13, 'If thou turn away thy foot from (going about on) the sabbath, from doing thy pleasure on my holy day; and call the sabbath a delight, the holy one of the Lord honourable; and shalt honour him. . . .'

lxvi. 5, 'Hear the word of the Lord, ye that tremble at his word; Your brethren that hated you, that cast you out for my name's sake, said, Let the Lord be glorified: but he shall appear to your joy, and they shall be ashamed.'

It is obvious that some of these passages are identical with those regarded as prophetic of Christ and Christianity. But they exactly reflect the Messianic expectations and the teaching of the New Covenant Party. We come now to some passages marked by other symbols.

Isa. vii.8, 'For the head of Syria is Damascus.'

viii. 16, 'Bind up the Testimony, seal the Law among my disciples.'

viii. 19, 'And when they shall say unto you, Seek unto them that have familiar spirits . . . should not a people seek unto their God?'

ix. 2, 'The people that walked in darkness have seen a great light.'

xi. 11, 'In that day the Lord shall set his hand again the second time to recover the remnant of his people . . .'

xxviii. 15, 'Because ye have said . . . we have made lies our refuge, and under falsehood have we hid ourselves.'

xxix. 13, 'Forasmuch as this people draw near me with their mouth . . . but have removed their heart far from me, and their fear towards me is taught by the precept of men.'

xxix. 21, 'That make a man an offender for a word.'

xxxiii. 1, 'And when thou shalt make an end to deal treacherously, they shall deal treacherously with thee.'

xl. ii, 'Speak ye comfortably to Jerusalem . . . that her warfare is accomplished, that her iniquity is pardoned.'

xliii. 14, ' . . . and the Chaldeans, whose cry is in the ships.'

xliv. 1, 'Yet now hear, O Jacob my servant; and Israel, whom I have chosen.'

xlv. 1, 'Thus saith the Lord to his anointed . . .'

xlviii. 20, 'Go ye forth of Babylon, flee ye from the Chaldeans.'

xlix. 5, 'Though Israel be not gathered, yet shall I be glorious.'

xlix. 8, 'In an acceptable time I have heard thee . . . and will give thee for a covenant of the nations.'

li. 7, 'Hearken unto me ye that know righteousness, the people in whose heart is my law; fear ye not the reproach of men.'

lii.7, 'How beautiful upon the mountains are the feet of him that bringeth good tidings.'

liii. 1, 'Who hath believed our report?'

liii. 5, 'But he was wounded for our transgressions, he was bruised for our iniquities.'[1]

---

[1] This passage is doubtful because of discoloration of the margin.

Among other passages we may note *Isa.* iii. 1; v. 30; vii. 20; viii. 8; xi. 15; xxi. 12 or 13; xxx. 1; xli. 1, 4, 16, 21; xlii. 12; xlv. 11; xlix. 1; lxi. 9; lxiii. 5; lxiv. 12 or lxv. 1; lxvi. 4.

Here again some of the passages were employed as proof texts by Christians as well as by the Qumran Community. In the case of certain of these texts, primed by the *Damascus Document* and the *Habakkuk Commentary*, we can almost write the explanation ourselves. We can see what would be held to refer to the Teacher of Righteousness and to the Wicked Priest, what to the Romans, or to the sojourn of the sect in the land of Damascus, what to the Elect Ones themselves. Perhaps it is with reference to such markings of the sacred books that Philo says of the Essenes that they expounded them 'by means of symbols'. If we are correct in suggesting that the signs have to do with prophetic exegesis we have an important piece of evidence relating to the last period of the Community's existence, where it appears to begin to link on to the Judaeo-Christians.

But the *Book of Isaiah* offers us a further link with the Nazarenes (the Judaeo-Christians). This is found in Jerome's *Commentary on Isaiah.* He claimed to have been in contact with the Nazarene Community at Aleppo in Syria, and in several places in this work he gives us the interpretation which the Nazarenes put on passages. He does not offer us exact quotations, and we must therefore exercise caution in considering the accuracy of what he states. But it is at least obvious that the Nazarenes employed the same method of exegesis as the Commentators of the New Covenant Community. It is also to be noted that out of six passages where Jerome gives the interpretation of the Nazarenes no less than four are identical with marked passages in the *Isaiah* scroll.

On *Isa.* viii. 14, 'A rock of offence to both houses of Israel.'

> The Nazarenes, who receive Christ but have not given up observing the old Law, interpret the two families of Shammai and Hillel, from whom sprang the Scribes and Pharisees, and of whom, they assert, Akiba, teacher of the proselyte Aquila, carried on the sect, and after him Meir, who succeeded Johanan ben Zaccai, and after him Eliezer (ben Hyrkanus), and after him Tarphon, and again Jose the Galilean, and so up to Joshua at the taking of Jerusalem (135 A.D.). Shammai and Hillel arose in Judea not long before the Lord was born, of whom the former they (the Nazarenes) interpret (by a wordplay) as 'Devastator' and the latter as 'Profane', because by their traditions and Mishnah (*Deuterosis*) they had defiled the ordinances of the Law.

On *Isa.* viii. 19, 'And when they say unto, Seek unto them that have familiar spirits, and unto wizards, etc.'

The Nazarenes explain this passage as follows: 'When the Scribes and

Pharisees say that you should hearken unto them, who do everything for their belly's sake, and who mutter in their incantations after the fashion of wizards in order to deceive you, answer them thus: It is no marvel that you follow your traditions; every nation consults its idols. We, therefore, need not consult you dead about the living things, for God has given us a magic of our own, the Law and Testimony of Scripture, which if you do not follow it you will never have the light, but the darkness will always oppress you as it passes over your land and your doctrine; as also those who are deceived by you will see themselves in error, suffering a hunger for the truth. Then shall they fret themselves and be angry and curse you, whom they thought of as gods and kings. And they shall look towards heaven and earth in vain, and shall abide in darkness and be unable to escape your insidiousness.'

On *Isa.* ix. 1-2, 'Zebulun and Naphtali . . . the people that walked in darkness.'

The Hebrews who believe in Christ interpret these passages as follows : 'Of old these two tribes of Zebulun and Naphtali were taken captive by the Assyrians and were led away into a strange country, and Galilee was deserted; but as the Prophet said, they should be relieved by him (Christ), who should bear the sins of the people.' Afterwards not only the two tribes, but the remnant who dwelt beyond Jordan and in Samaria, were likewise led away into captivity. And this they (the Nazarenes) affirm the Scripture to say: 'In the selfsame region whose population had been led captive and had started to serve the Babylonians, and which was first tormented by the darkness of error, that same land should be the first to see the light of the preaching of Christ.' And it was from thence that the Gospel was spread abroad to all the nations of the world.

On *Isa.* ix. 4, 'For thou has broken the yoke of his burden.'

The Nazarenes, whose opinions I have quoted above, endeavour to explain this passage as follows: 'At the coming of Christ and at his preaching they were illumined. The first region to be delivered from error was that of Zebulun and Naphtali, and the burdensome traditions of Judaism were lifted from their neck.'

On *Isa.* xxix. 20-21, 'That watch for iniquity . . . that make a man an offender for a word.'

The Nazarenes testify against the Scribes and Pharisees, wherein they fail through their Mishnah, who first deluded the people through their very bad traditions: they watched day and night in order to deceive the simple, and caused men to sin through (misrepresenting) the word of God, so that they should deny the Messiah.

On *Isa.* xxxi. 6-8, 'Turn ye unto him from whom the children of Israel have deeply revolted. For in that day every man shall cast away his idols. . . .'

The Nazarenes explain this passage as follows: 'O children of Israel, who by very evil counsel deny the Son of God, turn back to him and to his apostles; for if you do so you will cast away all idols which were formerly a sin to you, and the Devil shall fall down for you, not by your mighty men but by the mercy of God, and the young men who at one time fought for him (the Devil) shall be discomfited by the Church, and all his strongholds and rock shall pass away. Philosophy also, and all perverse doctrine shall turn its back at the sign of the Cross. This indeed is the mind of the Lord, that it should be so, whose fire and flame is in Zion and his brazier in Jerusalem.'

As we have said, allowance has to be made for some inaccuracy and interpreting on Jerome's part. But even so, there is a distinct likeness to the exegetical methods of the New Covenant Community. The preoccupations of the Nazarenes, as shown by their comments, are not the same. They are concerned with the Scribes and Pharisees, while the others are concerned with the Romans, the Wicked Priest, and the Teacher of Righteousness. If the Nazarene *Commentary on Isaiah* was a written one it probably dates from the end of the second century or beginning of the third. From about the same period may be dated the midrashic work *Sifre*, in which in one passage the maligned Rabbinists retorted in the same vein.

I will render vengeance to mine adversaries (*Deut.*xxxii.41), these are the Cuthim (Samaritans) . . . and 'I will recompense them that hate me,' these are the Minim (Sectaries); and thus God saith (*Ps.*cxxxix.21-22), 'Do I not hate them which hate thee, O Lord? I hate them with a perfect hatred; they have become mine enemies.[1]

At the very beginning of these studies we have given a small part of the considerable evidence that in the second and third century in Palestine there was extensive controversy and bitter hostility between the Nazarenes and Rabbinists, and here we have a reflection of it in the flinging of texts by one side against the other. We are not here so much concerned with these polemics, however, as with the exegetical methods revealed by this literature. I have not been able to find any justification from this viewpoint in dating the Commentary in the *Damascus Document*, and its fellow in interpretation the *Habakkuk Commentary*, any earlier than the first century A.D., the conclusion we have reached on other grounds.

The *Habakkuk Commentary* especially has to be dated as late as is practically possible, for in the time of its writer the sands should already have run out, as was felt by some of the New Testament writers (*II Tim.* ii; *II Pet.* iii;

[1] *Sifre*, 140a. Cp. also the employment of this method in the Targums and early Midrashim.

I Jn. ii. 18). The passage in *II Pet.* is particularly interesting because it seeks to explain the delay of the Second Advent of Christ and the Consummation of the Age. Believers were disturbed by this delay, which is alluded to elsewhere in the parable of the faithful servant (*Matt.* xxiv. 48). 'Peter' urges that the delay is due to the long-suffering of God, who is not slack concerning His promises. To the same effect the Commentator on *Habakkuk* (ii. 1-3), writes: 'And God told Habakkuk to write what is to befall the Last Generation; but the Consummation of the Time He did not make known to him. And where he says "that he who runs may read it," the reference is to the Righteous Teacher to whom God made known all the secrets of the words of His servants the Prophets. "For the vision is yet for an appointed time, but at the end it shall speak and not lie." The explanation is that the Last Time will be prolonged, and will transcend (or exceed) all that the Prophets have said; for the secrets of God are wonderful. "But if it delays, wait for it; for it will surely come, and will not tarry." This refers to the Men of Truth who practise the Law, whose hands never relax from the service of the Truth, in having the Last Time extended (or delayed) for them; for all the Times of God will come in their due season, just as He decreed of them in the secrets of His prudence.'

CHAPTER EIGHT

The Men of the Caves

SINCE I have expressed the view with some positiveness that the Commentary material of the Qumran sect is relatively late, and could not have originated before Daniel's Time of the End was believed to have commenced towards the close of the first century B.C., it is essential to interpose at this point additional evidence in support of this opinion. We have considered various lines of argument; that the *Damascus Document* itself speaks of a protracted period amounting to several generations intervening between the original initiative early in the second century B.C. and the time when the commentator is writing; that this is also signified by the stages denominated as that of 'the Priests', 'the Levites', and 'the Sons of Zadok', the latter being 'the Elect at the End of the Days'; that the End of the Days, on the interpretation of Daniel's reckoning, was found to have begun at the earliest near the end of the first century B.C.; that the type of prophetic exegesis found in this literature could not be older, with the *Habakkuk Commentary* revealing a consciousness that the expected Consummation had already been unduly delayed.

In the extremely complex kind of investigation to which the Dead Sea Scrolls give rise with their mysterious hints and allusions a great deal depends upon cumulative evidence. Information has to be sought over a very wide area and brought to bear on the problem. Scholars have patiently been performing this task, so that now there is much supplementary material available as a foundation on which to build.

A very fruitful subject of inquiry has been the traces of such literature as has been found at Qumran in the Jewish Karaite writings of the ninth and tenth century A.D. These references have been seen to link up with the report of Timotheus, mentioned in the last chapter, that about 800 A.D. a hoard of Hebrew manuscripts had been discovered by Jews in a cave near Jericho. The documents utilised by the Karaites in the subsequent century and a half are attributed to the *Magharriyah* ('the Men of the Caves'), because as the Karaite author Kirkisani explains their books were found in a cave (*maghar*). It is as certain as anything can be that the vast quantity of manuscripts recovered about 800 A.D. belonged to the same community as the present Dead Sea Scrolls. From the report of Timotheus it is seen that they included a collection of psalms and Biblical works, and Kirkisani makes reference to a *Book of Zadok*, a *Book of Yadua*, the works of the Alexandrian (almost certainly Philo), and many strange commentaries on the Scriptures (evidently similar to the *Habakkuk* and fragments of other commentaries from Qumran). To these may be added the *Damascus Document* which came to light in the old Karaite synagogue at Cairo. Except for the copies of the latter published by Schechter in 1910,[1] we do not know what may have survived. It is highly probable that some of the books either in copies or translation eventually reached Russia,[2] and may in part be represented by Slavonic texts such as those of the *Book of the Secrets of Enoch*, *Apocalypse of Abraham*, *Testaments of the XII Patriarchs*, *Vision of Isaiah*, *Life of Adam and Eve* and others known by name like the *Pentitence of Jannes and Jambres* and the *Book of Eldad and Medad*.

The value of the Karaite allusions was seen immediately the *Damascus Document* was published under the title *Fragments of a Zadokite Work*. Dr. Schechter had noted Kirkisani's reference to a sect in possession of a *Book of Zadok*, later united to the Dositheans, and Dr. Charles in the introduction to his translation in 1912 has this to say:

> Our book . . . was most probably called 'The Book of Zadok' or some such designation. We draw this inference from the statements of Kirkisani, a Karaite scholar, who wrote in the tenth century A.D. and appears to have had our book or one closely resembling it before him. In his Kitab al-Anwar ('Book of Lights') he states (1) that Zadok was the first to attack the Rabbinites. This is true of our author, who attacks fiercely the Pharisees of his time. Kirkisani further states (2) that Zadok absolutely forbade divorce; so our author in vii. 1; (3) that Zadok did not support by proofs the laws he had laid down save in the case of his forbidding a man to marry his niece—the daughter of his brother or sister—on the ground that these connexions were already prohibited in Lev. xviii. 13, being analogous to the forbidden connexion of a man with his aunt on the father or mother's side; so in our author vii. 9-10. It is worth observing also that in i. 1*a* there is a play on the name Zadok, also that the Zadokites ascribed to a Zadok the merit of having rediscovered the Law, vii. 6.

[1] *Documents of Jewish Sectarians*, vol. i.

[2] Dupont-Sommer refers to a study by H. Gregoire, *Les Gens de la Caverne, les Qaraites et les Khazars* in *Le Flambeau* (Brussels, 1952), in which the Belgian scholar has pointed out that the Karaite document, known as *The Cambridge Anonymous*, has inserted into the history of the conversion of the Khazars to Judaism a curious passage where ancient Hebrew MSS. discovered in a cave are mentioned. The Khazars were in alliance with the Byzantines, and there was a large Karaite community in Constantinople. On the activities of the Karaite Zacharias of Kiev see Eisler, *The Messiah Jesus*, p. 155ff.

Who this Zadok was can hardly be determined. In v. 7 'the Priests and the Levites and the sons of Zadok' are mentioned. From the explanation of these words in vi. 1-2 it is clear that the Priests and Levites represent the original founders of the Party, and that the expression 'Sons of Zadok' designates their spiritual successors 'at the end of the days'.

We shall return to these Zadokite intimations in the *Damascus Document;* but a brief look at the Karaite data will be helpful. I regret that I am dependent here on a few published articles and recent books, as I have not had the opportunity to study the older authorities, especially Harkavy, *Le-Korot ha-Kittot be-Israel,* who identified the Men of the Caves with the Essenes.

It appears that Kirkisani reveals that the Men of the Caves were opposed to anthropomorphisms and held that the world was produced by an angel. Some of his information came from a previous Karaite author David ibn Mirwan, who wrote a book on the various Jewish sects, and notably from the Karaite Benjamin ben Moses al-Nahawendi (early ninth century). Nahawendi declared that God created (1) The Glory (*Kabod*), (2) The Throne (*Kisse*), (3) an Angel (*Malach*). It was the Angel who created the world and acted (like the Angel Metatron) as the Divine representative and intermediary between God and Man. These views may derive from the writings of the Men of the Caves. *Enoch* introduces us to such an angelic figure in the person of the Son of Man.

> At that hour that Son of Man was named in the presence of the Lord of Spirits and his name before the Head of Days. And before the sun and the signs were created, before the stars of heaven were made, his name was named before the Lord of Spirits. He will be a staff to the righteous . . . and he will be the light of the Gentiles and the hope of those who are troubled of heart. All who dwell on earth will fall down and bow the knee before him and will bless and laud and celebrate with song the Lord of Spirits. And for this reason has he been chosen and hidden before Him before the creation of the world and for evermore. And the wisdom of the Lord of Spirits hath revealed him to the holy and righteous . . . because they have hated and despised this world of unrighteousness, and have hated all its works and ways in the name of the Lord of Spirits: for they are saved in his name and he is the avenger of their life (xlviii. 3-7).

Here we have the beginning of the Angel-Messiah concept afterwards taken over by the Judaeo-Christians and associated by them with Jesus in whom was incarnated the Messiah Above through the entrance into him of that Spiritual Being in the likeness of a dove. Epiphanius tells us that the Ebionites say that this Christ Above 'is a manlike figure, invisible to men in general'. 'They deny that he was begotten of God the Father, but say that he was created, as one of the archangels, yet greater, and that he is lord of angels and of all things made by the Almighty.' (*Panarion,* xxx).

These ideas also bring us close to the Essenes and to the Qumran sect, and Nahawendi is known to have been strongly under the influence of the writings of the Men of the Caves.

Teicher has shown[1] from the Karaite writers Hassan ben Massiah and Sahl ben Mazliah how widespread was the knowledge of the 'Zadokite' literature in the ninth and tenth centuries pre-eminently, affecting the teaching and practices not only of the Karaites themselves but also of the Rabbanites in matters as diverse as vegetarianism, methods of calendration and levitical purity. As Sahl says in a letter: '(the true knowledge of the Law) was revealed to us and became certain as soon as we read the writings of the sages of the Second Temple.'

It is evident that these sages were flourishing in the first century A.D. if, as it would appear, they possessed the works of Philo of Alexandria, who wrote during the first half of that century. This brings us back to Zadok, to whom Kirkisani attributed teachings comparable to those found in the *Damascus Document*. It is not to be dismissed that at least the testamentary work may have been entitled the 'Book of Zadok', as Charles proposed on the basis of Kirkisani's reference; and certainly the Qumran sect applied to the Elect in the End of the Days the term 'Sons of Zadok.' This period of the End of the Days we have shown to have commenced near the end of the first century B.C.

But who was this Zadok? Was he someone known by this name? Did the name help to conceal the identity of someone else? Or was the name employed because of relationship of the sect with the old Zadokite high priestly line which went out of office with the coming of the Maccabees?

The Qumran sect has been shown to have had its origin among the Chasidim of the old pre-Maccabean priesthood, to whom they applied the words of *Ezekiel* xliv. 15 that the Zadokite priesthood should minister in Divine things because 'they kept the charge of My Sanctuary when the children of Israel went astray from them'. The sect venerated Zadok, to whom, with probable reference to Hilkiah the high priest (II *Ki*. xxii. 8), they attributed the finding of the Book of the Law. The opening of the copper scrolls recovered from Qumran Cave Three has now provided an additional allusion. The scrolls refer to the distribution over an area of some fifty miles between Hebron and Mount Gerizim of a vast hoard of buried treasure, including vessels of incense concealed 'below the southern corner of the portico at Zadok's tomb and underneath the pilaster in the exedras'. The tomb is presumably that of the Biblical Zadok of the time of David, and not that of a leader of the sect. It is

[1] '"Zadokite" Writings in the Ninth and Tenth Centuries' *Journal of Jewish Studies*, Vol. ii, No. 2 (pp. 87-91).

significant that the text of the copper scrolls is stated to be in colloquial Mishnaic Hebrew, unlikely to be earlier than the late first century A.D.

We have to consider, however, whether there was any other reason why the Qumran sect should have applied to themselves the name 'Sons of Zadok' in the latter part of the first century B.C. It could be that in the history of the sect there was an important fresh development at this time heralding the beginning of the Time of the End, a time of special excitement and Messianic import. There is indeed evidence of this in both Jewish and Christian traditions of the origin of the Sadducees, where there has clearly been some understandable confusion between the Sadducees and Zadokites.

According to *Aboth R. Nathan* the famous Jewish teacher Antigonus of Socho (third cent. B.C.) had two pupils Zadok and Boethus, and these became respectively the founders of the sects of Sadducees and Boethusians. But the Boethusians were a high priestly family, connected with the Sadducees, deriving from Boethus or his son Simon made high priest by Herod 25-24 B.C. If, then, Zadok was the contemporary of Boethus, the tradition must really concern the Zadokites, since the Sadducees were already in existence under that name a century earlier. If this was all the evidence it would not amount to much; but we find the *Clementine Recognitions* making the same kind of mistake. 'The (Jewish) people,' it says, 'was now divided into many parties, ever since the days of John the Baptist . . . The first schism was that of those who were called Sadducees, which took their rise almost in the time of John. These, as more righteous than others, began to separate themselves from the assembly of the people' (Bk. I. liii-liv). The earliest date for the beginning of John's activities according to certain sources is the reign of Archelaus (3 B.C.-6 A.D.). So 'almost in the time of John' means about 25-20 B.C. The *Recognitions* do not mention Zadok: they make Dositheus the founder of the sect, followed by Simon (Magus); but they also quote the saying attributed to Antigonus of Socho. This is interesting, because in the Mishnaic tract *Pirke Aboth* the saying is again given in the name of Antigonus, and it is then said that one who received the tradition from him was Joseph ben Joezer, the priestly Chasid executed under the wicked high priest Alcimus.[1]

Elsewhere, both in the *Clementine Recognitions* and *Homilies*, Dositheus and Simon Magus are found among the immediate disciples of John the Baptist, and upon his death became in turn leaders of the Baptist sect. This led Eisler to make John the founder of the Zadokites and to indentify him with the Teacher of Righteousness of the *Damascus Document*.

Eisler quotes from a life of John the Baptist, purporting to have been written

[1] Above p. 18.

by a disciple Mark, where John advises his followers to 'go forth from the cities', i.e. into the wilderness, and he links this with the statement in the *Recognitions* about the Sadducees (Zadokites) 'segregating themselves from the people'.[1]

Had Eisler lived to learn about the contents of the Dead Sea Scrolls he would have found ample material with which to support his opinion, since the *Manual of Discipline*, with reference to these times, gives a specific injunction 'to take to the wilderness' to prepare there the way of the Lord, employing the same Biblical prophecies applied to John the Baptist in the Gospels.[2]

It cannot be said categorically that the Zadokite development around 25 B.C. had no connexion with an individual called Zadok; but it seems preferable to suppose that such a person was assumed to have founded the Zadokites at this time because the sect made use of the Biblical references and prophetic intimations attaching to the name in relation to their activities in what was believed to be the beginning of the End of the Days. This period gave rise to great messianic excitement, of which the coming of John the Baptist was only one manifestation. 'From the days of John the Baptist until now the kingdom of heaven suffereth violence, and the violent take it by force' (*Mt.* xi. 12). 'The people was now divided into many parties, ever since the days of John the Baptist' (*Recog.* Bk. I, liii). 'Israel did not go into captivity until twenty-four varieties of sectaries had come into existence' (T. J. *Sanh.* 29c). Lists are given by Justin Martyr (*Dialogue with Trypho*, lxxx), and Hegesippus (Euseb. *Eccles Hist.* Bk. IV, xxii). This multiplication of groups of the Elect in the crucial Time of the End is exactly what we should expect to have happened. It was the time to take to the wilderness, to separate from the ungodly, to write and store away appropriate books, as was done by the Men of the Caves, perhaps also to hide away treasure ready for the Wars of Messiah.

---

[1] *The Messiah Jesus and John the Baptist*, p. 254f.
[2] *Man. Disc.* viii. 12-16; ix. 16-20.

CHAPTER NINE

The Priestly Messiah

WE HAVE seen reason to believe that the *Damascus Document* speaks of two Teachers of Righteousness, who, if the various considerations we have brought forward are correct, may have been separated by some two hundred years. The first Teacher, who appeared about 175 B.C., is a rather shadowy figure, seemingly a priest and chasid, who organised the emigration to the land of Damascus, founded the Community of the New Covenant and drew up its rules. It may have been partly because of him that there developed an expectation of the ultimate Teacher, 'the Teacher of Righteousness in the End of the Days' identified perhaps with the looked-for Messiah. It is this final Teacher, whether or not held to be the Messiah, about whom so much is said in the *Habakkuk Commentary*.

It was quickly observed by a number of scholars that there are striking likenesses between the career of Jesus and that of the Teacher of Righteousness as portrayed in the *Habakkuk Commentary*, and it has even been suggested that Jesus may consciously have modelled himself in certain respects on a pattern created by the experiences of the earlier Teacher of Righteousness. Leaving this question aside, it may well be true that in Chasidic circles there had been handed down traditions regarding the original Teacher of Righteousness which helped in shaping expectations of the second Teacher. We know how parallels were drawn by the Rabbis between the expected Messiah and Moses, because the Messiah was regarded as the 'Prophet like unto Moses'. As Moses appeared, and was hid, and appeared again, so would the Messiah appear, and be hid, and appear again. As Moses brought down manna from heaven, so would the Messiah. As Moses made a spring of water to rise, so would the Messiah. We may therefore, perhaps, learn a little more about the first Teacher not only from what is said in the *Habakkuk Commentary* about the second Teacher, and in the New Testament about Jesus, but also from the older Chasidic literature and other sources.

In this chapter we propose to deal with the subject of the Priestly Messiah. Why did there develop a belief that the Messiah would be a priest?

It is plain from the *Habakkuk Commentary* that the Teacher to whom it refers was regarded as a priest, for *Hab.* i. 5 is explained as relating to the treacherous, the violent ones, at the End of Days, 'who will not believe when they hear all that will befall the Last Generation by the mouth of the Priest whom God placed in the house of Judah to explain all the words of His servants the Prophets (and to expound from?) the book of God all that will befall his people Israel'.

When John the Baptist appeared many believed that he might be the Messiah. Since John was of priestly descent this could hardly have happened had there not been some expectation of a Priestly Messiah. Indeed some of his followers claimed that John had been the Messiah, and by the Mandaeans it was asserted that he was directly descended from Moses.[1]

We find also in the case of Jesus that it was felt necessary to prove that he was a priest, and indeed high priest, as in the *Epistle to the Hebrews.* 'And no man taketh this honour unto himself, but he that is called of God, as was Aaron. So also Christ glorified not himself to be made an high priest; but he that said unto him, "Thou art my son, to-day have I begotten thee." As he saith also in another place, "thou art a priest forever after the order of Melchizedek" ' (*Heb.* v. 4-6). The writer then goes on to argue: 'If therefore perfection were by the Levitical priesthood (for under it the people received the Law), what further need was there that another priest should rise after the order of Melchizedek, and not be called after the order of Aaron? For the priesthood being changed, there is made of necessity a change also of the Law. For he of whom these things are spoken pertaineth to another tribe, of which no man gave attendance at the altar. For it is evident that our Lord sprang out of Judah; of which tribe Moses spake nothing concerning priesthood. And it is yet far more evident: for that after the similitude of Melchizedek there ariseth another priest, who is made, not after the law of a carnal commandment, but after the power of an endless life' (vii. 11-16). While this writer is at pains to prove that Jesus was a priest in spite of his not being of Levitical descent, S. Ephraim the Syrian will have it that Jesus was in some sense a Levite. When Jesus sent Peter to catch a fish in order to pay the tribute money, the Pharisees went with him. 'And when he had drawn out the fish, which had in its mouth a stater, the symbol of dominion, those haughty ones were reproved and confounded, because they believed not that he was a Levite, to whom the sea and the fishes were witnesses that he is king and priest.'[2]

---

[1] *Sidra d'Yahya*, sect. 18.

[2] *Gospel Commentaries.* A reading to the same effect is found in one Gospel MS., Codex Algerinae Peckover. See also Hippolytus of Rome, *Comm. on the Blessings of Isaac, Jacob and Moses.*

Of James the brother of Jesus it was related that he wore the high-priestly frontlet and had the right to enter the Holy of Holies. Epiphanius says that James 'was of the lineage of David. . . . and moreover we have found that he officiated after the manner of the ancient priesthood. Wherefore also he was permitted once a year to enter into the Holy of Holies, as the Law commanded the High Priests, according to that which is written; for so many before us have told of him, both Eusebius and Clement and others. Furthermore, he was empowered to wear on his head the high-priestly diadem, as the aforementioned trustworthy men have attested in their memoirs'.[1]

The coming of a Righteous Priest could have been predicted from *Deut.* xviii. 15-19, 'the Prophet like unto Moses' (who was of Levitic descent); from *Ps.* cx. 4, 'the Priest after the order of Melchizedek'; from *Mal.* iii. 1-4, 'the Messenger of the Covenant who will purify the sons of Levi', who might possibly be identified with Elijah the Prophet (*Mal.* iv. 5-6); from *Daniel* ix. 24, 'The anointed holy one of holies', and from other passages. But it would certainly have stimulated such an expectation, and drawn attention to such passages, if some notable Righteous Priest had arisen in the early days of the Chasidic Movement.

Regarding Elijah the Prophet, called in the Talmud 'Elijah the Righteous', believed to herald the Messiah, it had become accepted that he was descended from Aaron. It is told of Rava bar Abuhu that he encountered Elijah in a Gentile cemetery. 'Is not my master a priest?' exclaimed the Rabbi, 'Why, then, dost thou stand in a cemetery?'[2]

Even more to this point is a passage in a later midrash. 'To that generation (in Egypt) thou didst send redemption through two redeemers, as it is said (*Ps.* cv. 26), "He sent Moses his servant and Aaron whom he had chosen." And also to this generation (in the Messianic Age) he sendeth two, corresponding to those other two. "Send out thy light and thy truth" (*Ps.* xliii. 3). "Thy light", that is the Prophet Elijah of the house of Aaron, of whom it is written (*Num.* viii. 2), "the seven lamps shall throw their light in front of the lampstand". And "thy truth", that is Messiah ben David, as it is said (*Ps.* cxxxii. 11), "The Lord hath sworn unto David (in) truth, he will not turn from it." And likewise it is said (*Isa.* xlii. 1), "Behold my servant whom I uphold." '[3]

We have already seen that scholars have paid considerable attention to

---

[1] Epiph. *Haeres.* lxxviii.

[2] *Bab. Mets.* 114b.

[3] *Midr. Tehill.* xliii. 1. In another midrash we are offered four Messianic personalities, corresponding to the four carpenters of *Zech.* i. 20-21: these are Elijah, a Messiah of Manasseh, a Messiah of Ephraim (the Anointed of War), and the Great Redeemer of the line of David (*Num. R.* 14).

the evidence that the Jewish sect of Karaites in the ninth and tenth century exhibited in doctrine and practices a striking relationship to the old New Covenant Community, and Dupont-Sommer mentions a prayer which the Karaites still recite,[1] and which in effect links the Teacher of Righteousness with Elijah, and by inference with the Messiah. The prayer runs: 'And may God send us the Teacher of Righteousness to guide the hearts of the fathers towards their children.'

These considerations suggest a fresh possibility. In spite of what I have said above about the Messiah from Aaron and Israel in the *Damascus Document*,[2] could the commentator not mean two persons, a Messiah from Aaron and a Messiah from Israel? *Test. Damasc.* does seem to think of laity and priests separately when it says that God 'caused to spring forth from Israel and Aaron a root of His planting . . . and *they* had understanding of their iniquity'.[3] The *Manual of Discipline*, ix. 11, actually uses the plural: 'until there comes a prophet and Messiahs of Aaron and Israel'.

But even if the writer means only one person it could well be that he is fusing two into one, combining the expectations of the priestly and lay redeemer as was done in the case of Jesus, presenting us, so to speak, with a composite Messiah.

The Teacher of Righteousness of the Karaite prayer is an Elijah figure, and already in the Book of Ben Sira (*Ecclesiasticus*)[4] Elijah is given the redemptive task not only 'to turn the heart of the father unto the son', but also 'to restore the tribes of Jacob'. We have seen how the words of the Psalmist about the eternal priest after the order of Melchizedek were applied prophetically to the Messiah, and how Elijah was held to be descended from Aaron. We also find all these ideas curiously associated in the *Targum of Palestine*,[5] where it is said of Phineas the grandson of Aaron, 'Behold, I confirm to him My covenant of peace, and will make him an Angel (Messenger) of the Covenant, that he may ever live, to announce the Redemption at the End of the Days.' Here Phineas is identified with the Messenger of the Covenant of *Malachi* and given the Elijah rôle. Phineas and Elijah are actually regarded as one and the same in *Pirke de R. Eliezer*, xxix, xlvii, *Biblical Antiquities of Philo*, xlviii, and elsewhere.

In the Gospels it is John the Baptist, descendant of Aaron, who is identified with Elijah (*Lk.* i. 120; *Mk.* ix. 12-13), and in the late Hebrew *Josippon* and the

---

[1] *The Jewish Sect of Qumran and the Essenes*, p. 76.
[2] Above, p. 42f.
[3] Above, p. 15f.
[4] *Ecclus.* xlviii. 10.
[5] On *Num.* xxv. 12.

Arabic *Jusifus* John is called high priest. Eisler,[1] who notes this, accounts for this tradition by supposing that something of the kind originally stood in the Greek Josephus, but was afterwards struck out. But the tradition could have derived from Christian sources. There was the tradition that James the brother of Jesus had served as high priest, which we have already quoted from Epiphanius. There was also a tradition that John the Beloved Disciple had served in the same capacity. This is quoted by Eusebius[2] from a letter from Polycrates, Bishop of Ephesus, to Victor, Bishop of Rome, c. 196 A.D., who says: 'There is also John, who lay on the Lord's breast, who had been a priest who had worn the golden frontlet, and a martyr and a teacher. He sleeps at Ephesus.' If this James and John got confused with James and John the sons of Zebedee, who are made in *Lk.* ix. 54 to ask Jesus whether they might not call down fire from heaven 'as Elijah did', might not there also have existed a story of Elijah-John the Baptist as the Aaronic high priestly Messiah of the Daniel prophecy which got transferred to John the Beloved Disciple,assumed to be the son of Zebedee; John the son of Zebedee thus replacing John the son of Zechariah?

In the passage we have given from the Midrash on the *Psalms* two Messianic personalities are distinguished corresponding to Aaron and Moses: the first is Elijah and the second Messiah ben David. That this expectation was an ancient one we have given some reasons for believing, and obviously we should bring into the record what is said in the *Apocalypse of John* in the New Testament of the Two Witnesses (xi. 3-13). These Witnesses have the power to stop the fall of rain (like Elijah) and turn water into blood (like Moses). Eisler[3] pertinently quotes Prof. Benjamin Bacon for the interpretation of this passage.

> The two witnesses of verse 3-8a, who by the description of verses 5f. are Elijah and Moses *redivivi*, must be understood to represent disciples of Jesus . . . the reader is meant to understand that two Christian martyrs have fulfilled the well-known Jewish expectation that before the great day of judgement Moses (*al.*Enoch) and Elias will be sent from Paradise to preach repentance to the people and that Belial will set the cope-stone on his wickedness by putting the two witnesses to death. Who, then, were these two Christian martyrs? Originally (if we may judge by Mark x.35 ff.) the two sons of Zebedee.

It would take us too far afield to go into the development of the tradition of the Two Redeemers in the later and even medieval midrashic and apocalyptic literature. But we must briefly mention that on the basis of the old concept

[1] *The Messiah Jesus and John the Baptist*, p. 260.
[2] *Eccl. Hist.* III. xxxi. 2; V. xxiv. 7.
[3] *The Enigma of the Fourth Gospel*, p. 86.

of the priestly and secular Redeemers there was formulated the doctrine of the Messiah ben Joseph and the Messiah ben David. This doctrine had already found expression by the third century, for in the Talmud R. Dosa (c. 250 A.D.) is quoted on the subject. Messiah ben Joseph is the forerunner of Messiah ben David, destined to fall in battle against the enemies of Israel. In any case in the traditions, whether in battle or simply as a martyr, he is killed by Belial's agent, the arch-enemy of Israel, later identified as Armilus (Romulus—Rome). Why he is called Ben Joseph has not been satisfactorily explained. Some have supposed that an Ephraimite Messiah is meant, a Messiah of the Ten Tribes, but no warrant for this interpretation exists. It may possibly be accounted for by a Jewish borrowing from Christianity. The martyred Messiah of the Christians was Jesus ben Joseph. But as we shall see further on in our investigation there may be a still older tradition which helps to account for the term Ben Joseph. At any rate Messiah ben Joseph succeeds to the position of the Aaronic Messiah, and in his death at the hands of a minion of Belial he bears some resemblance to the Priestly Teacher of Righteousness of the *Habakkuk Commentary*. We are certainly entitled to ask, whether in this respect the story of the second Teacher does not reflect that of the first? Did the experiences of the first Teacher, persecution, and perhaps martyrdom, help to create a tradition which made it natural that the second Teacher, that John the Baptist, that Jesus, that the Two Witnesses of the *Apocalypse*, should be persecuted and slain?

A work which can assist us to answer this question is one which, so far as the present chapter is concerned, we have purposely ignored, the *Testaments of the XII Patriarchs*. The evidence which it affords cannot be regarded as conclusive because the original is not available; but since we have in Greek two rescensions for comparison with two Armenian rescensions we can to an extent distinguish between the purer text and the more corrupt. But even the better Armenian (A) text suffers from additions, some of them characteristically Christian, others not so certainly identifiable. Some of the most evidential eschatological passages are the very ones where a doubt exists.

The oldest stratum of the *Testaments* may belong to the end of the reign of John Hyrcanus (137-105 B.C.). The author is a priestly Chasid like the author of *Jubilees*, and he finds in the combination of the regal and high-priestly office by the early Hasmonean rulers the fulfilment of the highest destiny of the house of Levi. He pictures a golden age under such government with certain features which might be held to reflect what is recorded of John Hyrcanus (*Levi.* xviii; *Jud.* xxiv-xxv). This golden age did not materialise, and the successors of Hyrcanus proved to be anything but ideal personalities.

Faced with the corruption and evil practices of the later Maccabees considerable additions were made to the *Testaments* between 70 and 40 B.C. which dealt with these circumstances and linked Judah with Levi in the expression of the Messianic Hope. 'And now, my children, obey Levi and Judah, and be not lifted up against these two tribes, for from them shall arise unto you the salvation of God. For the Lord shall raise up from Levi as it were a High Priest, and from Judah as it were a King: he shall save all the race of Israel' (*Sim.* vii. 1-2). Here and in comparable passages (*Napht.* viii. 2-3; *Jos.* xix. 11) the Messiah would seem to be one person descended from Levi and Judah. I can find no trace in additions to the *Testaments* of distinct Levite and Judean Messiahs. We should also note the possibility that this combination of a Messiah from Levi and Judah might have been made much later still in the Christian interest; for there remains hardly one Messianic passage in the *Testaments* that has not been tampered with so as to make it apply to Jesus.

I take this to be true even of the passage which it is suggested might apply to a pre-Christian Teacher of Righteousness. This passage reads as follows (the speaker is the Patriarch Levi): 'And now I have learnt that for seventy weeks ye (my descendants) shall go astray, and profane the priesthood, and pollute the sacrifices. And ye shall make void the Law, and set at naught the words of the Prophets by evil perverseness. And ye shall persecute righteous men, and hate the godly; the words of the faithful shall ye abhor. [And a man who reneweth the Law in the power of the Most High, ye shall call a deceiver; and at last ye shall rush (upon him) to slay him, not knowing his dignity, taking innocent blood through wickedness upon your heads.] And your holy places shall be laid waste even to the ground because of [him] (true text, it). And ye shall have no place that is clean; but ye shall be among the Gentiles a curse and a dispersion until He (i.e., God) shall again visit you, and in pity shall receive you [through faith and water]' (*Levi.* xvi. 1-5).

It is certainly tempting to think of the first words within square brackets as pre-Christian, even if, as Charles says, they have been worked over by a Christian scribe. The temptation is the greater in that the words do not necessarily relate to someone regarded as the Messiah. If the words are not interpolated they must refer to some very highly regarded righteous godly man, whose rejection and murder emphasised the general apostasy. In his note on the passage[1] Charles asks whether the words could refer to the pious Onias who refused to pray for either of the warring factions lead by Hyrcanus II and Aristobulus II, and was stoned to death (Joseph. *Antiq.* XIV. ii. 1-2), or to the murdered High Priest Onias III. (*II Macc.* iv. 33-36)?

[1] *Testaments of the XII Patriarchs*, pp. 59-60.

The words 'And a man who reneweth the Law in the power of the Most High' are certainly intriguing, since this is the function of the original Teacher of Righteousness in the testamentary section of the *Damascus Document* which tells of his appearance about 175 B.C. On the other hand the whole of the bracketed words could be a Christian interpolation, and 'renewing the Law in the power of the Most High' may be a reflection of the teaching of Jesus in *Matt.* iv. 17-19, as 'taking innocent blood through wickedness upon your heads' is reminiscent of *Matt.* xxvii. 24-25. Against the view that the words are authentic and early is the fact that the whole passage is introduced by a reference to the Seventy Weeks of Daniel. As understood later this period was not regarded as having expired until near the end of the first century B.C. In our passage there is no direct connexion with the terms of the Daniel prophecy, unless we are to think of the murdered sage as the anointed one who is cut off, and is no more, of *Dan.* ix. 26. This is possible, but not very probable, unless it is agreed that our author is looking back to the time of Antiochus Epiphanes, and treating the Daniel prophecy in its original sense as having been fulfilled in those days. Again, the whole passage reads quite coherently and consistently without the bracketed words.

Excluding this one doubtful reference to a pre-Maccabean Teacher of Righteousness, it would appear from the *Testaments* that between the extreme dates of composition 137-40 B.C., allowing for all Jewish additions to the text, no new Messianic figure had arisen to the knowledge of the various writers who might be conceived to answer to the description of the Teacher of Righteousness of the *Habakkuk Commentary*.

In the salient Messianic sections in *Levi* and *Judah* the Messianic Prince is expected to come after the punishment of the Hellenizing priesthood of the time of Antiochus Epiphanes. These sections it seems to me must be taken together, and we shall therefore quote from both.

> And in the fifth week (of the seventh jubilee) they shall return to their desolate country, and shall renew the house of the Lord. And in the seventh week shall come priests (who are) idolaters, adulterers, lovers of money, proud, lawless, lascivious, abusers of children and beasts. And after their punishment shall have come from the Lord, the priesthood shall fail. Then shall the Lord raise up a new priest. And to him all the words of the Lord shall be revealed; and he shall execute a righteous judgment upon the earth for a multitude of days. And his star shall arise in heaven as of a king, lighting up the light of knowledge as the sun the day. And he shall be magnified in the world. He shall shine forth as the sun on the earth, and shall remove all darkness from under heaven, and there shall be peace in all the earth. . . . The heavens shall be opened, and from the temple of glory shall come upon him sanctification, with the Father's voice as from

Abraham to Isaac. And the glory of the Most High shall be uttered over him, and the spirit of understanding and sanctification shall rest upon him. And he shall give the majesty of the Lord to His sons in truth for evermore; and there shall none succeed him for all generations for ever.... In his priesthood shall sin come to an end, and the lawless shall cease to do evil.... And he shall give to the saints to eat from the tree of life, and the spirit of holiness shall be on them. And Belial shall be bound by him, and he shall give power to His children to tread upon the evil spirits. And the Lord shall rejoice in His children, and be well pleased in His beloved ones for ever. Then shall Abraham and Isaac and Jacob exult, and I will be glad, and all the saints shall clothe themselves with joy. (*Levi*, xvii. 10–xviii. 14).

And now I have much grief, my children, because of your lewdness and witchcrafts, and idolatries which ye shall practise . . . and ye shall mingle in the abominations of the Gentiles. For which things' sake the Lord shall bring upon you famine and pestilence, death and the sword . . . the laying waste of the land, the enslavement of yourselves among the Gentiles . . . until ye turn unto the Lord with perfect heart repenting and walking in all the commandments of God, and the Lord visit you with mercy and bring you up from captivity among the Gentiles. And after these things shall arise the star of peace, and he shall walk with men in meekness and righteousness. And the heavens shall be opened unto him, and the blessings of the Holy Father will be poured down upon him. And He shall pour down upon us the spirit of grace. And ye shall be His true children by adoption, and ye shall walk in His commandments first and last. And the sceptre of my kingdom shall shine forth; and from your root shall arise a stem; and from it shall grow up the rod of righteousness unto the Gentiles, to judge and to save all that call upon the Lord. And after these things shall Abraham and Isaac and Jacob arise unto life, and I and my brethren shall be chiefs of the tribes of Israel: Levi first, I the second, Joseph third . . . And ye shall be the people of the Lord, and have one tongue; and there shall be no spirit of deceit of Belial, for he shall be cast into the fire for ever. (*Jud.* xxiii. 1–xxv. 3).

The parallelism of these passages is undeniable. Our difficulty with them is that in their present form the Messianic doctrine has reached an advanced stage, too advanced to have been written at the time of the Maccabean revolt. Sixty years later, as Charles proposes, comes within the bounds of possibility; and while it may be true that some features remind us of what is said in Josephus of John Hyrcanus, almost the whole description could have been built up from passages in the *Psalms* and the Prophets. We should need to suppose that by about 107 B.C. the Messianic study of the Old Testament had already resulted in the compilation of a series of proof-texts. All that it is safe to say is that when these sections were written no other catastrophe had overtaken Israel to diminish or replace the memory of the sufferings under Antiochus Epiphanes.

The picture of the Messiah in the later additions to the *Testaments* is not materially changed. The corruption of the Maccabean priest-kings is dealt with, leading to willingness to associate Judah with Levi in the Messianic Hope by making certain changes in the text. No attempt was made to expunge the references to the Priestly Messiah, only to find room for a Messiah from Judah (the Davidic Messiah). Confusion was bound to result, since it could no longer be clear whether two persons were to be expected, or one who might fulfil in himself both expectations. It would appear to have been considered by some that one way of getting round this difficulty was to apply the Hope of a Levitic Messiah to Elijah redivivus as forerunner of the Davidic Messiah. Subsequently, another line of interpretation created Messiah ben Joseph. One thing at least is plain, there is no evidence in the *Testaments* or in other apocalyptic and pseudepigraphic writings of the first century B.C. of the recognition of any Messiah who had already come. This weighs heavily against the view of Dupont-Sommer that the Messianic Teacher of Righteousness of the *Habakkuk Commentary* lived about 75-62 B.C. We can rule out the whole of the period 137-40 B.C. No one corresponding to him appears in the *Testaments*, the later sections of *Enoch*, or the *Psalms of Solomon*.

Even so, there may well have been handed down among the Chasidim the recollection of that noble Teacher of Righteousness who appeared among them in the days of the Hellenizing priesthood early in the second century B.C. There could have been a legend of his martyrdom at the hands of a Wicked High Priest. Such a legend could have helped to colour later Messianic anticipations, so that the idea of a suffering Messiah became strengthened by it, and Messiah ben Joseph emerged from it. Such a tradition could find fulfilment in the experiences of John the Baptist, of Jesus, of the Teacher of Righteousness of the End of the Days, even of others.

For support for such a hypothesis we are not dependent on the doubtful reference in *Test. Levi.* If there is one thing that can be said in favour of the genuineness of that reference it is that it can be interpreted as applying to someone who is not the Messiah. At every stage of the *Testaments* until the Christian overworking of the text the coming of the Messiah is still future, whereas this 'man who reneweth the Law in the power of the Most High' is an historical person who has wickedly been done to death. We have one other relevant passage in the *Testaments*, and this is less open to criticism since it relates neither to Levi nor Judah. The passage is found in *Test. Benj.* iii:

> Do ye also, therefore, my children, love the Lord God of heaven and earth, and keep His commandments, following the example of the holy and good man Joseph. For until his death he was not willing to tell regarding himself; but Jacob, having learnt it from the Lord, told it to him.

> Nevertheless he kept denying it. And then with difficulty he was persuaded by the adjurations of Israel. For Joseph also besought our father that he would pray for his brethren, that the Lord would not impute to them as sin whatever evil they had done unto him. And thus Jacob cried out: 'My good child, thou hast prevailed over the bowels of thy father Jacob.' And he embraced him, and kissed him for two hours, saying: 'In thee shall be fulfilled the prophecy of heaven, which says that the blameless one shall be defiled for lawless men, and the sinless one shall die for godless men.'

The Patriarch Joseph does not really qualify as fulfiller of such a prophecy; but he was regarded as the antetype of a righteous man killed by the godless, a veritable suffering Ben Joseph. The passage in some texts has quite naturally been heavily interpolated to make it prophetic of Jesus. Obviously we have to seek further light on this concept and trace out the traditions of this Joseph personality. But already we begin to have a glimpse of two streams descending associated respectively with the Priestly Messiah and the Righteous Sufferer, which finally converged and became united.

To complete the picture presented in this chapter, it is deserving of serious consideration that somewhat parallel ideas are found in Samaritan eschatology.[1] In the *Clementine* literature the sects of Baptists and Samaritans are brought together, and Josephus is witness that in the first century A.D. the Samaritans were definitely infected by the prevailing messianic expectations, for a candidate for the rôle of Taheb appeared during Pilate's governorship.[2] Moreover the treasure described in the copper scrolls from Qumran is stated to have been buried in part in Samaritan territory. The Samaritans naturally expressed their messianic hope in terms of their own background and tradition, but it is an open question to what extent this has been influenced by the beliefs of the Jewish eclectic groups.

Certain it is that the Samaritans came to believe in a world to come. In the *Yom al-Din* that world is deduced from the fact that the Hebrew Bible begins with the letter *Bet*, the numerical value of which is two, thus signifying God's creation of two worlds, this world and the world to come. In the *Shira Yetima* of Abisha ben Phineas reference is made to the 'friends of Moses' of the Last Days, who are 'the Elect Ones', who have been chosen by God from all nations; while in the *Hilluk* it is declared that God has reserved to Himself the knowledge 'of the number of days until the Appointed Day which is the Day of the End,' the Day of Resurrection (the Upstanding).

But above all we have the Samaritan hope of the advent of the Taheb or

---

[1] All the references are given in Gaster, *Samaritan Eschatology*, a work which I was privileged to assist in editing.

[2] Jos. *Antiq.* XVIII. iv. 1.

Shaheb, the Restorer, the Prophet like unto Moses, and the promise in *Deuteronomy* of this Prophet is made the Samaritan Tenth Commandment. The Taheb is not exactly a Messiah, but he is to perform messianic functions, inaugurating the era of the return of God's favour to Israel, the *Rahuta*. He will be Prophet, Priest, and King over 'the Second Kingdom.' In his time will be fulfilled the promise to Phineas, whose righteous priestly seed has been kept hidden away in absolute purity and sanctity during the period of the Fanuta (the turning away of God's favour); and these will be brought back by God to perform their office, just as the lost original Scroll of the Law will be revealed from its hiding place. The Taheb, the perfect man, restorer of God's favour, will come from the desert. He will be of the tribe of Levi. His birth will be announced by the rise of a new star in the heavens which will continue for ever. At the same time a high priest of the line of Phineas will appear, who like Enoch had been translated to heaven, and he will serve in the New Temple on Mt. Gerizim. At the age of 120 years the Taheb will die, and will be buried by the sacred mount; but over his grave the star of his advent will continue to shine.

Such in brief are the Samaritan traditions of one who, as in the *Testaments of the XII Patriarchs*, 'renews the Law in the power of the Most High,' and whose 'star arises in heaven as of a king.'

CHAPTER TEN

The Legend of Ben Berechiah

WE HAVE come a long way from the point at which our investigation started; but now we can begin to work back to it. It has been necessary to wander far afield, and we have still much ground to cover even on our return journey. We had to reach on the evidence a consciousness of distance, of a considerable lapse of time between the beginning of the Chasidic Movement when the first Teacher of Righteousness appeared and the latest era of the New Covenant Party in the End of the Days when the second Teacher of Righteousness was anticipated. We have seen no signs on the way in the literature we have examined of any consciousness of the advent and ministry of such a figure between the first half of the second century B.C. and the first half of the first century A.D. Here it may be objected that as yet we have hardly touched the evidence of the *Habakkuk Commentary* upon which the hypothesis of Dupont-Sommer and other scholars mainly rests that the Teacher flourished in the first half of the first century B.C. We shall not neglect to give that work full examination in its place; but it is hardly favourable to the theory if we cannot find in the apocalyptic and pseudepigraphic books which cover and describe the intermediate period from the view-point of the Saints any reference to such a person as the Teacher of Righteousness, who is stated to have appeared in the days of the decadent Maccabean rulers. The additions to the *Testaments* of this period do not mention him. The *Assumption of Moses* in its description of the same period knows nothing of him. The *Psalms of Solomon* written only a short time after the Teacher is assumed to have been active has never heard of him. Are we to suppose that this man was of such insignificance that he was only of consequence to a small sect, so that no record of him got into the books which were its spiritual inheritance? Surely, that is most improbable if the Teacher did indeed live at the time suggested by this theory, and if the sect formed part of those we have known as the Essenes.

The position is quite different if we accept the statement in the *Damascus Document* that about 176 B.C. a Teacher of Righteousness was sent to the repentant remnant of Aaron and Israel 'to lead them in the way of God's heart.' This Teacher was not the Messiah. The doctrine of a Messiah had not developed at this time. But it is by no means excluded that the remembrance of the experiences of this Teacher handed down among the Chasidim helped to shape their Messianic doctrine, especially in the concept of a suffering Just One. Thus there could be built up an expectation of the Teacher of Righteousness of the End of the Days, who would be a Messianic figure, and whose life and death would be a reflection and a fulfilment of the almost legendary life and death of the original Teacher. We may not succeed in identifying the ultimate Teacher of Righteousness, who is described in the *Habakkuk Commentary*. But at least if we have to think of his advent in the first century A.D. there is no lack in the records of the period of likely candidates.

Our first concern, then, must be to learn from legend and tradition all we can of the concept of a Teacher of Righteousness. In the last chapter, the typical Righteous Sufferer of the Old Testament was the Patriarch Joseph, who was regarded by the Chasidim as pre-figuring someone known to them. 'In thee (Joseph) shall be fulfilled the prophecy of heaven, which says that the blameless one shall be defiled for lawless men, and the sinless one shall die for godless men' (*T. Benj.* iii. 8). The prophecy referred to may be that of *Isa.* liii. Obviously, even in retrospect, it could not relate to the Patriarch, who died peacefully in his bed and in no sense vicariously. The writer therefore means us to understand a Joseph-type of person to whom the prophecy could well have been applied. This person could be regarded, as was the Patriarch, as the *Zaddik gamur*, the perfect righteous man. Of the Patriarch it was said by the Rabbis,[1] that he was well-versed in the Torah, that he was a Prophet, and that the Holy Spirit dwelt in him from his childhood to the day of his death. In *Jubilees* it is stated that the Day of Atonement was instituted because of him: 'And the sons of Jacob slaughtered a kid, and dipped the coat of Joseph in the blood, and sent it to Jacob their father on the tenth of the seventh month. . . . For this reason it is ordained for the children of Israel that they should afflict themselves on the tenth of the seventh month—on the day that the news which made him weep for Joseph came to Jacob his father—that they should make atonement for themselves with a young goat on the tenth of the seventh month, once a year, for their sins' (xxxiv. 12-18). Is this curious story another indirect reference to the Teacher of Righteousness?

Some leading Chasid was certainly killed in the early days of the Movement.

[1] See JE art. Joseph.

To this fact reference is made in the *Visions of Enoch*: 'And I saw until those sheep were devoured by the dogs and eagles and kites, and they left neither flesh nor skin nor sinew remaining on them till only their skeletons stood there: their skeletons too fell to the earth and the sheep became few. . . . But behold lambs were borne by those white sheep, and they began to open their eyes and to see, and to cry to the sheep. But the sheep did not cry to them and did not hear what they said to them, but were exceedingly deaf, and their eyes were exceedingly and forcibly blinded. And I saw in the vision how the ravens flew upon those lambs and took one of those lambs, and dashed the sheep in pieces and devoured them. And I saw till horns grew upon those lambs, and the ravens cast down their horns; and I saw till a great horn of one of those sheep branched forth, and their eyes were opened . . . and it cried to the sheep and the rams saw it and all ran to it. . . . And those ravens fought and battled with it and sought to destroy his horn, but they had no power over it' (xc. 4-12).

Charles successfully interpreted the main features of this vision. The dogs, eagles and kites are the oppressing Philistines, Macedonians and Egyptians, while the sheep represent Israel. The lambs borne by the white sheep are the Chasidim who called unavailingly on the people to repent. The ravens are the Syrian Seleucids, who killed one of the Chasids and proceeded to persecute and destroy the Israelites. The lambs then grew horns, that is to say, the Chasidim took up arms; but the ravens (the Syrians) overcame them. Then, however, a great horn, Judas Maccabaeus, branched forth from the sheep, and called to the people, who rallied to him. The Syrians did their utmost to destroy Judas and his followers in battle; but they failed.

The question that concerns us is, who was the murdered Chasid? Charles identifies him with the High Priest Onias III, treacherously murdered by the representative of Antiochus Epiphanes at Daphne near Antioch (*II Macc.* iv. 34). This identification may well be correct, though, as Charles says, 'We should, perhaps, have expected Onias III to be symbolized by a white sheep rather than by a lamb. The writer may have gone back for a moment to the symbolic meaning of this term in lxxxix. 45; but it is more likely that it is used loosely as including Onias among the Chasids.'[1] The date of the murder of Onias, 171 B.C., is entirely consistent with the information given in the *Damascus Document* of the appearance of the Teacher of Righteousness about 176 B.C. Without at present considering this identification, we at least have the information that a notable Chasid perished at the period our researches have indicated.

[1] *The Book of Enoch*, p. 251.

Onias III was not the only famous Chasid of whose murder we have memories, who lived at this time. In our account of the Chasidim[1] we quoted the midrashic story of the martyrdom of the Chasid and Priest Joseph ben Joezer for which the Wicked High Priest Alcimus was responsible, as was the Wicked High Priest Menelaus for the death of Onias. Here we should note how the tradition has attached itself to one of the name of Joseph, in keeping with the Joseph cycle, who is described as having perfectly carried out the will of God. Was Joseph ben Joezer a Priest and a Chasid as the Rabbis relate? Or has the tradition merely attached itself to a famous scholar Joseph, known to have taught in the period of which the records told?

Finally, among the Joseph references we must include a heavily Christianised work the *Ascension of Isaiah*. The author gives a list of the Minor Prophets, who have treated of the Messianic Age, in the following order, Amos, Hosea, Micah, Joel, Nahum, Jonah, Obadiah, Habakkuk, Haggai, Zephaniah, Zechariah, Malachi. To these he adds Joseph the Just and Daniel.[2] Who is this stranger prophet who so singularly appears between Malachi and Daniel (165 B.C.)? No other apocryphal books are mentioned in the list. It is certainly curious that Joseph the Just is found also among the prophets in the position we should expect and bearing a name we should expect.

Whether on the basis of traditions regarding some particular Just One, or otherwise, by the time the *Wisdom of Solomon* was written a pen portrait could be made of the Righteous Sufferer:

> Let us lie in wait for the righteous man,
> Because he is of disservice to us,
> And is contrary to our works,
> And upbraideth us with sins against the Law,
> And layeth to our charge sins against our discipline.
> He professeth to have knowledge of God,
> And nameth himself servant of the Lord.
> He became to us a reproof of our thoughts.
> He is grievous unto us even to behold,
> Because his life is unlike other men's,
> And his paths are of strange fashion.
> We were accounted of him as base metal,
> And he abstaineth from our ways as from uncleanness.
> The latter end of the righteous he calleth happy;
> And he vaunteth that God is his father.
> Let us see if his words be true,
> And let us try what shall befall in the ending of his life.
> For if the righteous man is God's son He will uphold him,

[1] Above, p. 18.
[2] *Ascension of Isaiah*, edition and translation by R. H. Charles, p. 39.

And He will deliver him out of the hand of his adversaries.
With outrage and torture let us put him to the test,
That we may learn his gentleness,
And may prove his patience under wrong.
Let us condemn him to a shameful death;
For he shall be visited according to his words.[1]

It is apparently from some such Wisdom source that a quotation put into the mouth of Jesus is taken. Two different versions are given in *Matthew* and *Luke*, the words being credited in the latter to the 'Wisdom of God'. These words introduce us to another strange tradition, the legend of Ben Berechiah.

Behold, I send unto you prophets and wise men and scribes;
And some of them ye shall kill and crucify . . . and persecute . . .
That upon you may come all the righteous blood shed upon earth,
From the blood of Abel the righteous
Unto the blood of Zechariah son of Berechiah,
Whom ye slew between the temple and the altar. [2]

Here Zechariah ben Berechiah is named as the last great Zaddik wickedly done to death. A variant reading in the *Gospel of the Hebrews* makes him the son of Jehoiada in the time of King Joash, in accordance with what is stated in *II Chron.* xxiv. 18-21: 'And they left the house of the Lord God of their fathers, and served groves and idols: and wrath came upon Judah and Jerusalem for this their trespass. Yet He sent prophets to them to bring them again unto the Lord; and they testified against them: but they would not give ear. And the Spirit of God came upon Zechariah the son of Jehoiada the priest, which stood above the people, and said unto them, "Thus saith God, why transgress ye the commandments of the Lord, that ye cannot prosper? Because ye have forsaken the Lord, He hath also forsaken you." And they conspired against him, and stoned him with stones at the commandment of the king, in the court of the house of the Lord.'

The reading 'son of Berechiah' would seem to refer to the post-exilic prophet Zechariah, the son of Berechiah, the son of Iddo, reputed author of the canonical *Book of Zechariah*. Gaster proposed to get round the difficulty by suggesting that chapters ix to the end of the *Book of Zechariah* were in fact the work of the earlier murdered prophet Zechariah son of Jehoiada. Further

[1] *Wisd. Sol.* i. 12-20. The work is believed to have been written in Egypt in the first half of the 1st century B.C.
[2] *Matt.* xxiii. 34-35. Cp. *Lk.* xi. 49-50, where the words are in the third person. The quotation in *Matthew* seems to have been influenced by *Matt.* x. 17-18.

to complicate the circumstances, whether based on fact or the Zechariah tradition, Josephus[1] gives an account of an eminent man of Jerusalem, Zechariah son of Baris (or Bariscaeus), murdered by the Zealots in the Temple after a mock trial in 68 A.D., while The Armenian Text of Epiphanius' *Homilies* speaks of a Zacharias son of Barek as chief priest in the time of Antipater father of Herod.

Like the authors of the Gospels the Rabbis make much of the death of Zechariah, attributing the destruction of Jerusalem by Nebuchadnezzar to the murder of this Zaddik. The Jewish legend is found in both the Palestinian Talmud (*Taan.* 69a-b) and the Babylonian Talmud (*Sanh.* 96b).

> R. Jochanan said, Eighty thousand priests were killed for the blood of Zechariah. R. Judah asked R. Acha, Whereabouts did they kill Zechariah, in the Court of the Women, or in the Court of Israel? He answered, Neither in the Court of Israel, nor in the Court of the Women, but in the Court of the Priests. And it was not done to his blood as is done to the blood of a ram or a kid. Concerning the latter it is written, 'And he shall pour out its blood, and cover it with dust.' But concerning the former it is written, 'Her blood is in the midst of her; she set it upon the top of a rock, she poured it not upon the ground.' And wherefore? 'That it might cause fury to come up to take vengeance.'
>
> They committed seven wickednesses in that day. They killed a Priest, a Prophet, and a Judge; they shed the blood of an innocent man; they polluted the Court; and that day was the Sabbath, and the Day of Atonement. When therefore Nebuzaradan (Nebuchadnezzar's general) went up thither, he saw the blood bubbling: so he said to them, What meaneth this? They said, It is the blood of calves, lambs and rams, which we have offered on the altar. Bring then, said he, calves, lambs and rams, that I may try whether this be their blood. They brought them and slew them, but that blood still bubbled, while their blood bubbled not. Declare unto me this matter, said he, or I will tear your flesh with iron rakes. Then said they unto him, This was a Priest, a Prophet, and a Judge, who foretold to Israel all these evils which we have suffered from you, and we rose up against him, and slew him. But I, said he, will appease him. He brought the Rabbis, and slew them upon that blood; and yet it was not pacified: he brought the children out of the school, and slew them upon it; and yet it was not quiet: he brought the young priests, and slew them upon it, and yet it was not quiet. So that he slew upon it ninety-four thousand, and yet it was not quiet. He drew near to it himself, and said, O Zechariah, Zechariah, thou hast destroyed the best of thy people; would you have me destroy all? Then it was quiet, and bubbled no more.

This legend must be of some antiquity, for it is found in early Christian literature. There it is related of Zechariah, father of John the Baptist. It is

[1] *Wars*, IV. v. 4.

found in the *Gospel Commentaries* of S. Ephraim the Syrian (c. 373 A.D.) in words that reflect some older account: 'Others say, that Zechariah, when his son was demanded of him during the slaughter of the infants, because he had preserved him by flight into the desert, was slain before the altar, as the Lord said.' A clear parallel to the Talmudic story is given in the *Life of John the Baptist*, composed by Serapion, an Egyptian bishop, c. 385-395 A.D. The text was edited and translated from two MSS. by Dr. A. Mingana.[1] The relevant passage is as follows: 'Let us now proceed and commemorate the holy Zecharias, the martyr, and relate to you a few of his numerous merits. I should wish to praise your true life, but I fear to hear a reproof from you, similar to that you made to the blessed Elizabeth. I am full of admiration for you, O pious Zecharias! In the time when the soldiers of Herod came to you and asked you, saying, Where is your infant son, the child of your old age? you did not deny the fact and say, I have no knowledge of such a child, but you simply answered, His mother took him into the desert. And when Zecharias uttered these words to the soldiers concerning his son, they killed him inside the Temple, and the priests shrouded his body and placed it near that of his father Berechiah in a hidden cemetery, from fear of the wicked (king); and his blood boiled on the earth for fifty years, until Titus son of Vespasian, the Emperor of the Romans, came and destroyed Jerusalem and killed the Jewish priests for the blood of Zecharias, as the Lord ordered him.'

How did this legend of the bubbling blood originate, which is known both to the Rabbis and the Church Fathers? In the Gospels the crime against Zechariah, the last Just One, is associated with that of the first Just One, Abel; and so in our legend the idea of the bubbling blood seems to depend on a midrashic interpretation of *Gen.* iv. 10, where God says to Cain: 'The voice of thy brother's blood crieth unto me from the ground.' The common features in the story as given are: (1.) the foul murder of an innocent man in the Temple; (2.) he is a priest and a prophet; (3.) his blood boils or bubbles, thus crying out for vengeance; (4.) the enemy commander slaughters the priests; (5.) this happens on the eve of the destruction of Jerusalem.

In both forms of the story the victim is Zechariah (either the son of Berechiah or Jehoiada). But we are at liberty, because of the other details, to consider this name as a disguise, one of the two Prophets Zechariah being taken as an anticipation of the martyred Just One in view of the account in *Chronicles*. The quotation as it stands in the Gospels seems to imply that 'Zechariah' is the very latest outstanding Zaddik. And here again vengeance for his death, and that of all the previous righteous ones, is to fall on a single

[1] *Bulletin of the John Rylands Library*, July 1927.

generation in one terrible catastrophe. In the legend of the boiling blood the catastrophe in the one case is the destruction of Jerusalem at the time of the first Temple, and in the other case at the time of the second Temple. The historic Zechariah the son of Jehoiada was murdered a long time before the fall of Jerusalem at the hands of the forces of Nebuchadnezzar, and thus the sense of immediacy is lost, while Zechariah the son of Berechiah the son of Iddo prophesied after the Exile and there is no evidence that he met a violent end. We are reminded of *Rev.* vi. 9-11: 'And when he had opened the fifth seal, I saw *under the altar* the souls of them that were slain for the word of God, and for the testimony which they held: and they cried with a loud voice, saying, How long, O Lord, holy and true, dost Thou not *judge and avenge our blood* on them that dwell on the earth? . . . And it was said unto them, that they should rest for a *little season*, until their fellow-servants also, and their brethren, that should be killed as they were, should be fulfilled.'

In Zechariah, therefore, we may have an antetype, comparable to the Joseph antetype, of one who, in the words of the *Testament of Benjamin*, would fulfil 'the prophecy of heaven, which says that the blameless one shall be defiled for lawless men, and the sinless one shall die for godless men'. It is the 'Wisdom of God' which declares this, as it is the *Wisdom of Solomon* which sets before us the tortured end of the righteous man at the hands of the wicked.

'Let us lie in wait for the righteous man, because he is of disservice to us', says the *Wisdom of Solomon*. These words are based on the Greek LXX version of *Isaiah* iii. 10: 'Woe to their soul, for they have devised an evil counsel against themselves, saying against themselves, Let us bind the just, for he is inconvenient to us: therefore they shall eat the fruits of their works.'

Pursuing this matter, we come to the account given of the death of James the Just, brother of Jesus, where the same text is quoted. The passage is extracted by Eusebius from the Fifth Book of the *Commentaries* of Hegesippus. We need not here give the whole extract. James had been invited by the Scribes and Pharisees to stand on a wing of the Temple to offer testimony which would restrain the people from believing in Christ. Instead he encouraged his audience to believe in Jesus. Thereupon his sponsors decided to kill him. 'And they cried out, "Oh, oh, the Just himself is deceived," and they fulfilled that which is written in Isaiah, "Let us take away the Just, because he is offensive to us; wherefore they shall eat the fruit of their doings."' After stoning James, a fuller finally beat out his brains with a club. 'Thus he suffered martyrdom, and they buried him on the spot where his tombstone is still remaining, by the Temple. Immediately after this, Vespasian invaded and took Judea.' Eusebius then continues: 'Such is the more ample testimony of Hegesippus, in which he fully coincides with Clement. So admirable a man indeed was James, and so celebrated by all for his justice, that even the wiser part of the Jews were of opinion that this was the cause of the immediate siege of Jerusalem, which happened to them for no other reason than the crime against him. Josephus also has not hesitated to superadd this testimony in his works: "These things," says he, "happened to the Jews to avenge James the Just, who was the brother of him that is called Christ, and whom the Jews had slain, notwithstanding his pre-eminent justice." '[1]

We cannot fail to see here the influence of a tradition which had turned into a prophecy. When Hegesippus wrote (c. 180 A.D.) the tradition had already become applied to the historical figure of James the Just, and the works of Josephus had been interpolated accordingly. James is the Just One killed in the Temple (he had previously been described as a priestly figure), in vengeance for whose death divine justice decreed the desolation of Jerusalem at the hands of Vespasian. It was the Fifth Book of Josephus's *Jewish War*, under its old name of *The Capture* (of Jerusalem) in which, apparently, this statement was inserted,[2] and Origen read it in his copy in the third century:

> Although not believing in Jesus as the Christ, Josephus, when searching for the true cause of the fall of Jerusalem, ought to have said that the persecution of Jesus was the cause of its ruin, because the people had killed the prophesied Messiah; yet as if against his will and not far from the truth he says that this befell the Jews in revenge for James the Just, who was the brother of Jesus the so-called Christ, because they killed him, although he was a perfectly just man.[3]

So now the tradition embodied in the legend of Ben Berechiah has attached itself to James the Just, and what had been handed down regarding the martyred Just One finds its ultimate fulfilment in him. There is no smoke without fire. The memory of some distinguished blameless sufferer of the first half of the second century B.C., alluded to but never named, must have been very strong to create both legends and prophecies to be fulfilled in the Last Days. The memory related to the death of a famous Chasid, Prophet and Priest, reflected in the *Vision of Enoch*, in the tradition of Joseph ben Joezer in *Genesis Rabbah*, in the Joseph prophecy in the *Testament of Benjamin*, in the passage on the righteous sufferer in the *Wisdom of Solomon*, in the Ben Berechiah story in the *Talmud* and in the *Life of John the Baptist*, in the

[1] *Eccl. Hist.* Bk. II. xxiii.
[2] See Eisler, *The Messiah Jesus and John the Baptist*, pp. 140-141.
[3] *C. Cels.* Bk. I. xlvii. The statement is absent from the extant Greek text of Josephus's *Jewish War*.

function assigned to Messiah ben Joseph, and the application of the prophecies to James the Just.

The memories, the traditions and the legends, working with the writings of the Prophets and Chasidic faith in the high destiny of the priesthood, became responsible for the twin expectation that in the End of the Days there would arise a Suffering Teacher of Righteousness and a Suffering Messiah, Priest, Prophet, Precursor, whatever it might be. Joseph the Just merges with Elijah the Just. Zechariah Ben Berechiah (or Jehoiada) the Just finds fulfilment in James the Just. Elijah the Just is realized in John the Baptist, the Suffering Messiah in Jesus ben Joseph the Just or a future Ben Joseph, in whatever way one might feel that there had come to pass 'what is written'. So Jesus is made to speak of both himself and John the Baptist: 'And they asked him, saying, Why say the scribes that Elijah must first come? And he answered and told them, Elijah verily cometh first, and restoreth all things; and how *it is written* of the Son of Man, that he must suffer many things, and be set at naught. But I say unto you, That Elijah is indeed come, and they have done unto him whatsoever they listed, as *it is written* of him' (*Mk*. ix. 11-13).

Always the Great Crime precedes the Great Catastrophe. 'Which of the prophets have not your fathers persecuted? And they have slain them which shewed before of the coming of the Just One; of whom ye have been now the betrayers and murderers' (*Acts*. vii. 52); 'that upon you may come all the righteous blood shed upon the earth, from the blood of righteous Abel unto the blood of Zechariah son of Berechiah, whom ye slew between the temple and the altar. Verily I say unto you, all these things shall come upon this generation' (*Matt*. xxiii. 35-36). The blood of Zechariah brings the Catastrophe of Nebuchadnezzar. The blood of the first Teacher brings the Catastrophe of Antiochus Epiphanes. The blood of Jesus, or James the Just, or the last Teacher of Righteousness, brings the Catastrophe of Titus and Vespasian.

But we are not yet finished with the legend of Ben Berechiah, and the light that can be thrown on the first Teacher of Righteousness.

CHAPTER ELEVEN

Taxo

ONE of the most important books that have come down to us from the Jewish pietists is the *Assumption*, or more properly the *Testament of Moses*. The author, writing early in the first century A.D., gives an outline of Jewish history in the form of a prophecy by Moses delivered to Joshua as a parting charge, and he is a valuable witness because he particularly surveys the period from the time of the Hellenizers down to his own day. He regards himself as living in the Time of the End, and expects the Consummation in the fairly near future.

As we have already seen[1] the book begins significantly enough with the handing over to Joshua of the prophetic script. Moses addresses his successor: 'Receive thou the writing that thou mayst know how to preserve the books which I shall deliver unto thee. And thou shalt set these in order and anoint them with oil of cedar and put them away in earthen vessels in the place which He made from the beginning of the creation of the world, that His Name should be called upon until the day of repentance in the visitation wherewith the Lord shall visit them in the Consummation of the End of the Days' (i. 16-18).

We may pass over chapters ii-iv, which are devoted to a brief coverage of events from the entrance into Canaan down to the resettlement after the Babylonian Exile, and come directly to chapters v-ix. These we shall here reproduce as a continuous text without chapter and verse divisions employing Charles's translation.[2]

> And when the times of chastisement draw nigh and vengeance arises through the kings who share in their guilt and punish them (the Jews), they themselves also will be divided as to the truth. Wherefore it hath come to pass: 'They will turn aside from righteousness and approach iniquity, and they will defile with pollutions the house of their worship,'

---

[1] Above p. 11.

[2] *The Assumption of Moses* by R. H. Charles, edition of 1897. The critical and explanatory notes are excellent.

and 'they will go a whoring after strange gods.' For they will not follow the truth of God, but some will pollute the altar with the very gifts which they offer to the Lord, (they) who are not priests but slaves, sons of slaves.[1]

And many in those times will respect the persons of the rich, and be greedy of gain, and wrest judgment on receiving presents. And on this account their colony (i.e. Jerusalem) and the borders of their habitation will be filled with lawless deeds and iniquities: they will forsake the Lord: they will be impious judges: they will be ready to judge for money as each may wish.[2]

And there will come upon them a second visitation and wrath, such as has not befallen them from the beginning until that time, in which He will stir up against them the King of the kings of the earth and one that ruleth with great power (i.e. Antiochus Epiphanes), who will crucify those who confess to their circumcision: and those who conceal it he will torture and deliver them to be bound and led into prison. And their wives will be given to the gods among the Gentiles and their young sons will be operated on by the physicians in order to bring forward their foreskin. And others amongst them will be punished by tortures and sword, and they will be forced to bear in public their idols, (which are as) polluted as are the (shrines) that contain them. And they will likewise be forced by those who torture them to enter their inmost Sanctuary, and they will be forced by goads to blaspheme with insolence the Name, finally after these things the laws and what they had above their altar.

Then in that day there will be a man of the tribe of Levi, whose name will be Taxo,[3] who having seven sons will speak to them exhorting (them): 'Observe, my sons, behold a second ruthless (and) unclean visitation has come upon the people, and a punishment merciless and far exceeding the first. For what nation or region or what people of those who are impious towards the Lord, who have done many abominations, have suffered as great calamities as have befallen us? Now therefore, my sons, hear me: for observe and know that neither did (our) fathers nor their forefathers tempt God, so as to transgress His commands. And ye know that this is our strength, and thus we will do. Let us fast for the space of three days and on the fourth let us go into a cave which is in the field, and let us die rather than transgress the commands of the Lord of lords, the God of our fathers. For if we do this and die, our blood will be avenged before the Lord.'[4]

[1] The Hellenizing priesthood.

[2] Ch. v ends here, and the next two paragraphs represent viii and ix, which as Charles shows are misplaced in the MS.

[3] On the basis of a passage in the Samaritan *Legends of Moses*, which here seems dependent on our work, where it is said: 'his name shall be called "Zealot of the Community,"' Charles inclines to regard *Taxo* (transliterated חקסא) as a corruption of הקנא 'the Zealot.' He rightly draws attention to the words of Mattathias (*I. Macc.* ii. 27) and to the martyred seven sons in *II Macc.*vii. He concludes that *Taxo* represents those who were zealous for the Law.

[4] The transposition of viii-ix may have caused the loss of some lines here at the end of ix, for the transition back to vi and vii—next two paragraphs—is rather abrupt.

Then there will be raised up unto them kings bearing rule (i.e. the Hasmoneans), and they will call themselves high priests of God: they will assuredly work iniquity in the holy of holies. And an insolent king (i.e. Herod) will succeed them, who will not be of the race of the priests, a man bold and shameless, and he will judge them as they shall deserve. And he will cut off their chief men with the sword, and will destroy (them) in secret places, so that no one may know where their bodies are. He will slay the old and the young, and he will not spare. Then the fear of him will be bitter unto them in their land. And he will execute judgments on them as the Egyptians executed upon them, during thirty and four years, and he will punish them. And he will beget children, who succeeding him will rule for shorter periods.[1] Into their parts cohorts and a powerful king of the west will come (i.e. Varus, Roman legate of Syria), who will conquer them: and he will take them captive, and burn a part of their Temple with fire, (and) he will crucify some around their colony.[2]

And when this is done the times will be ended, in a moment the (second) course will be (at hand), the four hours will come. They will be forced. . . .[3] And, in the time of these, scornful and impious men will rule, saying that they are just. And these will conceal the wrath of their minds, being treacherous men, self-pleasers, dissemblers in all their own affairs and lovers of banquets at every hour of the day, gluttons, gourmands . . . devourers of the goods of the poor, saying that they do so on the ground of their justice, but (in reality) to destroy them, complainers, deceitful, concealing themselves lest they should be recognised, impious, filled with lawlessness and iniquity from sunrise to sunset, saying: 'We shall have feastings and luxury, yea we shall drink our fill, we shall be as princes.' And though their hands and their minds touch unclean things, yet their mouth will speak great things, and they will say furthermore: 'Do not touch me lest thou shouldst pollute me in the place where I stand. . . .'[4]

As has been pointed out in the notes, chapters viii and ix have been misplaced in the MS, and their proper position is after chapter v, as in this translation. But there may have been a reason for the misplacement, because if the two chapters are left where they actually come in the text the next words following the end of our quotation will be the opening of viii: 'And there will come upon them a second visitation and wrath, such as has not befallen

[1] Archelaus ruled for ten years, and the author evidently assumed that Philip and Antipas would also not reign as long as Herod. This is why Charles fixes on the date of composition as lying somewhere between 9–30 A.D.

[2] See Joseph. *Wars*, II. v. 1–3.

[3] The text here is defective, but a few words remain which Charles does not translate, though he quotes the restorations of other scholars. From these words and the expression 'the four hours' it is to be assumed that the reference is to the watches of the night before the dawn.

[4] The author may be castigating the Pharisees as well as the Sadducean hierarchy.

them from the beginning until that time.' An editor, perhaps a Christian, may in this way have wanted to bring in the 'visitation and wrath' of 70 A.D., though the terms are strictly inapplicable. The final chapter x, which we have not quoted, is in fact devoted to an apocalyptic description of the coming of the Kingdom of God, closely akin to elements of what is known as 'the Little Apocalypse' in the Synoptic Gospels (*Matt.* xxiv. 29; *Mk.* xiii. 24-25; *Lk.* 25-26). Charles has remarked upon the use of this work by New Testament writers, and has particularly drawn attention to its influence on the speech put into the mouth of Stephen in the *Acts of the Apostles*. That speech itself is in the form of an outline of the history of Israel (*Acts* vii) ending with the coming of the promised *Zaddik* (the Just One).

We are specially interested in what is said of the period of the 'second visitation and wrath' in the time of Antiochus Epiphanes. It is to be observed that there is no reference, as in older works, to the heroic exploits of the Maccabees. But we are given the kind of exhortation which the priest of Modin is said to have uttered in the *First Book of Maccabees*, here voiced by 'a man of the tribe of Levi' mysteriously called Taxo. Surely we have every right to suspect that this late tradition may allude to the original Teacher of Righteousness!

The name is obviously a disguise, and comes to us in Latin, derived from Greek and ultimately from Hebrew. There can be no doubt that the book was first written in Hebrew. Therefore we must visualize the name in its Hebrew form, and Charles's suggestion of HaQana הקנא 'the Zealot', which by a scribal error became *Taqsa*, is not at all convincing. Helped by the Hagu or Hago of the *Damascus Document*, we can readily see that the natural Hebrew original of Taxo would be Tachu or Tacho (תחו).[1] 'To disclose the secret of this name we turn once more to the *Atbash* cipher, which we employed so profitably in the first stages of our investigation, and, behold, a genuine Hebrew name appears! תחו converts by *Atbash* into אסף (Asaph). A new and surprising name becomes available to us, even if this too should prove to be another alias of the anonymous Teacher.

Furnished with this fresh clue we have to set to work to explore its possibilities. We can see at once how the name links up with the material in our last chapter, for the best known Asaph was the Levite Asaph ben Berechiah, the singer, founder of a choral guild called the Sons of Asaph. Another Ben Berechiah!

Now it is an extraordinary fact that in the Biblical records Asaph and his

---

[1] Assuming TAXO to represent a Greek TAXΩ. Compare the name Ham (חם), Gr. XAM.

choir are exclusively mentioned in the late priestly books of *Chronicles*, *Ezra* and *Nehemiah*, compiled in the third century B.C. The books of *Kings* make no reference to Asaph, his choir, and those associated with him. In one place in *Chronicles* Asaph is curiously called a seer, and in the Septuagint a prophet (*II Chron*. xxix. 30). It is by no means impossible, therefore, that the description was inserted by the Chasidim in allusion to one with whom they associated the name of Asaph. In Jewish and Mohammedan legend Asaph ben Berechiah is a princely figure, the confidant of King Solomon. Moreover he knew the Ineffable Name of God, and had the power to perform wonders by means of the Name.[1] There also exists a work, the origin of which is unknown, variously entitled *Sefer Asaf*, *Midrash Refu'ot*, and *Sefer Refu'ot*. It is a medical treatise, and its author is said to have been Asaph the Younger, Asaph the Physician, Asaph the Sage, and even Asaph ben Berechiah the Astronomer. The introduction ascribes the origin of medicine to Shem the son of Noah,[2] and it is interesting to find in *Jubilees*: 'And we explained to Noah all the medicines of their diseases, together with their seductions, how he might heal them with herbs of the earth. And Noah wrote down all things in a book as we instructed him concerning every kind of medicine' (x. 12-13). All that Noah wrote he gave to Shem (x. 14), and in due course the ancient scripts were handed on by Jacob to Levi: 'And he gave all his books and the books of his fathers to Levi his son that he might preserve them and renew them for his children until this day' (xlv. 16). Thus is explained how the Chasidim, and so the Essenes, came to be in possession of works attributed to the ancestors of the race, by knowledge of which they could heal the sick and predict the future. This is confirmed by Josephus. 'They (the Essenes) display an extraordinary interest in the writings of the ancients, singling out in particular those which make for the welfare of soul and body; with the help of these, and with a view to the treatment of diseases, they make investigation into medicinal roots and the properties of stones' (*Wars*, II. viii. 6.). 'There are some among them who profess to foretell the future, being versed from their early years in holy books, various forms of purification and apophthegms of prophets; and seldom, if ever, do they err in their predictions' (II. viii. 12). Linked with this tradition is the name of Asaph, seer, sage, physician and astronomer.

Before we discuss other matters of consequence connected with the name of Asaph, it will be well to follow this line of thought a little further, as far indeed as the available material will take us.

Additional references to the writings of Noah are found not only in

[1] Rappoport, *Myth and Legend of Ancient Israel*, Vol. III, pp. 97, 200, 204.

[2] See JE. art. *Asaph ben Berechiah*, Vol. II, p. 162; A. Mingana, *Some Judaeo-Christian Documents in the John Rylands Library*, pp. 20–21.

Jubilees, but in some fragments of a *Testament of Levi* in Aramaic and Greek which Charles regards as an original source both of this Testament in the *Test. XII Patriarchs* and of *Jubilees*.[1] In the first, Abraham delivers an injunction to Isaac that sacrificial meat is not to be eaten after the second day; 'for thus I have found it written in the words of Enoch, and in the words of Noah' (*Jub*. xxi. 10), and in the second, Levi speaks of the prohibition of the eating of blood; 'for so my father Abraham commanded me; for so he found in the writing of the Book of Noah, concerning the blood.' Fragments of the *Book of Noah* have come to light at Qumran.[2] There is also a late Syriac *Book of Shem*, which may best be described as Old Shem's Almanac: it is only of consequence because of the introduction to the Asaph medical treatise, and because in the same Syriac MS. which contains the *Book of Shem* there is an extract from another work which mentions Asaph.[3] This latter is a quotation from a Greek writer called 'Andronicus the Wise, the Philosopher and the Learned.' Mingana thinks he is likely to have been the astronomer Andronicus Cyrrhestes, who died about 100 B.C., and who is credited by Vitruvius with the setting up of the octagonal marble tower at Athens now known as the Temple of the Winds. The quotation deals with the signs of the Zodiac and includes the following passage:

> Asaph the writer and the historian of the Hebrews explains and teaches clearly the history of all these (signs), but does not write and show them with Greek names, but according to the names of the sons of Jacob. As to the effects and influences of these στοιχέια he, too, enumerates them fully without adding or diminishing anything, but in simply changing in a clear language their names into those of the Patriarchs. He begins then in the Aramaic language and puts at the head Taurus, which he calls 'Reuben'. After it comes Aries, which they call 'Simeon'. After it comes Pisces, which they call 'Levi'. After it comes Aquarius, which they call 'Issacher'. After it comes Capricorn, which they call 'Naphtali'. After it he sketches a rider while shooting, and calls him 'Gad', and he is analogous with the Kirek (?) of the Greeks. After it comes Scorpio, which he calls 'Dan'. After it he mentions Libra, which he calls 'Asher'. After it he mentions Virgo, whom he calls 'Dinah'. After it (comes) Leo, which he calls 'Judah'. Then he sketches Cancer, which he calls 'Zebulun'. After it he mentions Gemini, whom he calls 'Ephraim and Manasseh'.

Mingana makes it clear that the Asaph referred to cannot be the historian Josephus, whose name is transcribed in Syriac as *Yusiphus*, and he suggests that 'there might have been a Jewish astronomer, historian and physician

[1] *Testaments of the Twelve Patriarchs*, pp. lxviii-lxxiv, 232.
[2] *Qumran Cave* 1, p. 84f.
[3] Mingana, *op. cit.*, pp. 20-33.

called Asaph living in the centuries immediately preceding or following the Christian era. His works having been lost, his surviving name might have been prefixed to some later literary productions, in order to enhance their credit.' That is an interesting guess in view of the revelation of the name in the *Assumption of Moses*, of which Mingana was unaware, and the date at which Taxo-Asaph lived. It is difficult not to presume the identity of this man with the Teacher of Righteousness, who otherwise must have been his contemporary.[1] Two such distinguished 'Zealots of the Law', erudite Chasids, of whom the traditions tell, while not impossible is not very likely. The Teacher of Righteousness, as reflected in the *Habakkuk Commentary*, was also a seer like Asaph. He was a 'priest whom God placed in the house of Judah to explain all the words of His servants the Prophets (and to expound from) the book of God all that will befall His people Israel' (i. 5). To him 'God made known all the secrets of His servants the Prophets' (ii. 1-3).

Early in our inquiry we pointed out that in *II Macc.* ii. 14 Judas Maccabaeus is credited with having 'gathered together for us all those writings that had been scattered by reason of the war that befell.'[2] This he would not have done himself, and must have delegated the responsibility to a supremely competent person or persons. The expression 'gathered together' is in Hebrew 'asaph' and the name itself means 'The Collector.' Could it be that one of the reasons why the Teacher of Righteousness was called Asaph was because he performed this function? *Jubilees*, as we have seen, entrusts to Levi the preservation and renewing of the sacred books *until this day*. The name Asaph is also connected with Joseph (*Gen.* xxx. 23-24), and we have found rabbinical stories attaching the recollection of a martyred Chasid and Priest to Joseph ben Joezer, a prominent scholar of the time.[3] We have also found a reference in the *Ascension of Isaiah* to a book of *Joseph the Just*, placed after *Malachi* and before *Daniel* (165 B.C.). The one who at least acquiesced in the execution of Joseph ben Joezer, if he was not actually responsible for it, was the wicked High Priest Alcimus. It was this Alcimus who betrayed the Chasidim when they came to him for redress.[4] 'And he spake with them words of peace, and sware unto them, saying, "We will seek the hurt neither of you nor your friends." And they gave him credence: and he laid hands on threescore men of them, and slew them in one day, according to the word which he wrote, "The flesh of thy saints (did they cast out), and their blood did they shed round about

[1] It probably has no significance that the verb *asaph* 'to gather in' is selected in the *Damascus Document* to indicate the death of the Unique Teacher. But it may be noted.

[2] Above p. 9.

[3] Above p. 18.

[4] Above p. 18.

Jerusalem; and there was no man to bury them" ' (*I Macc.* vii. 5). The word which who wrote? Why be so evasive? The text is taken from *Ps.* lxxix. 2-3. Why not say Asaph? For this is one of the twelve psalms attributed to Asaph in the Biblical Collection.

The Asaphite psalms are those numbered l (50), and lxxiii-lxxxiii inclusive. At least two of these, lxxiv and lxxxiii, have been placed by scholars in the Maccabean period. It is questionable whether any of them are of much higher antiquity. The dating of these psalms now becomes a matter of great importance in view of the discovery of the Asaph of the *Assumption of Moses*, and because of the collection of so-called *Thanksgiving Psalms* at Khirbet Qumran. Also to be recalled is the report of Timotheus, Metropolitan of Seleucia in the ninth century, of the find of some two hundred 'Psalms of David' in a cave near Jericho,[1] and the text of the *Psalms* discovered in a jar at Jericho in the reign of Antoninus son of Severus and used by Origin in his Hexapla.[2] Was the choral guild of Asaph closely identified with the Chasidic Movement? The text of the Asaphite psalms would certainly suggest that it was; for the whole spirit and attitude of the Movement is reflected in them.

I do not propose to discuss this question in detail. But some points may briefly be touched upon as representing fruitful lines for further inquiry.

Ps. lxxxiii, last of the Asaphite psalms, speaks of a confederacy against Israel, which includes Edom and Moab, Ammon and Amalek, the Philistines with the inhabitants of Tyre, and Assur. These are among the enemies of Israel prophesied against in the late section of *Jeremiah* (xxv- and xlvi-li). In the war of Esau against Jacob described in *Jubilees* xxxvii there is a similar list, which it has long been seen refers to the Syrians and their allies against whom the Maccabees fought (*I Macc.* v). The list comes up again as the Host of Belial in the *War of the Sons of Light with the Sons of Darkness* found among the Dead Sea Scrolls, and this work contains battle and victory hymns.

Both the *War of the Sons of Light* and the *Thanksgiving Psalms* have distinct points of contact with the hymns in the *Gospel of Luke*, and the *Thanksgiving Psalms* are also reflected in some of the so-called *Odes of Solomon*. Asaph ben Berechiah is placed in the reign of Solomon, who was anointed by Zadok. It is not surprising, therefore, that collections of hymns subsequently appear among the pietists bearing names like the *Psalms of Solomon* and *Odes of Solomon*.

The Asaph of the *Assumption of Moses* has seven sons. This puts the 'Sons of Asaph' in a new context like 'the Sons of Zadok.' It should be noted what is said in *Test. Levi* xviii: 'Then shall the Lord raise up a new priest. And to him all

---

[1] Above p. 48.
[2] See Euseb. *Eccl. Hist.* Bk. VI. xvi.

the words of the Lord shall be revealed . . . He shall give the majesty of the Lord to his sons in truth for evermore.' This passage follows a reference to the seventh week in which there will be an apostate priesthood (xvii. 11), comparable with chapters iv and v of *Assumption of Moses* before the coming of Taxo-Asaph.

We also read in *Enoch* xciii. 9-10: 'And after that in the seventh week will a generation arise and many will be its deeds, and all its deeds will be apostate. And at its close will the Elect of Righteousness of the Eternal Plant of Righteousness be elected to receive the *sevenfold* instruction regarding His whole creation.'

Without any knowledge of the name Asaph entering into the study of the Dead Sea Scrolls, Dupont-Sommer[1] has considered that the Teacher of Righteousness may have been a psalmist, composer of at least one of the recovered *Thanksgiving Psalms* which seems to speak of the Teacher's tribulations.

Whatever may lie behind the disguise or pseudonym of Asaph, everything with which it connects agrees in time and circumstances, and can be related to all we are learning of the origin and history of the New Covenant Party. Tradition, legend, and even intentional mystification, may prevent us from seeing as clearly as we would wish, but cannot wholly conceal what we are so anxious to discover.

---

[1] *The Dead Sea Scrolls*, p.70.

CHAPTER TWELVE

The Habakkuk Commentary

WE COME now at last to the most enlightening of the Dead Sea Scrolls on matters of detail, the *Habakkuk Commentary*. We have frequently dipped into this work in the course of our investigation; but have reserved lengthier consideration of its contents until this point so as not to detract from the weight of evidence which so clearly placed the original Teacher of Righteousness in the first half of the second century B.C. The arguments we have employed in chapters v, vi, vii, viii and ix make it highly probable that the *Habakkuk Commentary* was written in the first century A.D. and envisages events that were very recent, and that the hero of the work is the second Teacher of the *Damascus Commentary*, 'the Teacher of Righteousness of the End of the Days.' Except in so far as the experiences of the second Teacher could be expected prophetically to reproduce what was traditionally remembered of the first Teacher, which indeed would help to identify him to the faithful as 'the one who should come', he is not—unless by transmigration of soul—the same person. The Teacher of the *Habakkuk Commentary* is so closely related to circumstances within the immediate knowledge of the commentator, that it seems improbable that he should be someone who lived very much earlier, while we have given reasons for believing that the kind of exegesis represented by the *Commentary* is not older than the first century A.D. We shall see that the most natural interpretation of the commentator's explanations confirms this. What difficulties have arisen over interpretation and dating are due in no small measure to the assumption that the Teacher of Righteousness referred to was the original founder of the Party instead of the Expected One who would be like him. Except in respect of this likeness we may no longer be dealing with the former Just One, who has come before us as the 'Son of Berechiah'—Zechariah, Asaph or Joseph—the Prophet, Priest and Judge who arose at the time of the Wrath that followed the Great Apostasy of the Hellenizers. In the interval generations had elapsed, the Party had undergone many trials and vicissitudes, built up its discipline and its literature. Here, in the *Habakkuk Commentary*, we meet with it in the fateful period of the End of the Days, unexpectedly prolonged, awaiting eagerly in the light of events the ultimate Deliverance. It is the confusion of the two periods and the two Teachers which has forced some scholars to do such violence to the material, and produced the hypothesis of a single Teacher in the first half of the first century B.C.

The book consists of an exegetical interpretation of the prophecies of Habakkuk. The author works steadily through the first two chapters, quoting short passages and adding to each the application of its terms. The words of the Prophet, as given, do not always agree with the Massoretic Hebrew text. Some may be better readings; but in a few cases it looks as if the alteration has been made deliberately to suit the requirements of the author's exegesis. For example, *Hab.* ii. 15 is quoted as למען הבט אל מועדיהם 'in order that God may look at their feasts' instead of למען הביט על מעוריהם 'that thou mayst look on their nakedness.'

The author does not state in so many words the time of which he is writing, but he gives more than adequate indications. At i. 6, on the text, ' "For, lo, I raise up the Chaldeans, that bitter and hasty nation," the explanation is that this refers to the Kittim, who are swift and mighty in battle . . . ' The commentary for nearly the whole of the rest of this chapter relates to the Kittim under various aspects, and the details given, as Dupont-Sommer[1] and others have plainly shown, make it certain that the Kittim are the Romans. This may be accepted as one assured result of the study of the work. But which period of Roman history is in the writer's mind has not been so generally agreed upon. I follow Teicher in regarding two passages as conclusive on this point.[2]

The first passage is the commentary on *Hab.* i. 11. ' "Then the wind has veered and he has passed away, and that one has made his strength his god." This refers to the Kittim, who under instruction from the House of Idolatry come in succession one after another. The rulers (governors) come one after another to destroy the people (or peoples).' On this passage Teicher says: 'The expression, "House of Idolatry," refers, I submit, to the Imperial Palace, a place of idolatry, since the Emperor was the object of a divine cult, and the passage in the Scroll means accordingly that the procurators of Judea sent out by

[1] *The Dead Sea Scrolls*, pp. 29-31. While largely using Dupont-Sommer's translation, I have carefully checked his rendering with the Hebrew, in a few cases with somewhat different results.

[2] J. L. Teicher, *The Habakkuk Scroll, Journal of Jewish Studies*, Vol. V, No. 2, p. 51.

the Emperor ruined the country—a concise and apt description of the Roman procurators in Palestine before the outbreak of the Jewish War.'

I believe it to be correct that the House of Idolatry here means the Imperial regime, the idolatrous character of which was featured in apocalyptic imagery and nearly brought the Jews to open war when Gaius Caligula had attempted to have his statue as Jupiter set up in the Temple at Jerusalem. As for the Roman procurators sent one after another, it is only necessary to mention the names of Cuspius Fadus, Ventidius Cumanus, Felix, Porcius Festus, and Albinus. 'But,' as Josephus says, almost echoing the words of our commentator, 'his successor, Gessius Florus, made Albinus appear by comparison a paragon of virtue. The crimes of Albinus were, for the most part, perpetrated in secret and with dissimulation; Gessius, on the contrary, ostentatiously paraded his outrages upon the nation, and, as though he had been sent as hangman of condemned criminals, abstained from no form of robbery or violence . . . He stripped whole cities, ruined entire populations, and almost went the length of proclaiming throughout the country that all were at liberty to practise brigandage, on condition that he received his share of the spoils.' It was in no small measure due to the conduct of these governors, culminating in Florus, that the Jews rose in revolt against the Romans.[1] Both the development of the Imperial cult and of the system of governors were features of the reign of Augustus (27 B.C.–14 A.D.).

The second passage is the commentary on *Hab.* ii. 8a. ' "Because thou hast spoiled many nations, all the residue of the peoples shall spoil thee." This refers to the last priests of Jerusalem, who amassed wealth and plunder by preying on the peoples. But in the Last Days their wealth and plunder will be given into the hand of the Kittim; for they are "the residue of the peoples." ' Dupont-Sommer, in the interests of his theory that the Teacher of Righteousness lived in the time of Aristobulus II and Hyrcanus II, takes the Last Priests to mean the Hasmoneans. But the Hasmoneans could not be so described, though it could be said that they were the last kings who were priests. Teicher, unfortunately, goes right off the rails in support of his own theory that the New Covenant Party represents the Judaeo-Christians, and that the Teacher of Righteousness is Jesus and the Wicked Priest is Paul. Accordingly, he has to conclude that the Last Priests of Jerusalem were the ministers or teachers of the Jerusalem Church, 'who have come to an agreement with Paul and accepted the collections from the Gentile Churches ("the booty of the

---

[1] The Slavonic Josephus includes two invectives against the Romans: 'They are insatiable in receiving; but if anyone gives them more to-day, to-morrow they want still more' Josephus, Vol. III, Appendix, (Loeb Classical Library).

Gentiles").' Both scholars agree, however, that the passage means that the Romans will get possession of funds amassed at Jerusalem.

Without any theorising at all, the plain sense of the passage is that the Last Priests of Jerusalem means the last officiating High Priests, whose treasure will fall into Roman hands. It is a prophecy either just before the event or in retrospect. The only other time when the words 'Last Priests' would be applicable would be when the Hasmoneans took the high priesthood away from the line of former holders. When the *Testaments of the XII Patriarchs* and the *Assumption of Moses* speak of apostate priests they mean the ruling High Priests. Why should the writer of the *Habakkuk Commentary* be supposed to mean Christian ministers? The natural inference is that the Temple is about to be or has been destroyed by the Romans. Historical facts fully confirm what the commentator says. We know from the pages of Josephus of the enormous treasure held in the Temple due to the costly gifts of non-Jews as well as Jews. Of the Last High Priests he tells how Ananias 'increased in glory every day, and this to a great degree . . . for he was great at amassing money . . . He also had servants who were very wicked, who joined themselves to the popular bullies, and went to the threshing-floors, and took by force the tithes that belonged to the priests, and did not refrain from beating such as would not give these tithes to them. So the other Chief Priests acted in the same manner as the servants of Ananias, without anyone being able to prevent them' (*Antiq.* XX. ix. 2). Josephus also accuses the High Priest Ananus son of Annas of taking bribes) *Life*, 39). How the Roman soldiers plundered Jerusalem and the Temple area is told by Josephus in *Wars*, VI. v-viii. He further relates how a priest Jesus son of Thebuthi, and the Treasurer of the Temple Phineas, bought their pardon from Titus by handing over the rich treasures of the Temple and of the High Priests (VI. viii. 3.).

The author of the *Habakkuk Commentary* is therefore aware of the depredations of the Roman procurators and of the treasure amassed by the High Priests falling into the hands of the Roman forces. The natural presumption is that he is writing not long before the fall of Jerusalem in 70 A.D., or very shortly after and that is the view we shall accept unless it is shaken by the clear implication of any other passage.

At this point we must consider a most important evidential passage from fragments of a *Nahum Commentary* from Qumran Cave Four, which reached me only just in time for inclusion in this volume.[1] The text, which expounds

[1] This is published by J. M. Allegro, 'Further Light on the History of the Qumran Sect,' *Journal of Biblical Literature*. Mr. Allegro kindly allowed me to study an infra-red photograph of the fragment.

the closing verses of *Nahum* ii, is very defective; but I render it approximately as follows:

> . . . a habitation of the wicked of the Gentiles. 'Where the lion, even the old lion, stalked, there too the cub, [and none made them afraid.' This is to be explained of Demetrius, king of Javan, who sought to enter Jerusalem on the advice of those who practise flatteries, [. . . and none made afraid] the kings of Javan from (the time of) Antiochus down to the rise of the rulers of the Kittim. But afterwards [. . .] will tread down [. . .]. 'The lion tears in pieces enough for his cubs and strangles for his lionesses' prey' [. . . This is to be explained] of the young lion of wrath who with his mighty men and his advisers will strike [. . . 'And he will fill with prey] . . . and his den with ravin.' This is to be explained of the young lion of wrath [. . .] death (?) by (or together with) those who practise flatteries, who will hang up men alive [. . . more than was ever done (?)] in Israel in time gone by; for the man hanged alive [is called (?) . . .] 'Behold, I am against thee [saith the Lord of Hosts, and I will burn up in smoke thy multitude], and thy young lions the sword shall devour. And I will cut off [from the land] his prey [. . .]. '*Thy multitude*, they are the troops of his army [. . .]. His *young lions*, they are [. . .]. And *his prey*, it is the wealth which the priests of Jerusalem amassed, which [. . . from] Ephraim, Israel shall be given [into . . .].

The striking fact about this passage is that it gives us names, though they are those of kings. There seems to be little doubt that Antiochus is Epiphanes, and that Demetrius is a subsequent Seleucid ruler. Allegro is in favour of Demetrius III, Eucaerus, called in by the rebellious Pharisees to assist them against Alexander Jannaeus. But Josephus does not tell us that this Demetrius attempted to enter Jerusalem. If the 'old lion' is Antiochus Epiphanes or his predecessor Seleucus IV, it is to be inferred that 'the cub' is much more immediately related, and is more likely to be the son of Seleucus, namely Demetrius I, Soter, who reigned (161-150 B.C.) when Alcimus was high priest. This was a time of persecution for the Chasidim, and we have already proposed that the migration to the land of Damascus took place c. 159. It was on the advice of 'those who practise flatteries,' in this case a deputation consisting of Alcimus and his supporters, who went to Demetrius to persuade him to proceed against Judas Maccabaeus at Jerusalem (*I Macc.* vii). It was as a result of this that some of the Chasidim were massacred, fulfilling the words of Asaph. Demetrius made another attempt against Jerusalem with forces under Bacchides and Alcimus in the same year (161 B.C.) and Judas was slain in the resultant battle (*I Macc.* ix).

The continuation of the passage brings us down to Roman times, and to circumstances of that period indicated by 'after' or 'afterwards.' We then come to the young lion (*kephir*) of wrath, who with his armed forces attacks Israel, and crucifies Jews. The prey he seizes is, as in *Hab. Comm.*, the wealth amassed by the priests by their depredations. Allegro, favouring Dupont-Sommer's dating of events, inclines to the view that the lion of wrath is Alexander Jannaeus, known to have crucified 800 Pharisees. But surely the position of the commentator is that the lion figures are foreign rulers, those of the Kittim having succeeded those of Javan. We should then regard him as a Roman. The *Assumption of Moses* twice refers to crucifixion of Jews carried out by alien rulers. First there was Antiochus Epiphanes, 'the king of the kings of the earth . . . who will crucify those who confess to their circumcision'; and second Varus (4 B.C.), 'a powerful king of the west, who . . . will crucify some around their colony.' If I have been correct in applying the language of the *Habakkuk Commentary* to the war with Rome of 67-70 A.D., then the reference in the *Nahum Commentary* must be to this still later situation. I therefore take the 'young lion of wrath' to be Titus.[1] Josephus tells a terrible story of the famine stricken inhabitants of Jerusalem leaving the besieged city in quest of food and being captured and tortured by the Romans at the rate of five hundred or more daily. 'The soldiers out of rage and hatred amused themselves by nailing their prisoners in different postures; and so great was their number, that space could not be found for the crosses nor crosses for the bodies.'[2]

The new evidence seems thus to confirm the conclusion I had tentatively reached from an examination of the *Habakkuk Commentary*. The writer of the *Nahum* passage, like other seers, *Revelation, Apocalypse of Ezra, Baruch, Sibylline Oracles,* foretells the doom of Rome in due time. The only other reference to the 'lion of wrath', a fragment of a *Hosea Commentary*, also makes him contemporary with the 'last priest.'

The writer of the *Habakkuk Commentary* believed himself to be living in the Last Days in which these events occurred. The New Testament writers also regarded the first century A.D. as the Last Days (*II Tim.* ii; *II Pet.* iii; *I Jn.* ii. 18). The passage in *II. Pet.* iii is specially interesting, because the writer of the epistle seeks to explain the delay in the Second Advent of Christ and the Consummation of the Age. Believers were disturbed by this delay, which is alluded to elsewhere in the parable of the faithful servant (*Matt.* xxiv. 48). 'Peter' urges that the delay is due to the longsuffering of God, who is not slack concerning His promises. This again is in line with our commentator on *Habakkuk*. On *Hab.*ii.1-3 he writes: ' . . . And God told Habakkuk to write what is to befall the Last Generation; but the Consummation of the Time He did not

[1] Paul uses the expression 'I was delivered out of the mouth of the lion' with reference to the satisfactory outcome of his first defence before Nero (*II Tim.* iv. 17). Cp. *Ps.* xxii. 21, and Jos. *Antiq.* XVIII. vi. 10 where Tiberius is referred to as 'the lion.'

[2] *Wars* V. xi. 2.

make known to him. And where he says, "that he who runs may read it," the reference is to the Righteous Teacher to whom God made known all the secrets of the words of His servants the Prophets. "For the vision is yet for an appointed time, but at the end it shall speak and not lie." The explanation is that the Last Time will be prolonged, and will transcend (or exceed) all that the Prophets have said; for the secrets of God are wonderful. "But if it delays, wait for it; for it will surely come, and will not tarry." This refers to the Men of Truth who practise the Law, whose hands never relax from the service of the Truth, in having the Last Time extended for them; for all the Times of God will come in their due season, just as He decreed of them in the secrets of His prudence.[1] The commentator, then, is conscious of delay, and he goes on to explain the words, 'But the just shall live by faith" (*Hab.* ii. 4), by saying: "This refers to all who practise the Law in the house of Judah, whom God will deliver from the House of Judgment (i.e. the Last Assize) because of their tribulation, and their faith in the Righteous Teacher." '

With the foregoing we should associate the comments on *Hab.* i. 4-5, ii. 5-6 and ii. 17. The manuscript covering i. 4-5 is very defective, but the commentator speaks of those 'who act treacherously with the Deceitful Man (or Man of Untruth)' in respect of the New Covenant and the Righteous Teacher, not believing God's Covenant. He explains i. 5 of the treacherous, the violent ones, at the End of the Days, 'who will not believe when they hear all that will befall the Last Generation by the mouth of the Priest whom God placed in the house of Judah to explain all the words of His servants the Prophets (and to expound from) the book of God all that will befall His people Israel.' Here again the Righteous Teacher is a Priest, and an interpreter of the Prophetic Scriptures. The Man of Untruth, perhaps to be identified with the Prophesier of Untruth (ii. 12-13), we have already encountered in late sections of the *Damascus Document*. He may well be the same as the one described in the *Habakkuk Commentary* as the Wicked Priest or Priest who rebelled. But it is best to reserve judgment on this matter. As to 'the treacherous, the violent ones,' who appear in our next passage as 'violent men who rebelled against God,' there is perhaps less uncertainty. They may tentatively be identified with the Zealots and Sicarii who involved Judea and Jerusalem in civil strife, and refused to credit warnings of impending judgment on Israel, so stimulated were they by false prophecies and so confident that they would triumph over the Romans.

Josephus writes of these 'violent ones' in *Wars*, II. xiii. 2-6, and tells how eventually c. 58 A.D. 'the impostors and brigands, banding together, incited

[1] Cp. *Apoc. Bar.* xliv. 7, 14-15.

numbers to revolt, exhorting them to assert their independence, and threatening to kill any who submitted to Roman domination and forcibly to suppress those who voluntarily accepted servitude. Distributing themselves in companies throughout the country, they looted the houses of the wealthy, murdered their owners, and set the villages on fire. The effects of their frenzy were thus felt throughout all Judea, and every day saw this war being fanned into fiercer flame.' The final madness of the Zealots in Jerusalem during the war with Rome is too well known to require quotation.

The *Apocalypse of Baruch*, also written after the destruction of Jerusalem, seems to refer to these Zealots when it says: 'Then zeal will arise in those of whom they thought not, and passion will seize him who is peaceful, and many will be roused in anger to injure many, and they will rouse up armies in order to shed blood, and in the end they will perish together with them' (xlviii. 37).

We come then to the comments on *Hab.* ii. 5-6 and ii. 17. The first reads: ' "Yea, also, riches will make treacherous the mighty man, and he will not stop, for his appetite is as wide as Sheol and he is as insatiable as death . . . " This refers to the Wicked Priest, who was called by the Name of Truth at the commencement of his office. But when he ruled Israel his heart was lifted up and he forsook God, and he betrayed the statutes because of riches, and he despoiled and amassed the riches of violent men who rebelled against God. And he took the riches of peoples to increase his iniquitous guilt, and followed abominable ways in every kind of foul impurity.'

The second passage is as follows: ' "For the violence inflicted on Lebanon shall return upon thee, and the oppression exercised against the cattle shall fan (the flame), because of the human blood which has been shed and the violence which has been inflicted on the country, on the city, and on all that dwell therein." This refers to the Wicked Priest, to reward him for the recompense he has repaid to the poor; for "Lebanon" is the Party of the Community, and "the cattle" are the simple of Judah who practise the Law. And God shall condemn him to destruction, even as he purposed to destroy the poor. And when it is said, "because of the blood shed in the city and the violence inflicted on the country," "the city" refers to Jerusalem, in which the Wicked Priest has done abominable deeds and has profaned the Sanctuary. As to "violence inflicted on the country" ("the country") means the towns of Judah in which he robbed the poor of their substance.'

Here the Wicked Priest becomes corrupted by his high office. The expression 'when he ruled Israel' has historical significance, for it was after Archelaus (A.D. 6) that 'the government became an aristocracy, and the high priests were entrusted with a dominion over the nation' (Joseph. *Antiq.* XX. xi. 1). The story is one we have already examined in its essentials: the Zealots and brigands pillaged the rich, and the procurators and chief priests seized the spoils of the brigands. We have also seen how the chief priests robbed the poor priests, and the particular Wicked Priest is here accused further of persecuting and seeking to destroy the poor saints, even to shedding blood in Jerusalem and profaning the Sanctuary.

We have the evidence of the *Acts of the Apostles* of the way in which the chief priests attempted to suppress the Judaeo-Christians, and according to Christian tradition their leader James the Just was murdered in the Temple area. In Josephus the death of James and some of his associates is laid at the door of the High Priest Ananus. We shall have more to say about this later; but the commentator's words are certainly consistent with events in Judea in the period before the war with Rome. The heart of the Wicked Priest was lifted up when he ruled Israel, and to the same effect Josephus says that 'this younger Ananus, who took the high priesthood, was a bold man in his temper, and very insolent' (*Antiq.* XX. ix. 1).

It is to be noted that the *Apocalypse of Baruch*, which we have quoted, in the passage immediately following reference to the Zealots, continues: 'And it will come to pass at the self-same time, that a change of times will manifestly appear to every man, by reason of which in all those times they were polluted and practised oppression, and walked every man in his own works, and remembered not the law of the Mighty One.[1] Therefore a fire will consume their thoughts, and in flame will the meditations of their reins be tried; for the Judge will come and will not tarry. Because each of the inhabitants of the land knew when he was committing iniquity, and they have not known My Law by reason of their pride' (xlviii. 38-40).

Even more to the point and to an extent parallel with the *Apocalypse of Baruch* is the New Testament *Epistle of James*. 'Go to now, ye rich men, weep and howl for your miseries that shall come upon you. Your gold and silver is cankered, and the rust of them shall be a witness against you, and shall eat your flesh as it were fire. Ye have heaped treasure together for the Last Days. Behold, the hire of the labourers who have reaped down your fields, which of you is kept back by fraud, crieth; and the cries of them which have reaped are entered into the ears of the Lord of hosts. Ye have lived in pleasure on the earth, and been wanton; ye have nourished your hearts, as in a day of slaughter. Ye have condemned and killed the just; and he doth not resist you. Be patient

---

[1] Cp. *Hab.Comm.* 'He forsook God and betrayed the statutes.'

therefore, brethren, unto the coming of the Lord . . . Grudge not one against another, brethren, lest ye be condemned: behold, the Judge standeth before the door' (v. 1-9). Elsewhere we read: 'Hearken, my beloved brethren, hath not God chosen the poor of this world rich in faith, and heirs of the kingdom which He hath promised to them that love Him? But ye have despised the poor. Do not rich men oppress you, and draw you before the judgment seats? Do they not blaspheme that worthy name by the which ye are called' (ii. 5-7).

We know how 'the poor' (*Ebionim*) became a descriptive term applied to the Judaeo-Christians; but it would in fact cover all communities of Essene type who embraced a voluntary poverty. The poor with whom the commentator is concerned is the Party of the Community, and their oppressor and persecutor would inevitably meet with his just reward.

Continuing our quotations we will now select three other passages with associated ideas.

' "Woe to him that buildeth a town with bloodshed, and stablisheth a city by iniquity! Behold, can this be from the Lord of hosts that the people should toil for the fire's benefit, and that the peoples should wear themselves out for the benefit of nothingness?" This refers to the Prophesier of Untruth, who has led many astray to build his city of falsehood with bloodshed, and establish a testimony with untruth, for the sake of its glory (or, in the service of his glory)[1]; so that many might toil in the service of his falsehood, and devise deceitful practices, that their labour might be in vain, in order they should come to the Judgment of Fire for having reviled and reproached God's Elect Ones' (ii. 12-13).

Dupont-Sommer speaks without justification of *re*building, and without warrant from the text introduces the word 'new' before glory. Thus, in keeping with his theory, he is able to make the passage refer to the rebuilding of the walls of Jerusalem under Hyrcanus II, and to new glory which Jerusalem enjoyed. It is not by any means certain that the commentator is thinking here of Jerusalem, or of an actual city. Rather does he appear to be speaking metaphorically of an edifice of lies built up by the Prophesier of Untruth to serve his own ends, thus leading his wretched dupes to their damnation in assisting him in his fell designs against God's Elect. We may introduce here the comment on *Hab.* ii. 15: ' "Thou hast sated thyself with ignominy rather than with glory. Drink, thou also, and stagger. The cup in the right hand of the Lord turns towards thee, and shame shall be on thy glory." This is explained of the Priest whose shame has exceeded his glory. For he has not circumcised the

[1] The text has בעבוד כבודו. We should read either בעבור כבודה or בעבוד כבודו.

foreskin of his heart, but has followed the ways of drunkenness to quench his thirst. But the cup of God's anger shall swallow him up . . . ' Called to the glory of the high priesthood the Wicked Priest has become drunk with power and lust for riches. Retribution awaits him.

We come now to what is probably the most difficult passage in the whole scroll. ' "Woe unto him that giveth his neighbour drink, pouring out his anger, even strong drink, in order that God may look at their feasts." This refers to the Wicked Priest who persecuted the Teacher of Righteousness to swallow him up in his place of exile. But at the time of the Day of Atonement festival of rest, he shone forth to them to swallow them up and make them stumble on the Fast Day, their sabbath of rest' (ii. 15).

In the first place the text of *Habakkuk* is altered so as to change the sense in a way that destroys the meaning the context requires. The substitution of 'in order that God may look at their feasts' for 'in order that thou mayst look upon their nakedness' must be intentional. This surely rules out the view taken by some scholars that the 'he' who 'shone forth' can be the Wicked Priest. We are intended to see a reversal of the circumstances, a come-back by the Righteous Teacher. Here I must agree with Dupont-Sommer. But I cannot follow him when he makes this 'appearance' an apparition of the martyred Teacher, nor when he imagines that this was associated with some great catastrophe that befell the Jews on the Day of Atonement, namely the capture of Jerusalem by Pompey on the Fast Day in 63 B.C.[1] Nothing is said about the taking of the city by the Kittim, who for the commentator are the Romans.

The only way I can see of extracting something approaching Dupont-Sommer's interpretation is by supposing that 'he' here means God. In saying that God 'shone forth' the commentator could have had in mind *Ps.* xciv, where the same word is used.[2]

> O God, to whom vengeance belongeth, *shine forth.*
> Lift up Thyself, thou Judge of the earth:
> Render a reward to the proud.
> Lord, how long shall the wicked,
> How long shall the wicked triumph?
> . . . .
> Yet they say, The Lord shall not see,

[1] Dupont-Sommer continues to adhere to his theory in *The Jewish Sect of Qumran and the Essenes*, pp. 32-37. Indeed he is forced to do so, since this passage in the *Habakkuk Commentary* is the foundation of his whole hypothesis about the date of the Teacher of Righteousness.

[2] Cp. *Damascus Document*, B. ix. 49, 'And as for all those who have broken down the landmark of the Law amongst those who have entered into the covenant, when *there shall shine forth the glory of God* to Israel, they shall be cut off from the midst of the camp . . . '

Neither shall the God of Jacob regard it.
. . . .
They gather themselves together against the soul
of *the Just*,
And condemn the innocent blood.
But the Lord is my defence;
And my God is the rock of my refuge.
And He shall bring upon them their own iniquity,
And shall cut them off in their own wickedness;
Yea, the Lord our God shall cut them off.

In the *Seder Olam*, xxx (ed. Neubauer), as also in the Talmud, it is stated that this psalm was being sung by the Levites on the day the Temple was destroyed by the Romans in 70. A.D.

But I do not think it is at all necessary to resort to such a strained interpretation of the commentator's language as that it relates to any capture of Jerusalem. In one of the so-called *Thanksgiving Psalms* there is, as Dupont-Sommer himself has noted, a close parallel to our passage. The Teacher of Righteousness seems to be the speaker and declares:

For I was an object of scorn to them
and they did not esteem me when Thou wast strengthened in me!
For I was driven from my country, as the bird from its nest,
and all my companions and acquaintances were thrust far from me,
and they treated me as a useless thing.
And they, interpreters of lies and seers full of guile,
they formed against me plots of Belial,
bartering Thy Law, which Thou hast engraved on my heart,
for the flatteries which they address to Thy people.
And they prevented the thirsty from drinking the draught
of Knowledge,
and when they were thirsty they made them drink sour wine:
so that God saw their error,
so that they were in madness at their (feasts,
so that they were taken in their nets.[1]

Here the Teacher, or the psalmist personating him, speaks of exile, a plot for his destruction that failed, the plotters entangled in their own net, in madness at their feasts. The *Thanksgiving Psalms* have been given this title from the opening words, true of the one just quoted, 'I will give thanks unto Thee, O Lord.' Now in the collection called *The Odes of Solomon* there is a psalm in many ways similar which begins in the same way, and which we may quote in part.

[1] *The Dead Sea Scrolls*, p. 74.

I will give thanks unto Thee, O Lord, because I love Thee;
O Most High, Thou wilt not foresake me, for Thou art my hope:
Freely I have received Thy grace, I shall live thereby.
My persecutors will come and not see me:
A cloud of darkness shall fall on their eyes;
and an air of thick gloom shall darken them:
and they shall have no light to see, that they may not take hold upon me.
Let their counsel become thick darkness,
and what they have cunningly devised, let it return upon their own heads:
For they have devised a counsel, and it did not succeed:
They have prepared themselves for evil, and were found to be empty.[1]

The interesting thing regarding this Ode is that much of it is found used in the Gnostic *Pistis Sophia*. Likewise the *Thanksgiving Psalm* speaks of 'Knowledge' (i.e. Gnosis). It is assumed that in the Ode the Messiah is the speaker, as again in another Ode:

They who saw me marvelled at me, *because I was* persecuted,
And *they supposed that I was swallowed up;*
for I seemed to them as one of the lost.
But my oppression became my salvation;
And *I was their reprobation* because there was no zeal in me.[2]

Evidently, in the light of the recovered Dead Sea Scrolls, the *Odes of Solomon* need to be carefully looked at again. But to return to our passage in the *Habakkuk Commentary* : it says little more than what is given in these poems. The Wicked Priest persecuted the Righteous Teacher and attempted to destroy him in his place of exile. It is not said that the attempt succeeded. Instead the Teacher suddenly confounded his persecutors by appearing before them on the Day of Atonement.

It is impossible in a case like this, except by a stretch of imagination, to pin the commentary to any known historical event. But if fresh possibilities are to be considered we may think of the persecution of the Judaeo-Christians under Cuspius Fadus and Tiberias Alexander mentioned in the Old Russian text of Josephus. 'But when these noble governors saw the falling away of the people, they determined, *together with the Scribes*, to seize them . . . for fear lest the little might not be little, if it ended in the great . . . They sent them away, some to Caesar, others to Antioch to be tried, *others they exiled to distant*

[1] *Ode* 5, J. Rendel Harris, *The Odes of Solomon*, p. 94. See also 'The prayer of Jesus the son of Sirach' (*Ecclus.* li). This too begins 'I will give thanks unto Thee, O Lord,' and deals with deliverance from enemies. Was this psalm added from one of the collections in the possession of the saints?

[2] *Ibid. Ode* 28.

lands.'[1] It probably relates to this time when Eusebius says, that 'the rest of the apostles, who were harassed in innumerable ways *with a view to destroy them*, and *driven from the land of Judea*, went forth to preach the gospel to all nations.'[2] James the Just, head of the Nazarenes, had not been executed at this period (45-50 A.D.), and may well have been in temporary exile. The possibility is worth mentioning, first because an attempt on his life is related in the *Clementine Recognitions*. According to this story he was left for dead, and apparently taken to Jericho.[3] Second, there is a tradition that James 'was permitted to enter the Holy of Holies once a year (i.e. on the Day of Atonement), as the Law commanded the high priests.'[4] Further, since he was said to have officiated as high priest, he could well have 'shone forth' or 'appeared all resplendent' on such an occasion in 'the robe of glory'[5] worn by the high priest. Third, as we shall discuss in the next chapter, James was eventually the victim of the High Priest Ananus. Admittedly this line of thought gives a Christian emphasis, but again and again in the material associations with Primitive Christianity appear, and have to be taken seriously into account.

---

[1] Replacing *Wars*, II. xi. 6. Josephus, Vol. III, Thackeray's translation (Loeb Classical Library), pp. 651-2.

[2] *Eccl. Hist.* III. v.

[3] *Recog.* I. lxx-lxxi.

[4] Epiphanius, *Haeres.* lxxviii.

[5] *Ecclus.* I. 11, but see the whole description in this chapter.

CHAPTER THIRTEEN

I Will Repay

We shall deal now with the fate of the Wicked Priest as this is depicted in the *Habakkuk Commentary*. We have already been told categorically by the commentator that retribution will overtake him. 'The cup of God's anger shall swallow him up' (ii. 15). 'God shall condemn him to destruction, even as he purposed to destroy the poor' (ii. 17).

The Wicked Priest had plotted against the Righteous Teacher and the Elect Ones, oppressed and persecuted them. His crowning enormity appears to have been that he finally succeeded in compassing the death of the Righteous Teacher. This is to be inferred from the comment on *Hab*. i. 13: ' "Wherefore lookest thou upon them that deal treacherously, and holdest thy tongue when the wicked swalloweth up the more righteous than he?" This refers to the house of Absalom and its counsellors, who were silent when the Teacher of Righteousness was convicted (or punished), and failed to aid him against the Man of Untruth who flouted the Law in front of all the people.'

Again Dupont-Sommer jumps to conclusions in the interests of his theory. He at once identifies the Absalom of the text with the Absalom, uncle and father-in-law of Aristobulus II, mentioned as having been captured by the Romans in 63 B.C. (Jos. *Antiq*. XIV. iv.4). He regards 'such a precise indication' as conferring 'a quasi-evidential character' on his proposed identification of Aristobulus with the Wicked High Priest, the Man of Untruth.[1] The very fact that the commentaries of Qumran so rarely give names ought to have made it obvious that 'the house of Absalom' is an allegorical expression with which we may compare 'the house of Peleg' of the *Damascus Document*. Teicher rightly draws attention to the story of Absalom (II. *Sam*. xiii. 20), who temporarily, in the case of the outrage to his sister Tamar, connived at an iniquity,

[1] *The Dead Sea Scrolls*, pp. 36-37.

and using the same word as in *Habakkuk* advised her to 'hold her peace.'[1] Teicher, however, following his own theory, makes the comment relate to the outrage to the Church (the Teacher of Righteousness collective) when the Jerusalem elders kept silent and gave Paul the right hand of friendship when he had informed them of the nature of the gospel he was preaching to the Gentiles. This is quite fantastic. What we are told is that the Absalomites failed to intervene when the Wicked Priest illegally passed judgment on the Teacher of Righteousness. The natural presumption is that 'the house of Absalom and its counsellors' were members of the Sanhedrin, perhaps Pharisees, who should never have permitted the conviction of the Master.

In thinking of such a situation the illegal trial of Jesus under the High Priest Caiaphas at once comes to mind, though in this case we are at least told of Joseph of Arimathea 'that he had not consented to the counsel and deed of them' (*Lk*. xxiii. 51). In view of the indications we have found in the Commentary, however, that the author is dealing with events approximately from 45-70 A.D., and because James the Just and the Epistle attributed to him have already come before us in the course of our studies, it is certainly deserving of attention that the circumstances of his death as given by Josephus exactly fit the commentator's words.

The High Priest concerned was Ananus son of Ananus. 'This younger Ananus,' writes Josephus, 'who took the high priesthood, was a bold man in his temper, and very insolent; he was also of the party of the Sadducees, who were very rigid in judging offenders . . . When, therefore, Ananus was of this disposition, he thought he had now a proper opportunity (to carry out his designs). Festus (the Roman procurator) was now dead, and Albinus (his successor) was but upon the road; so he assembled the Sanhedrin of judges, and brought before them the brother of Jesus, who was called Christ, whose name was James, and some others; and when he had formulated a charge against them as breakers of the Law, he delivered them to be stoned. But as for those who seemed the most moderate of the citizens, and such as were strict in the observance of the Law, they disliked what was done; they also sent to the king (Agrippa II), desiring him to send to Ananus that he should act so no more, for that what he had already done was not to be justified: nay, some of them went also to meet Albinus, as he was upon his journey from Alexandria, and informed him that it was not lawful for Ananus to assemble a Sanhedrin without his consent' (*Antiq*. XX. ix. 1).

Here we have an illegal conviction of a Teacher of Righteousness by an illegally convened Sanhedrin at the instigation of an inimical and high-handed

[1] *The Habakkuk Scroll, Journal of Jewish Studies*, Vol. V, No. 2, p. 57.

High Priest. As regards James the Just the protest was made, but not until after he had been killed. Nothing was done by any of the judges to oppose the conviction or stop the execution. 'The house of Absalom and its counsellors' were very ready to salve their consciences later when the evil deed had been done.

We have already seen that the illegal execution of James was regarded as so heinous a crime that, in reporting it, Hegesippus declared that immediately after this Vespasian invaded Judea. There was even read a testimony of Josephus to this effect, quoted by Origen, that the fall of Jerusalem in 70 A.D. was in retribution for the death of this perfectly just man. Origen expressed surprise that it should be James rather than Jesus to whose death the historian attributed the doom of the city.[1] All this we have to keep before us as we proceed.

If divine vengeance had to fall on anyone in particular manifestly it should be the Wicked Priest; and this is what we find in the next two passages we shall quote from the *Habakkuk Commentary*.

First we have *Hab.* ii. 8b. ' "Because of the blood of men, and violence on the land, on the city, and all that dwell therein." This refers to the Wicked Priest, whom—because of the Teacher of Righteousness and his counsellors[2]—God delivered into the hands of his enemies, to afflict him by beating (or, smiting) him to death (or, to his destruction) in anguish of soul, for the evil (conspiracy?) against His Elect.'

In his comment on *Hab.* iia the author had referred to the plunder accumulated by the last priests of Jerusalem falling into the hands of the Romans. Now he deals with the fate of the Wicked Priest himself. The two circumstances ought to be related in time as they are in position. If the wealth in the hands of the High Priests came to the Romans in 70 A.D. as the result of the war, the death of the Wicked Priest may also have happened in the course of the war. We have, therefore, every justification for considering what was the end of the High Priests Ananias son of Nedebaeus and Ananus son of Ananus, both of whom had persecuted the Christians, and both of whom as we have shown are accused of venality by Josephus.

Needless to say, Dupont-Sommer thinks of the death of Aristobulus, and Teicher of the martyrdom of Paul. It hardly seems worth challenging these opinions further.

We must, however, bring in the second passage from the Commentary. This covers the immediately preceding verse *Hab.* ii. 7. 'Will not thy tormentors rise up suddenly and torment thee and get inflamed, and wilt thou not

[1] For the quotations see above p. 81.
[2] Cp. Josephus, 'James and some others.'

become their prey? . . . (This refers to) the Priest who rebelled (MS. defective here)[1] who was punished by evil judgments, and they inflicted upon him the most horrible tortures and vengeance upon his physical body.' In making his comment, it should be noted that the author brings it into association with a text that speaks of a sudden uprising and anger of those who wreak their vengeance, and he must therefore have regarded these words as highly appropriate to the circumstances of the death of the Wicked Priest.

Regarding the fate of the High Priest Ananias, Josephus tells us of the violence and madness of the Zealots early in the revolt against Rome. 'The victors (over the Peace party) burst in and set fire to the house of Ananias the High Priest and to the palaces of Agrippa and Berenice; they next carried their combustibles to the public archives, eager to destroy the money-lenders' bonds and to prevent the recovery of debts, in order to win over a host of grateful debtors and to cause a rising of the poor against the rich, sure of impunity.' Two days later, 'the High Priest Ananias was caught near the canal in the palace grounds, where he was hiding, and, with his brother Ezechias, was killed by the brigands' (*Wars*, II. xvi. 6-9).

As to Ananus, Josephus relates how later in the war the Zealots invited the Idumeans to Jerusalem, and joined forces with them in a horrible massacre of the moderates. 'The fury of the Idumeans being still unsatiated, they now turned to the city, looting every house and killing all who fell in their way. But, thinking their energies wasted on the common people, they went in search of the Chief Priests; it was for them that the main rush was made, and they were soon captured and slain. Then, standing over their dead bodies, they scoffed at Ananus for his patronage of the people and at Jesus (son of Gamaliel, another High Priest) for the addresss he had delivered from the wall. They actually sent so far in their impiety as to cast out their corpses without burial' (*Wars*, IV. v. 2).

Josephus only had second-hand knowledge of the fate of the High Priests, and it may well be as regards Ananus and Jesus that their maddened murderers mutilated and ill-treated their bodies before casting them out unburied. Thus the words of the commentator would have received their fulfilment to the very letter.

---

[1] Dupont-Sommer would supply words towards the end of the two lines which are missing so as to make the passage read as if it were the Teacher of Righteousness who was struck by the Wicked Priest in the execution of iniquitous judgments, etc. He then remarks, 'From all the evidence this passage alludes to the Passion of the Master of Justice; he was judged, condemned, tortured. He suffered in "his body of flesh"; without doubt he was a divine being who "became flesh" to live and die as a man' (*Dead Sea Scrolls*, p. 34). It is quite clear that it is the Wicked Priest himself who is getting his deserts as the text commented on shows: 'Will not thy tormentors . . . torment thee.' Cp. 'For the violence on Lebanon shall return upon thee.'

But we are bound to qualify any judgment that now we know exactly what the commentator intended to represent; for while these historical incidents are entirely relevant they may only be employed to impart a quality of realism to what is actually prophetic of the future. There are some things which seem faithfully to answer to history, and yet will not square completely with history.

It is so with the end of the Wicked Priest, as with the fate of the Teacher of Righteousness. The Wicked Priest meets with the horrible punishment he is held to deserve. Yet those who execute it appear to be external rather than internal enemies, contrary to what happened in the case of the High Priests at the time of the war with Rome. We gather this from fragments of a commentary on *Ps.* xxxvii, given by Allegro as follows:

> ['The wicked watcheth, etc. (vv. 32-33)'. This is to be explained of the Wicked Priest who sent to the Teacher of Righteousness . . . .] to slay him [. . .] and the Law which he sent to him. But God 'will not le[ave him (the Teacher of Righteousness) in his hand'] nor ['condemn him when] he is judged'. But God will repay to him (the Wicked Priest) his recompense to give him into the hand of the terrible ones of the Gentiles[1] to do to him . . .
> 'The wicked have drawn out the sword'. This is to be explained of the wicked of Ephraim and Manasseh who will endeavour to stretch forth a hand against the Priest (the Teacher) and the men of his counsel during the Time of Testing which is coming upon them. But God will deliver them out of their hand and after that they (the wicked ones) shall be given into the hand of the terrible ones of the Gentiles for judgment.

The instruments of vengeance are here seen to be Gentile foes of Israel as in the references to *Ezekiel*, and the events are still future, taking place during that coming Time of Testing spoken of in *Rev.* iii. 10. The *Book of Revelation*, indeed, presents us with the same kind of phenomenon, where recent and contemporary history, much of it relating to the war with Rome, is used as a foundation for the portrayal of the future events visualised by the seer.[2]

Punishment overtakes the wicked, but for God's people there is hope, and words of comfort are spoken. 'God will not destroy His people by means of the Gentiles. But it is by means of His Elect that God will execute judgment on all the Gentiles; and it will be at the time of their chastisement that all the sinful amongst His people will make atonement. Those who will have kept His commandments will be a rock to them . . . ' (On. *Hab.* i. 12).

Here again we enter the realm of the *Revelation*, and other later apocalypses

[1] See *Ezek.* xxviii. 7; xxx. 11.
[2] See my notes to the *Revelation* in *The Authentic New Testament.*

like those of *Baruch* and *Ezra*. Rome and her allies in their turn will feel the mighty hand of God. 'Here is the patience of the Saints: here are they that keep the commandments of God, and the faith of Jesus' (*Rev*. xiv. 12).

While it is still premature to reach any general conclusions, we can see that as far as these prophetic commentaries are concerned they would appear to derive much of their character and colouring from events which took place in the critical period which reached its climax in 70 A.D.

CHAPTER FOURTEEN

Opposing Forces

HAVING COME so far in our investigation, and before we go any further, we may well pause to consider what impressions we have received from the material we have been examining. What manner of people were they who produced and used this literature? Their high moral character and spiritual perceptiveness cannot be doubted. Yet we find them, childishly as it would appear, playing with ciphers and symbols having to do with no very profound secrets, and indulging in exegesis and interpretations of the most far-fetched and extravagant nature, which one would suppose they must have recognised as forced and often incredible. Were they really trying to pass off books obviously of no great antiquity purporting to be writings of the ancient fathers of the race as genuine traditions? Did they themselves actually place credence in their authenticity? Why should they constantly allude to historical persons from the beginning of the second century B.C. onwards and yet be so niggardly in naming them? What purpose was served by these thin, and frequently transparent, disguises? Did such dominant figures as the Righteous Teacher and his opponent the Wicked Priest or Man of Untruth represent single individuals, or were they composite characters built up from real persons but in combination fictitious? Certainly the effect of the portaiture of the Wicked Priest is that he is larger than life in his enormities, and the Righteous Teacher in his virtues. One feels that there must be a rational and convincing answer to such questions.

I must say that the major impression I have received from the pseudepigraphic and apocalyptic literature is of its dramatic quality. This finds its expression not only in the quite astonishing output of lyrical and poetic material, but in the treatment of events and conditions. Almost everything was dramatised by the people with whom we are dealing, including themselves, their communal discipline and organisation, and the details of their day-to-day lives. They were conscious that they were playing a leading part in the last Act of a stupendous Cosmic Drama begun in the dawn of time;

and this Act was regarded as having opened around the commencement of the second century B.C. in the Great Apostasy which gave rise to Chasidism.

On the subject of this Cosmic Drama I may be pardoned if I quote here some things I have said elsewhere. 'Originating in the primitive half-light of magical practises and beliefs, it was nourished by the protracted observation of heavenly and earthly phenomena and of the conduct of man himself. The developing mind of man confirmed and expanded his consciousness that there existed between himself and the universe a special and intimate relationship. "The stars in their courses fought against Sisera," and for Joshua the sun stood still.

'The artistry of priesthood gave to the Drama its ritual and literary expression, which described the eternal conflict between Order and Chaos, Light and Darkness, Good and Evil, the Divine Hero and the Dragon. There was perceived both a purpose of Creation and a plain of Redemption operating over a series of Ages—as Acts in the Drama—until with the final stroke of judgment the reign of harmony would ensue.

'All the time, as generation followed generation, the Drama was handed on while it was being played out by Sumerians, Babylonians, Persians and Jews, and from them spreading out in ever-widening circles to the east and the west. The changes, sufferings and visitations that overshadowed the life of man and affected both his communal and domestic affairs were consequent upon the cosmic struggle and reflected his participation in it. Man was the creature of destiny, and yet in some sense the master of it. To him, prompted by the *agathodaemon* (the good spirit), was granted the last word which would signalise the inevitable and ultimate triumph of right. By obedience to heavenly revelations in dreams and visions, laws and commandments, man could turn towards himself the better face of destiny, and even expedite that "far off Divine event to which the whole Creation moves." '[1]

'And so began the age of apocalypse, or revelation. An age which believed that upon itself had fallen the ends of all the ages, that it was to witness the consummation, the catastrophic curtain to the drama of humanity, must be something of a phenomenon in history. No other age that we know, unless indeed it be our own, has been so much impressed with its own finality, so greatly preoccupied with its own imminent disintegration . . . Prophets before this age had had apocalyptic moments, but never in the known traditions of man had there been such an outburst of religio-political ecstasy, which penetrated the guarded gates of heaven by its own intensity, and saw the fate of humanity mirrored in the crystal sea that surrounded the Throne.

[1] Schonfield, *Saints Against Caesar*, pp. viii-ix.

'No one who has read the apocalyptic writings can doubt the urge, the compulsion put upon the authors. "What thou seest, write in a book" is the barest statement of a command that would brook no refusal. They felt themselves pressed into service to convey the final warnings of God. Some of them question the justice of the Divine action, as if to find excuse for requesting a stay of execution of the sentence passed upon the world. Like Abraham seeking to save Sodom, they bargain down to the smallest shred of merit. But none of the writers doubts the terrible reality of the Wrath to Come. The emotional stress under which they laboured by the very urgency and desperation of their calling defies calculating analysis. The visions tumble over one another; there are abrupt transitions, for the action is continuous and one scene gives place to another with kinematic rapidity. There was a double strain both on heart and hand. Numerology is only one of the scribe's devices to record purposefully as well as rapidly: he employed appropriate round figures, meaningful abbreviations, but without occult significance unless so stated. The same principle applies to the theriology, the menagerie of queer beasts presented as typical of the qualities of men and kingdoms. The visions were subjective, the writing in a sense automatic, the phraseology and imagery often borrowed, but it is fitness rather than previous association that usually dictates their use.

'The apocalypses were of necessity pseudonymous, put forth in the names of ancient seers and patriarchs of Israel, and on that very account importing a sense of the miraculous and the revealed presence of God into an age of sophistication, worldliness and agnosticism. With a stroke of the pen the past was telescoped into the present, and what was once possible became possible again, because with God all things are possible.'[1]

One could say much more about the Cosmic Drama and its representation, but this already goes a long way towards answering some of the questions we have asked. We have the harking back to the beginning of things, the struggle for the control of the world, of man, and later of the soul of Israel, by the opposing spiritual forces. We have the contending of the Elect One and his elect ones with Beliar and his minions. We have the progression of the Ages, the divisions of times, the jubilees and weeks. We have the double stage of heaven and earth, with a Jerusalem and Temple above and below, with saints and seers ascending and angels descending, and a great business of messages passing and prophecies being recorded. We have the mapping of the compartments of heaven and hell, the keeping of a Book of Life above and a register of the faithful below. Finally, we have the triumph of the saints and the

[1] Schonfield, *Jesus: a Biography*, pp. 24-25.

destruction of the evildoers, the Last Assize, the new heaven and new earth. It is through the knowledge of the Cosmic Drama that we gain an insight into the working of the minds of the people we are studying, and can make sense of their literature, their methods and techniques. It is partly because the material and the circumstances have been examined too coldly and matter-of-factly that interpretations offered by scholars have sometimes been so wide of the mark.

Let us look briefly at some of the dramatic effects produced by consciousness of the Cosmic Drama. Outstanding is the portrayal of the opposing forces, typified on earth by the last protagonists, the Teacher of Righteousness and the Wicked Priest or Man of Untruth, and the War of the Sons of Light with the Sons of Darkness. The latter is a spiritual war, yet with all the realistic dramatic accompaniments of battle order, weapons, signals of advance and retreat, banners and slogans. It is as old as the conflict between Esau and Jacob, and as historically recent as the wars of the Maccabees with the neighbouring peoples. So it is a struggle on two planes, which is not history, and yet history is an integral part of it. The former, as we have suggested, no less personify principles, and are not simply individuals who can be exactly identified. Yet they come to life in distinguishable historical persons at crucial times within the period conceived as covering the last Act in the Cosmic Drama. These crucial times are the beginning of the Act in the first half of the second century B.C. and the End of the Days in the first century A.D. The leading characters are not named both because they represent principles and because historically at the relevant times details regarding them are drawn not from one person but from various individuals some of whom were contemporaries or near contemporaries. Even the secondary characters within the period are rarely named, though in their case quite definite and well-known persons are usually in the mind of the various authors.

We have to understand the methodology of the writers. Take, for instance, the subject of priestly corruption. Three periods are represented: (1) the period of the Hellenising priesthood, (2) the period of decadence of the Hasmonean priest-kings, and (3) the period of the arrogant Sadducean hierarchy. Each of these periods invited a 'visitation' and judgment, and the evildoings of the high priests in all of them could be described in almost identical terms. Thus, since there was such repetition of offences, what was said in denunciation of them in the first period could be taken up again as applying to the second, and yet again as applying to the third, making it difficult sometimes to be certain which period was particularly in view unless the context made it clear. We are dealing, so to speak, with an instrument with certain interchangeable parts, or to employ another metaphor, there are situations which form a joint stock in trade of these latter-day saints. Material written at different times could be united or associated without any clearly discernible join. That is why interpolations are often so hard to detect as such: they fit in so naturally and perfectly. There was nothing at all to stop one group of the pious from borrowing wholesale from another, whether predecessor or contemporary, and employing terms and descriptions with every appearance of accuracy and cogency in relation to persons and circumstances not necessarily identical and possibly removed in time a hundred years or more.

We have to consider that there was a tacit understanding about this common documentary property. As *Enoch* says: 'I know another mystery, that books will be given to the righteous and the wise to become a cause of joy and uprightness and much wisdom. To them the books will be given, and they will believe in them and rejoice over them, and then will *all* the righteous be recompensed who have learnt therefrom all the paths of uprightness' (civ. 12-13). In the same way in the *Assumption of Moses* the instruction is given for such books to be carefully preserved and safely stored that they should be available in 'the day of repentance wherewith the Lord shall visit them in the Consummation of the End of the Days' (i. 16-18).

No deception was intended, nor was there any self-deception, in attributing authorship to saints of the dim past. In the Cosmic Drama a real kinship was felt to subsist between the righteous of antiquity, who had been on the stage in the first Act, and those who only came on towards the end of the Drama. Essentially they were the same people whom the Drama had brought together. The ancients were the fellows of their ultimate kindred, with the same outlook, speaking the same language, and were still present in the prompter's box with the text of the prophetic script before them. Since the Elect constituted a divine fellowship, separate from the Evildoers, from the beginning to the end of Time, what was said in the names of the Fathers could be presumed to be what they actually would have said as being of the same order and family of the Sons of God.

The eclectic groups could take the same family view of one another. What united them far transcended anything that divided them. They were leagued in their struggle with the opposing evil forces. They could apply to themselves the same generic terms. They were collectively the Elect, the Righteous, the Saints, the Poor, those who adhere to the Covenant and keep the Commandments of God. And so, making common cause, they could support and sustain each other, share their goods and their books, offer each other solace and asylum, recount the same trials and sing the same praises, follow the leadership and example of the same idealised figures who served as their Lawgiver. Those things that appear so curious in their interpretations, so childish in their ciphers and symbolism, constituted a kind of sign language for mutual recognition and a hall mark of authentication. This is why they invested initiation with such solemnity, and made so much of their possession of profound secrets which must never be disclosed.

Eloquent of the attitude of the various groups towards one another is a passage in the *Psalms of Solomon* where we read: 'And Jerusalem did all things according as the Gentiles did in their cities to their gods . . . and there was none amongst them that did mercy and truth in Jerusalem. They that love the assemblies of the saints fled away from them; and they flew like sparrows who fly from their nests: and they were wandering in the wilderness, in order to save their soul from evil: and precious in their eyes was the sojourning with them of any soul that was saved from them (the apostates)' (xvii. 17-19).

The common cause of the Saints against the Evildoers inevitably created something approaching a theological Dualism of a Zoroastrian type, with the inimical spirit Beliar credited with somewhat greater power and authority than was warranted by a strict Monotheism and reflecting the venerable traditions of the Cosmic Drama. The Saints would have strongly repudiated any suggestion that they were other than staunch and even fanatical monotheists, and would have rejected out of hand the Gnostic Marcionite conception of the Demiurge. But under the stresses and strains of the period following the end of even limited Jewish political independence, when the expected End and Day of Wrath did not come and Evil seemed to triumph, there was a theological danger inherent in the position of the eclectic groups which the Rabbis clearly saw and endeavoured by all means to combat. I believe that this explains the hostility of the Rabbis towards the Minim (Jewish sectaries) and their *Giljonim* (apocalyptic literature) to which I have alluded in the first chapter of this book.[1]

Admittedly the expression Minim covers a very wide range of heretical opinion, with emphasis on particular beliefs at different times, and aiming at Essenes, Judaeo-Christians, Gnostics and many others. But in denouncing heresy (*minuth*) the Talmud attacks most keenly the doctrine of Two Powers in Heaven, which represents the extreme to which deviation from orthodoxy could be driven. That extreme belongs on the whole to a later period than we have been considering; but even in the first two centuries of the Christian era—the Mishnaic period—the risks of deviationism were recognized, and a class of people specified who, if not actually heretics, were at least 'over the border' (*chitsonim*).[2]

[1] Above pp. 5-6.

[2] *Meg.* iv. 8.

The Saints themselves were too full of the struggle between Light and Darkness, too busy reading the Signs of the Times, to be conscious of any difficulties in their theological position. For them there was only Black and White, Evil and Good, the Two Spirits and the Two Ways, though they held God to be supreme. In the *Manual of Discipline*[1] found among the Dead Sea Scrolls it is written:

And God assigned for man two Spirits
By which to walk until the season of His Visitation:
They are the Spirits of Truth and Perversion.[2]
In a spring of light is the source of Truth,
And in a fountain of darkness is the generation of Perverseness.
In the hand of the Prince of lights
Is the rule over all the sons of righteousness;
In the ways of light they walk.
And in the hand of the Angel of darkness
Is all the rule over the sons of perversion;
And in the ways of darkness they walk.
And it is because of the Angel of darkness
That all the sons of righteousness go astray;
And all their sins and all their iniquities and all their guilt
And the rebellions of their deeds are the effect of his dominion:
According to God's Mysteries, until the term fixed by Him.
And all the blows which strike them, and all the seasons of their distress,
Are the effect of the dominion of his hostility.
And all the spirits allotted to him
Make the sons of light to stumble.
But the God of Israel and His angel of truth.
Come to the aid of all the sons of light.
Yea, He hath created the (two) Spirits of light and darkness
And upon these He hath founded every work;
Upon their [counsels] every service,
And upon their ways [every visit]ation.
The one of them God loves for the duration of the Ages,
And in all its deeds He delights for ever.
As for the other He loathes its counsel
And all its ways He hates for ever . . .
In these (two Spirits) are divided all their armies from generation to generation,
And in their (two) ways they walk;

[1] I have followed Dupont-Sommer's translation, *The Jewish Sect of Qumran and the Essenes*, p. 121 ff.

[2] Perversion (עול 'avel). Playing on this word the Rabbis themselves interpreted Belial (Beliar) as בל־עול (B'li-'Ol, 'without yoke'), i.e. the Lawless One.

And all the retribution of their works is made by
their divisions,
According to each his own share,
According to whether he has much or little,
For all periods of the Ages.
For God has set these in equal parts until the last period,
And He has put eternal enmity between their divisions;
And abomination to Truth are the acts of Wrongdoing,
And an abomination to Wrongdoing are all the ways
of Truth.
And passionate strife (opposes one to the other) on the
subject of all their decrees,
For they do not walk together.

This teaching can be seen to have passed directly into Christianity; for it is found in the letters of Paul. 'Do not be ill-yoked with unbelievers. For what has righteousness in common with lawlessness? Or what fellowship has light with darkness? What harmony has Christ with Beliar? Or what share has the faithful with the faithless?' (*II Cor.* vi. 14–15). 'Behave as children of the light... and have no fellowship with the unfruitful works of darkness' (*Eph.* v. 8-11). 'All of you are children of the light and children of the day. We do not belong to the night or to darkness' (*I Thess.* v. 5).[1]

Except for the mention of the name of Jesus the following passage could have been written by any member of the Qumran community:

> So now you know what is the retarding factor, that the Lawless One may be revealed at his proper time. Indeed, the process (lit. mystery) of lawlessness[2] is already at work, only there is one who is retarding it until his removal. And then the Lawless One will be revealed, whom the Lord Jesus will consume with the breath of his mouth and annihilate with the radiance of his presence, that one whose coming is attended, in the way Satan works, by every kind of mendacious trickery practised on those who are perishing, because they have not welcomed the love of Truth so as to be spared. For that reason God will send them a spirit of delusion so as to believe the Lie, that all may be condemned who have not credited Truth, but have taken pleasure in Falsehood (*II Thess.* ii. 6-12).

In a Christian context the doctrine of the Two Ways reappears in the *Teaching of the XII Apostles*, being found much earlier in the *Testaments of the XII Patriarchs* (*T. Ash.* i. 3-9). So full is the New Testament of ideas and even quotations taken from this eclectic literature, that not only must a substantial

---

[1] Cp. also *II Thess.* i. 6-9 with *Damsc. Doc.* ii. 3-5.

[2] The expression 'mystery of iniquity' occurs in fragment 27 from Cave 1: *Qumran Cave* 1, Clarendon Press, p. 103. The False Prophet of the *Book of Revelation* also bears some resemblance to the Prophesier of Untruth of the Scrolls.

part of this literature be anterior to Christianity, but at least indirect contact must have existed in the formative period of the Church for the Christians to have had access to so much of it. The only alternative view that can be taken is Teicher's that the Qumran community and the Primitive Judaeo-Christians were identical. I believe Teicher's hypothesis to be quite untenable in the way he uses it, but I must go a long way with him in seeing a very close connexion between the two. There is another term used by both Jesus and Paul which seems to embrace all the groups of the Elect: it is 'those who are on the Inside', who are contrasted with 'those who are on the Outside'. Here again we have a description of the opposing forces.

A clear perception of these antitheses is essential, it seems to me, to a right historical understanding of the documents and the circumstances; and it was necessary to interpose it before summing up and setting out our conclusions.

CHAPTER FIFTEEN

Review of the Evidence

IN THE course of our investigation we have chiefly been concerned with internal and literary evidence, and this we now propose to review and analyse. Ultimately the external evidence and publication of further fragments of documents may clarify much that otherwise must remain uncertain and obscure, and may even prove decisive on certain matters. All that can be said at present with any assurance is that the site at Khirbet Qumran was occupied most of the time from about 100 B.C. to about 70 A.D., and to some extent until at least 135 A.D. The last period of occupation is the one which is crucial, since it has to be determined whether those who then dwelt at Khirbet Qumran were at all identical with the sect that had been there before, or embraced other elements, or were substantially a different sect which had taken over and acquired the literary inheritance of their predecessors by which they were greatly influenced, just as the later Karaites seem to have been influenced by the find of a hoard of documents in the caves at the beginning of the ninth century. How many of the documents were copied and some perhaps interpolated during that last period of occupation? And of even more consequence, how many books, if any, actually originated in this period? These questions are not yet answered by the external evidence. Palaeography indicates that some documents could have been copied in the early part of the second century. No more than this can yet be stated with any element of probability, and some scholars would still contest that any additions to the library of the caves were made after 70 A.D.

Before we proceed, however, it is proper to introduce at this point the phenomenon of the Elchesaites, known to us mainly from the writings of Hippolytus, Origen and Epiphanius. A certain Alcibiades of Apamea in Syria brought to Rome about 222 A.D. a book purporting to have been obtained from Parthia by a righteous man Elxai or Elkesai and to have been given out by him as a fresh revelation in the third year of the Emperor Trajan.[1] The work was highly prized by the Judaeo-Christian Ebionites in the regions east of the Jordan and the Dead Sea towards the end of the second century. That there was a person called Elxai, who founded the sect of Elchesaites, is regarded as improbable, in fact as mythical as Ebion the supposed founder of the Ebionites. The name is Hebrew (Aramaic) and interpreted as 'The Hidden Power'. The teachings of the sect, as Epiphanius declares,[2] represent an extraordinary mixture of Jewish, Christian and Pagan ideas; and this is what is so interesting, for here we have clear evidence of the fusion of doctrines derived from the Essenes, Judaeo-Christians, the Mandaeans of the Euphrates Valley, Pythagorean and other elements. The basic principles were strongly Jewish, since they embraced faithfulness to the Law and the observance of the Sabbath, and the turning towards Jerusalem in prayer.[3] But there was opposition to animal sacrifice, vegetarianism, a good deal of abracadabra (astrology, magic, etc.), belief in the arche-typal man (the Angelic Son of Man and the Kabbalistic Great King) incarnated in Jesus, baptism, the transmigration of souls, and so on. We can trace anterior connexions with the Essenes and the New Covenant Party, and posterior connexions with the Ebionite Clementine literature and the eschatology of the Samaritans. The Elchesaites and their associations, therefore, establish that in the first half of the second century there had taken place a considerable fusion of tenets of the various sectarian groups. A Christo-Essenism had developed with admixture from other sources, setting in train the creation of a number of new sects of Gnostic type according to the particular inclinations and affiliations of their founders. Thus when Dupont-Sommer distinguishes Pythagorean and Mazdaean features in the Dead Sea Scrolls, and Teicher stresses their Ebionite characteristics, both these scholars are only confirming an evolutionary process for which we have to allow. At no point in the history of the New Covenant Saints was there a dead stop in doctrine, and from the first century A.D., and especially in the circumstances following the fall of Jerusalem, the permutation and combination of tenets went forward merrily and fully justified the concern both of the Jewish Rabbis and the Christian Fathers, champions of their respective orthodoxies.

What, also, are we to make of those strange Jewish Gipsies the Rechabites?

[1] He is said by Epiphanuis to have joined the Ossenes (Essenes).

[2] *Haeres.* liii. 1.

[3] Cp. *Odes of Solomon:* 'No man, O my God, changeth Thy Holy Place; and it is not possible that he should change it and put it in another place' (*Ode* iv). See also Irenaeus on the Ebionites: 'They even adore Jerusalem as if it were the house of God' (*Adv. Haeres.* I. xxi. 2.).

They claimed descent from Jonadab the son of Rechab, and according to *Jer.* xxxv they continued to obey the commands of their ancestor, not to drink wine, not to build houses, not to cultivate vineyards or fields. The Talmud identifies the Rechabites with the Potters (*yotsrim*) of *I Chron.* iv. 3 'because they observed (*natseru*) the commands of their ancestor (*Baba Bathra* 91b), thus apparently reading *notsrim* (Nazarenes) for *yotsrim*. Nazarenes and Nazarites, Baptists and Essenes, 'Keepers' of Secrets and 'Observers' of the pure Laws, all enter into the strange medley.

In later times the Rechabites are said to have married their daughters to priests, and their grandsons officiated as priests in the Temple (*Yalk. Jer.* 323). It was a Rechabite priest, according to Hegesippus, who appealed to the murderers of James the Just to desist. As far on as the twelfth century Benjamin of Tudela describes them as flourishing in Arabia, among them ascetics, eating no meat and abstaining from wine, dressing always in black, living in caves or in low huts. Even as recently as the nineteenth century, the missionary Dr. Wolff speaks of 60,000 of them near Mecca, still observing the pure Mosaic laws. What relationship may once have existed between these priestly cave-dwellers and the priestly Men of the Caves at Qumran?

Our problem is to get behind all this exotic incoherence, and define as far as we can the stages of growth, recognising that before the branches came there was a main stem from which they ultimately proceeded. We must not, therefore, be beguiled by subsequent developments and coincidences into imagining that they give us the key to the secrets of the Dead Sea Scrolls. We must treat them as exhibiting in varying degrees inherited likenesses traceable to a parent stock.

It would have been quite easy as our inquiry progressed to have introduced a great deal of additional supplementary material closely related to the subject, but not I believe adding anything of real consequence nor detracting from the worth of any of the evidences adduced, and only causing bewilderment and a difficulty in seeing the wood for the trees. The ramifications are enormous, and one could explore numerous by-paths with interest and enjoyment. One could also, to use the appropriate clichés, start quite a few hares and draw a number of red herrings across the trail. While extending the scope of the inquiry whenever there was a possible clue to be followed up, I have endeavoured to keep the investigation moving rather than dwell unduly on any feature.

In order to refresh the reader's memory and enable him to form his own judgment, whether or not this agrees with mine, I shall now briefly rehearse the contribution of each chapter.

Chapter I

In the Dead Sea Scrolls there is mentioned a highly prized work of reference in which the judges of the New Covenant Party were required to be expert. This is called the *Book of the Hagu*. By applying the ancient cipher known as *Atbash* to the inexplicable word Hagu sense was immediately obtained by its conversion into Tsoreph from the root Tsaraph, a word meaning 'proving' or 'testing'. Uses of this word were instanced in *Daniel* xii and *Malachi* iii of an apposite nature. Something was said about the period of testing for neophytes used by the New Covenant Party, the Essenes and Judaeo-Christians, and about a 'Time of Testing' mentioned in the Scrolls and the *Book of Revelation*.

The word threw light on a building called by the Rabbis *Bet-Nitsarphi*, evidently a centre of Jewish sectaries who used the apocalyptic literature and the Gospel. There was a rabbinical play on the word *Giljon* (apocalypse) and *Evangelion* (Gospel).

Chapter II

Assuming the correctness of the employment by the New Covenanters of the *Atbash* cipher, this invited reference to the oldest known use of it in *Jeremiah*. It was noted that the cipher only occurs in chapters widely recognised as late (perhaps second century B.C.) additions to the Prophet, and which are rearranged to form a complete section (xxvi-xxxi) in the Greek Septuagint. The prophecies concerned are directed among others against the Philistines, Edom and Moab, and the children of Ammon, traditional enemies of Israel, but significantly mentioned in *Psalm* lxxxiii, in the book of *Jubilees*, in *I Maccabees* (the peoples against whom Judas Maccabaeus fought), and in the *War of the Sons of Light with the Sons of Darkness* found among the Dead Sea Scrolls. This seemed to argue a family connexion between these works.

It was observed that Judas was described as having collected after the war the sacred books that had been scattered, and *Jubilees* states that the preservation and renewal of the books was committed to Levi (the priesthood) *until this day*. This could mean that the text of the Old Testament was finally edited by the pious priests and Levites (the Chasidim), who initiated a revolt against Hellenism in the first quarter of the second century B.C. and sided with Judas. The *Damascus Document* attributes the origins of the New Covenant Party and the advent of a Teacher of Righteousness to this period.

Jeremiah is treated as a specially significant figure in the records. It was he who first proclaimed a New Covenant and had a symbolic contract placed in an earthenware jar, as were the scrolls in the caves. He also, according to a tradition, caused the Tabernacle, and the Ark, and the altar of incense, to be hidden in a cave 'until mercy come'. Further, in a dream of Judas, Jeremiah is said to have handed him an invincible sword. It was pointed out that curiously enough the name Maccabee, probably meaning Hammerer, converts by *Atbash* into 'The Hand of God.' References to the concealment of books were also quoted from the *Assumption of Moses* and the *Apocalypse of Ezra*.

All these coincidences were unlikely to be fortuitous, and tended to confirm a relationship between the Chasidim and the beginnings of the New Covenant Party.

Chapter III

This led on to what we know of the history of the Chasidim. Their beginnings are obscure, but they may have been initially a group of zealots for the Law in the Jewish senate founded at the commencement of the second century B.C. (c. 196). The date is supported by the *Damascus Document*.

Strength was given to the Chasidic Movement by the Hellenistic way of life adopted by many Jews including the High Priests Jason and Menelaus. This apostasy was felt by the pious to invite a visitation of divine wrath, which manifested itself in the persecution by Antiochus Epiphanes. The *Assumption of Moses* and the *Damascus Document* concur in comparing this visitation with that of Nebuchadnezzar. The latter work describes the circumstances poetically and tells of a penitential movement by a remnant of Aaron and Israel which received a leader in a Teacher of Righteousness about 175 B.C. When the Maccabean revolt took place in 167 B.C. the Chasidim joined it. Later in 162 B.C. in the reign of Demetrius Soter a section of the Chasidim tried to make peace with his representatives Bacchides and Alcimus the High Priest, but the deputation was foully slain. Denunciations of this Wicked High Priest and his miserable end are quoted, and the martyrdom of a famous scribe 'the Chasid and priest' Joseph ben Joezer was cited in this connexion.

The *Damascus Document* speaks of an emigration of the Penitents of Israel to the land of Damascus, and with this we compared a passage in Josephus which tells of an emigration of the faithful at a time of further persecution about 160-159 B.C. when 'not a few . . . deserted their country, and went to the Macedonians' (i.e. to Syria, the land of Damascus). The *Damascus Document* says that a learned Scribe (the Student of the Law) was a leader of the Penitents, who entered into the New Covenant in the land of Damascus, and there laid down the precepts of the Party.

Under the name of Chasdanim the Chasidim are mentioned again in *V Macc.* in the reign of Hyrcanus I (134-103 B.C.) and in 71 B.C. in the time of Salome Alexandra. By this time they appear to be identified with the Essenes and are distinguished from the Pharisees and Sadducees.

Chapter IV

We now began a study of the *Damascus Document* and noted that the first part of the work is of a testamentary character written in the first person singular by one who addresses his readers as 'my children.' We are helped in dating this section by the fact that such testamentary literature (parts of *Enoch*, *Jubilees*, *I Maccabees*, *Testaments of the XII Patriarchs*) was developed in the period between approximately 120 B.C. and 70 B.C. What we have called for convenience *Testament Damascus* exhibits a kinship with other testamentary material, and its antiquity is vouched for by the fact that included in it are comments by a later writer (and also possible editorial interpolations) who employs the same type of exegesis found among the Dead Sea Scrolls in the *Habakkuk Commentary*. The commentator appears to be living in the time called 'the End of the Days' and is looking back over a lengthy period embracing several generations, years of sojourning and vicissitudes of his Party. The testamentary writer himself looks back to the Teacher of Righteousness who was before him. We therefore have to think of a considerable lapse of time between the original Teacher of Righteousness and the commentator writing at the End of the Days.

Chapter V

Continuing our study of the *Damascus Document* we considered much that appeared to be the work of the commentator. Between the emigration to the land of Damascus and his own time the commentator deals with a protracted period during which Belial was let loose against Israel, tempting the people through fornication, riches, and pollution of the Sanctuary. We compared what he says with other documents which show that this period coincided with the decadent days of the Hasmoneans from Alexander Jannaeus to Herod (102-40 B.C.). It is otherwise called by the commentator 'the Period of the Wickedness.' Things became so bad that the New Covenant Party formally severed itself from Judah. Adhering to the precepts of their Lawgiver they became a people apart (the house of Peleg—those who contracted out). But some went back on their allegiance to the New Covenant, and these renegades are castigated unmercifully, expunged from the register of the Community, and their lot will be with the ungodly. At the end we see the fully developed organization of the Party as we find it exemplified in the *Manual of Discipline*.

Chapter VI

Since so much is said in the *Damascus Document* and other books of the Party about the End of the Days it became important to discover when this time was supposed to have started. The *Assumption of Moses* holds that the End was to be expected not many years after 6 A.D. and the *Habakkuk Commentary* regards the End as having been delayed beyond the time anticipated.

We glanced at the archaeological evidence at Qumran, and saw that the numismatic finds pointed to a period of liveliest activity between 6 A.D. and 66 A.D. We also considered that Josephus's account of the movement of Roman forces during the war that followed permitted the view that books such as the *Habakkuk Commentary* could have been written at Qumran at least as late as 70 A.D. since the Community may not have been affected before the Roman attack on Masada in 73.

On the commencement of the Time of the End, the New Testament regards this as having already started in the days of John the Baptist and it should by rights have concluded long before the close of the first century A.D. The basis of the calculations was the prophecy of the Seventy Weeks in *Daniel*. This could be understood to give a terminal date towards the end of the first century B.C., and we quoted a discussion of the priests on this subject which is found in the Slavonic version of Josephus. Messianic excitement at this time is therefore easily explained, as the Messiah was identified with the Holy of Holies of the Daniel prophecy, and he might well be the same as the expected 'Teacher of Righteousness of the End of the Days' of the *Damascus Document*. As regards this last Teacher and the Messiah there are some mixed references in the texts of the *Document* due to interpolation, which at one time make these persons to be still future and at another to have already come.

These studies led to three broad conclusions: (1). the Time of the End began towards the close of the first century B.C. and was still in progress in 70 A.D.; (2). we could tentatively date the Commentary in the *Damascus Document* in the first quarter of the first century A.D. and the *Habakkuk Commentary* about fifty years later; (3). it was necessary to distinguish the original Teacher of Righteousness who appeared about 175 B.C. from the 'Teacher of Righteousness of the End of the Days.'

Chapter VII

Further to elucidate the question of the date of the *Damascus Document* and the *Habakkuk Commentary* we took up the subject of the study of prophetic fulfilment. This arose seriously at the time of the Maccabean revolt, but the kind of exegesis contained in the two works is not found before the first century A.D. when an intensive searching of the Scriptures began to be in evidence, and when of course the canon of the Old Testament was virtually closed.

We noted the development of Biblical exposition, the allegorical interpretations credited to the Essenes by Philo, and the curious marginal markings of some of the manuscripts among the Dead Sea Scrolls, in particular one of the recovered MSS. of *Isaiah*.

We looked at some of the *Isaiah* passages marked by symbols, and saw how eloquent they were of the teachings of the New Covenant Party and also of prophecies of interest to Judaeo-Christians.

This seemed to point to some kind of relationship subsisting between the two communities in the last period of the Qumran settlement. A further link was found in Jerome's *Commentary on Isaiah* in which he gives a number of interpretations of passages furnished by the Nazarenes (Judaeo-Christians). While the interests of the Nazarenes early in the third century differ from those of the New Covenant Party in the first, the family likeness in the method of exegesis is unmistakable. It also begins to be employed to an extent in the early Targums and Midrashim.

All these considerations force us to date the Commentary in the *Damascus Document* and the *Habakkuk Commentary* not earlier than the first century A.D. and as late as other circumstances will allow.

Chapter VIII

In confirmation of the dating we have provisionally assigned to the commentary documents we looked into the 'Zadokite' intimations equated with the period of the End of the Days, and this brought us to a consideration of a substantial find of manuscripts made in the area at the beginning of the ninth century.

The documents then discovered clearly belonged to the same sect as the Qumran people, and the Karaite authors of the ninth and tenth centuries made considerable use of these books of the 'Men of the Caves', so-called because their writings were found in a cave. The works mentioned included a *Book of Zadok*, a *Book of Yadua*, the works of the Alexandrian (Philo?), many strange commentaries on the Scriptures, and also a collection of Psalms. Certain of the tenets of the Men of the Caves cited by the Karaites bring us close to the beliefs of the Essenes.

We pursued the Zadok references in various quarters, the mention of the tomb of Zadok in the recently deciphered copper scrolls from Qumran, Jewish and Christian statements that the sect of Sadducees originated late in the first century B.C., associations with the followers of John the Baptist, and finally noted certain common ideas of 'taking to the wilderness' at a time of prevailing messianic excitement and expectation.

We had now differentiated between early and late material, and between an original Teacher of Righteousness and the ultimate Teacher. This made it possible to see that it could be the second Teacher and not the first who was the hero of the late *Habakkuk Commentary*. Even so, light might be thrown on the first Teacher by reason of a traditional pattern to which the experiences of the final Teacher would be expected to conform, and which partly served to identify him as the one who should come. In this respect scholars had already noted a certain likeness to the career of Jesus of the Teacher in the *Habakkuk Commentary*.

This invited attention to the expectation of a Priestly Messiah, which had made it possible for many to believe that John the Baptist, of priestly descent, was the Messiah, and had made it necessary for Christians to attempt to prove that Jesus was a priest. James the Just was also depicted as a priestly figure.

To back up this expectation there was the prediction of the Prophet like unto Moses, the Messenger who would purify the sons of Levi, the anointed Holy One of holies. There was also the heralding figure of Elijah, credited himself with being a priest. A midrash describes the final personalities of Elijah and the Messiah ben David as the ultimate redeemers corresponding to the first redeemers Moses and Aaron. A Karaite prayer links the Teacher of Righteousness with Elijah, and Jewish tradition made Elijah a reincarnation of Phineas the grandson of Aaron. There was the Aaronic Messiah predicted in the *Testaments of the XII Patriarchs*, and a Messiah or Messiahs from Aaron and Israel appear in the *Damascus Document* and the *Manual of Discipline*.

In all kinds of connexions the priestly Messiah and the two last witnesses were found to crop up, including the Two Witnesses of *Revelation* and the concept of a Messiah ben Joseph and a Messiah ben David. Ben Joseph was to be killed, and some tradition of a martyred Teacher of Righteousness seemed to be woven into the expectations.

We also looked at a passage in the *Testament of Benjamin* which applied to the Patriarch Joseph a prophecy 'that the blameless one shall be defiled for lawless men, and the sinless one shall die for godless men.' The Patriarch could not be held to qualify as fulfiller of such a prophecy, but it revealed a tradition of a Joseph-type of Righteous Sufferer which became mingled with the expectation of a Priestly Messiah. Finally, we saw how in the eschatology of the Samaritans there was the expectation of the priestly figure of the Taheb (the Restorer). Further examination of these ideas was essential.

Chapter IX

Throughout the period of the growth of a Messianic doctrine, from the days of the Maccabees down to the Time of the End, the pseudepigraphic and apocalyptic literature shows no trace of a figure answering to the requirements who appeared in the first half of the first century B.C. We have, therefore, to look to the beginning and end of the period, to the beginning for cause and to the end for effect. It is likely that the remembrance of someone who may be the first Teacher of Righteousness set in train the process which both created and defined the character of the expectation of the final Teacher. There was this tradition of the Joseph-type of suffering Just One mentioned not only in the *XII Patriarchs*, but also in *Jubilees*, where the Day of Atonement is said to have been instituted because of Joseph.

The *Visions of Enoch* tell of the killing of a notable Chasid in the time of Antiochus Epiphanes, and we have the midrashic account of the martyrdom of the Chasid and Priest Joseph ben Joezer at this period. Further in a list of the Minor Prophets the *Ascension of Isaiah* places a book of *Joseph the Just* between Malachi and Daniel. An account of a Righteous Sufferer is given in the *Wisdom of Solomon*, and in the Gospels of *Matthew* and *Luke* there is a prophecy that the blood of all the Just Ones from Abel to Zechariah son of Berechiah would fall on that generation. Who was this Ben Berechiah?

It could be held that he was really the Son of Jehoiada of *II Chron.* xxiv. 18-21, but legend while borrowing from the account of this murdered priest and prophet makes him a more important figure. The Talmud claims that the judgment on Israel in the time of Nebuchadnezzar was because of the death of Zechariah: 'they killed a priest, a prophet and a judge; they shed the blood of an innocent man; they polluted the Court of the Temple; and that day was the Sabbath, and the Day of Atonement.' The blood of the martyr bubbled until vengeance was complete, and then it rested. The very same legend is applied in Christian sources to the death of the priest Zechariah father of John the Baptist, where the blood bubbles until Titus destroyed Jerusalem.

Of the death of the Just One *Isa.* iii. 10 is quoted in the *Wisdom of Solomon*, and the text is also applied by Hegesippus to the death of James the Just, brother of Jesus. A testimony of Josephus is mentioned by Origen to the effect that the fall of Jerusalem in 70 A.D. was in vengeance for the death of James the Just. Always the Great Crime preceded the Great Catastrophe.

Chapter XI

There was still more to say about Ben Berechiah. The *Assumption of Moses* introduces at the time of the Maccabean revolt 'a man of the tribe of Levi, whose name will be Taxo.' This man exhorts his sons to die rather than transgress the commands of God, asserting that 'our blood will be avenged before the Lord.'

Applying the *Atbash* cipher to the mysterious name we found that Taxo converts into Asaph. The most notable person of that name is Asaph ben Berechiah, mentioned in the priestly books of *Chronicles, Ezra and Nehemiah.*

He was leader of the choral guild known as the Sons of Asaph, and credited with being a seer.

Legends about him are numerous, and a medical treatise exists said to have been written by Asaph the Younger, Asaph the Physician, and even Asaph ben Berechiah the Astronomer. This work ascribes the origin of medicine to Shem the son of Noah, and we traced this idea in *Jubilees* and the description of the Essenes, linking up with an Aramaic fragment of the *Testament of Levi* and a late Syriac *Book of Shem*. We also found a reference in a quotation from Andronicus the Philosopher to a work dealing with the Zodiac attributed to Asaph 'the writer and historian of the Hebrews.' This Andronicus could have been the astronomer Andronicus Cyrrhestes who died about 100 B.C., and this would be another pointer to the period of the first half of the second century B.C. The name Asaph is connected with Joseph, and thus fits in with the Joseph traditions we had dealt with earlier.

We noted then, in the murder of the Chasidim by the treacherous Alcimus reported in *I Maccabees*, that *Psalm* lxxix is quoted in a way that avoids naming the author. The psalm is in fact one of those credited to Asaph in the Biblical Collection. This group of Asaph psalms may belong to the Maccabean period, and the last of them (lxxxiii) has associations, as we saw in Chapter II, with the late section of *Jeremiah*, *I Maccabees*, *Jubilees*, and the *War of the Sons of Light with the Sons of Darkness*.

Moreover, among the Dead Sea Scrolls was a collection of so-called *Thanksgiving Psalms*, and other finds of psalms were made in the caves of the area in the third and ninth centuries. The original Asaph ben Berechiah was supposed to have lived in the time of Solomon, and this may explain why collections of psalms among the Saints bore the titles of *Psalms of Solomon* and *Odes of Solomon*.

Chapter XII

Having considered the evidence relating to the origins of the Chasidic movement we turned to what perhaps is the latest available testimony of the New Covenant Party to historical events, the *Habakkuk Commentary*. This contains numerous references to the Teacher of Righteousness and the Wicked Priest or Man of Untruth.

We found that many of the explanations given by the commentator tally with the records of Josephus, and that the incidents to which he is referring can be related to known circumstances immediately prior to and during the war with Rome. Much is made of the persecution of the Teacher and his followers at the hands of the Wicked Priest and his associates. The villain of the piece is an arrogant, corrupt and avaricious member of the Jewish hierarchy.

The wealth of the last priests of Jerusalem is described as falling into Roman hands. The author thinks very poorly of the Romans, who appear under the name of the Kittim, and in all the circumstances this was natural.

A recently published fragment of a *Nahum Commentary* may be understood as supporting the view that the circumstances of the war with Rome were present in the mind of the commentator. References to a 'lion of wrath' who was responsible for crucifixions may be applied to Titus.

There is not so much that is plainly evidential as regards the principal characters; but they are so vividly present that it is unlikely that the author can be dramatising persons and situations long before his own time. Since both his method of exegesis and certain things he says about the Romans and the way in which the End had been delayed carry conviction that he is writing late in the first century A.D. this seems to rule out any idea that he is speaking directly of things that happened in the previous century or still earlier.

Chapter XIII

The view just expressed is further confirmed by the passages in the *Habakkuk Commentary* which relate to the miserable fate of the Wicked Priest. Here again we found that Josephus was the best guide to the interpretation of the commentator's language, and that events prior to and in the course of the war with Rome fitted the requirements. The cumulative evidence was very striking indeed, and did not involve any strained or forced application of the terms used in the document. Retribution did overtake the arrogant High Priests when they were slaughtered by the Zealots and their allies. We had to allow, however, on the evidence of a Commentary on the *Psalms* that the end of the Wicked Priest and his supporters appeared to be future and their punishment to be in the hands of the Gentiles. A clear impression was received from the study of the *Habakkuk* and other commentaries that the New Covenant Party at this time reflected very closely the position of the Judaeo-Christians as found in the *Book of Revelation*.

Chapter XIV

At this point it was felt to be desirable to break away from the investigation of minute matters to consider the general character and atmosphere of the literature as a whole. What did it tell us about the people who wrote and revered these documents? We discerned the consciousness of a Cosmic Drama, of a struggle between the good and evil forces, culminating in triumph of right over wrong. We saw how there seemed to be a family relationship between the various eclectic groups, which enabled them to use each other's books and to give each other solace and support. Whatever their differences they were all on the same side, contending with the evildoers in generation after generation. In the course of discussion we introduced the Elchesaites and Rechabites. The circumstances at distinct periods could be depicted in analogous terms, and similarly the protagonists in the struggle. It was necessary, therefore, to be very careful in the matter of identifications, since the chief actors in the drama could to an extent be composite figures larger than life.

Preoccupied with the conflict between the opposing forces, set out in the doctrine of the Two Spirits and the Two Ways (*Manual of Discipline*, New Testament, and *Teaching of the XII Apostles*) there was a risk of theological dualism apparent to the early Rabbis and Church Fathers. And though the Saints were strict monotheists their emphasis on these antitheses was open to misinterpretation. To them the Drama was very real, and principles counted more than individuals. They were engaged in a spiritual war fast drawing to a close in the End of the Days, which was also the end of the Ages. To understand the allusions properly we have to enter into the Drama ourselves, and if we are too cold and matter-of-fact in our treatment of the material in its historical aspects our proposed solutions may be wide of the mark.

CHAPTER SIXTEEN

Observations

I SHALL now attempt an evaluation of the evidence presented in the foregoing pages, treating all tentative conclusions put forward as purely provisional and to be revised or set aside if necessary. I will begin with some general observations.

The nearest approximation to the ideas and way of life of the New Covenant Party is on the one side that of the Essenes as known to Philo and Josephus in the first century A.D., and on the other side that of the Primitive Judaeo-Christians of the same period. In both cases the points of resemblance are very striking indeed. Unfortunately, independent of the Dead Sea Scrolls, we have no contemporary quotations from Essene works nor from specifically Judaeo-Christian documents for purposes of exact comparison. There is also to be deplored the almost complete loss of the books extracted from the caves in the Qumran area at the beginning of the third and ninth centuries. Yet there do seem to be peculiarities about the New Covenant Party, or Party of the Community, which make it quite unsafe to identify it either with the Essenes or the Judaeo-Christians. In particular there is the question of terminology.

The New Covenant Party stressed entry into the Covenant, a Covenant made originally in the land of Damascus. It was specially concerned with a leader called the Teacher of Righteousness, and with persecution at the hands of a Wicked Priest or Man of Untruth. It had separated itself from Judah. These characteristics seem to reflect a narrower sectarianism than that of the Essenes in general, whose rule evidently allowed for some diversities of practice in different communities. If, of course, Essenism is used in an embracing and generic sense, then the New Covenant Party can be classified as Essene, though autonomous and with its special emphases. Identity with Judaeo-Christianity, at least before the destruction of Jerusalem, is a great deal less probable if the *Acts of the Apostles* is to be regarded as having historical authority. The early

Christians were exuberant publicisers of the name of Jesus and witnesses to his resurrection, whereas the New Covenant Party would not mention the name of their Teacher, and the fundamental doctrine of the Messiah's resurrection is totally absent. That there was contact cannot reasonably be doubted. The Church of Jerusalem would not otherwise have so quickly taken on an Essene colouring in its organization, neither would so much of the Party's doctrine and phraseology have found such ready acceptance. We are left in the dark as to what went on in the Christian Community of Jerusalem, why and how such a strongly Essene type of person like James the Just suddenly came to the fore in place of Peter. We know that many Pharisees and many priests came into the Church. There could have been an influx from the New Covenant Party as well, grouped about James (Jacob) and constituting a Jacobean-Ebionite section, and using the ideas of the Qumran Community. There are evidences which rather point in this direction, and they must be studied carefully in considering the last period of the Community's existence. We have seen how the letters of Paul were to an extent affected by the tenets and language of the New Covenanters, and he may have been protesting too much in *Gal.* ii. 6 that his conferences at Jerusalem added nothing to him. They did add something, though not touching his fundamental convictions; and Paul had a deep respect for the 'spiritual things' of the poor Saints at Jerusalem, of which through him the Gentiles had been made partakers (*Rom.* xv. 25-27). In fact, in his teaching, he revealed the hidden mysteries to his converts. On the other hand, Paul's attitude towards the Law and the Sabbath antagonised the Saints of Jerusalem, and anti-Paulinism comes out very strongly in Ebionitic literature. This, however, does not call for any endorsement of Teicher's theory that the Wicked Priest and Man of Untruth of the scrolls was Paul.

In looking at the material from the Qumran caves objectively I am impressed by certain things which have a definite bearing on the problem of date and associations, and which I have now touched upon only very briefly. First, there is the Community's preoccupation, almost an obsession, with the Last Days. The rule of the Community, as found in the *Manual of Discipline* and the *Damascus Document*, was on the showing of the documents a form of organization for the Last Days. Some of the descriptions are so dramatised and idealised that it is impossible to say to what extent the regulations set down were in force. We have details as exact and convincing, and yet as unreal, as the *War of the Sons of Light with the Sons of Darkness*. It would rather appear that the scribe, while building on a foundation of Essene practice, was imaginatively creating the structure for the Good Society of the Elect. In short, he was making a blue print of his own kind of utopia. The whole discipline and ritual is too grandiose, too elaborate, for us to suppose that the Qumran Community and any associated communities could ever have conformed to it. This view is confirmed by fragments 28a and b from Cave I.[1] In these not only are we told: 'This is the rule for all the Congregation of Israel in the Last Days,' but we also have an account of the ceremonial banquet when the Council of the Elect shall be in session, and the benedictions to be pronounced on the occasion. Here the chief priest (the Aaronic Messiah) has first place, then the priestly elders, then the Messiah of Israel as head of the lay dignitaries, who sit below him. This information is fatal to the theory that the New Covenanters can be indentified with the Ebionites. At least in origin they were quite distinct.

Further on the Last Days, we have the evidence of the *Damascus Document* and the *Habakkuk Commentary* that the commentators in these books, as well as in the recovered fragments of other comments on the Prophets, believed that the period called the End of the Days had already begun when they were writing. With the sacred books before them they could check by their system of exegesis the fulfilment of line after line in the records as external events demonstrated their truth. Yet they too seem to look beyond recent or contemporary history to a final and complete fulfilment of the prophecies. We have shown in Chapter vi how from the prophecy of Daniel's seventy weeks the conclusion was reached that the period called the End of the Days had begun towards the close of the first century B.C. The first century A.D. thus became a century of feverish messianic activity, established by the preaching of John the Baptist and of Jesus, and by Josephus's account of other Messianic figures and of the general excitement of the Jews because of prophetic intimations and revelations.

I therefore feel able to state as an assured result that the exegetical books of the New Covenant Community were mainly written during the first century A.D. I am not quite so certain about the *War of the Sons of Light* and the *Manual of Discipline*, but their style and character make this highly probable. It seems to me that we must give every possible weight to the outstanding difference between the literature which can be plainly labelled New Covenant Party by reason of kinship of ideas and expressions, and the general run of pseudepigraphic and apocalyptic literature. The testimony of the New Covenant documents to such books as *Enoch*, *Jubilees* and the *XII Patriarchs* establishes that they were written considerably earlier, so that by the time of the specifically New Covenant writings they already had the force of sacred scriptures. The

[1] *Qumran Cave I*, pp. 108–130.

peculiar nomenclature of the protagonists in the New Covenant documents nowhere appears in the older books.

What happened as the End Time dawned to give rise to the quite distinctive literature of the New Covenant Party? This is an all important question, especially since those called Essenes had been in existence at least as early as the reign of John Hyrcanus I.

We must look again at two passages in the *Damascus Document*, which I shall quote.

> The priests are the penitents of Israel who went forth out of the land of Judah; and the Levites are they who joined them. And the Sons of Zadok are the Elect of Israel called by name, that arise in the End of the Days. Behold the statement of their names according to their generations, and the period of their office, and the number of their afflictions, and the years of their sojournings, and the statement of their works.
>
> The first saints whom God pardoned both justified the righteous and condemned the wicked, and all they who come after them must do according to the interpretation of the Law in which the forefathers were instructed until the consummation of the period of these years, in accordance with the covenant which God established with the forefathers in order to pardon their sins. So shall God make atonement for them.
>
> But on the consummation of the period of these years they shall no more join themselves to the house of Judah: they shall everyone stand up against his net (i.e. the net of Belial). The wall shall have been built, the boundary have been far removed (vi. 1-8).

The second passage reads:

> The well is the Law, and they who digged it are the penitents of Israel who went forth out of the land of Judah and sojourned in the land of Damascus, all of whom God called princes; for they sought Him and His glory was not turned back in the mouth of one of them. And the Lawgiver is the Student of the Law, in regard to whom Isaiah said, 'He bringeth forth an instrument for His work.' And the nobles of the people are those who came to dig the well by the precepts in which the Lawgiver ordained that they should walk throughout the full period of the wickedness. And save them (i.e. these precepts) they shall acquire nothing until there arises the Teacher of Righteousness in the End of the Days (viii. 6-10).

I will add further passages from the *Habakkuk Commentary*.

On *Hab*. i. 5, the commentator speaks of the treacherous, the violent ones, at the End of the Days, 'who will not believe when they hear all that will befall the Last Generation by the mouth of the Priest whom God placed in the house of Judah to explain all the words of His servants the Prophets and to expound from the book of God all that will befall His people Israel.'

On *Hab*. ii. 1-3, the commentator writes: 'And God told Habakkuk to write what is to befall the Last Generation; but the consummation of the time He did not make known to him. And where he says, "that he who runs may read it," the reference is to the Righteous Teacher to whom God made known all the secrets of the words of His servants the Prophets.'

Whatever may yet have to be said about an earlier period of the Party's existence these passages seem to me to indicate a change. Down to the end of a certain period those called the first or former saints walked according to the instruction of the Old Covenant, as did their successors. But now there is a fresh development. At some subsequent period the Party severs itself from Judah. In the light of the second passage and the continuation of the first the period is at the close of that called 'the full period of the wickedness,' in which Belial is let loose against Israel. Thus we appear to have three periods mentioned: (1) that of the former saints, who may well be the original Chasidim; (2) that of their successors until the consummation of the period of the wickedness, which may have ended when the Time of the End began; and (3) that of the End of the Days, initiated by the severance from Judah. Now as regards the last period there was this fresh development. The precepts of the Student of the Law had served the Penitents of Israel until then. But we have what looks like a new teaching coming in eventually by the Teacher of Righteousness in the End of the Days. To this Teacher God made known all the secrets of the writings of the Prophets, though the treacherous, the violent ones' refused to credit his explanations and predictions.

If this is a correct interpretation, then the expected Righteous Teacher might conceivably have introduced the type of exegesis which his disciples followed in the New Covenant Party's Commentaries. It is to be noted what is said of Jesus, that after his resurrection he expounded to his disciples everything relating to himself in the law of Moses, the Psalms, and the Prophets (*Lk.* xxiv. 27. 44). It is also said of James the Just that he expounded the Prophets, his exegesis of *Amos* being not so unlike that of the New Covenant Commentaries (*Acts.* xv. 14-17). If the Commentaries reflect events that were contemporary and near contemporary, then there is an *a priori* case for believing that the New Covenant Commentaries were written during the crucial years of the first century A.D. I regard it as significant that just as there are substantial differences between the New Covenant literature and the previous pseudepigraphic and apocalyptic literature, so there are between the Party's documents and the apocalyptic writings that follow the fall of Jerusalem, such as the *Apocalypse of Ezra* and the *Apocalypse of Baruch*. It may fairly be argued that the Party's particular expression in the books peculiar to it was comparatively brief in point of time and localised in area.

The range and number of the books stored by the sect in the Qumran caves suggests an intensive and almost feverish activity of collecting, copying, composing and recording, as if these people were being driven by the consciousness that they were living in the Last Days, that the time was short, and that they must isolate themselves and make all essential preparations for the spiritual and organizational equipment of the Elect in the Messianic Era. There is much that favours this view.

We have just seen that the *Damascus Document* speaks of a withdrawal at the end of the period of the wickedness. At this time the Party separated from the house of Judah, and created a kind of iron curtain between themselves and the rest of Israel. The *Manual of Discipline* has passages which appear to relate to this.

> And when these things shall come to pass to the Community of Israel in these determined moments they shall separate themselves from the midst of the habitation of perverse men to take to the wilderness to prepare there the way of Him as was written: 'Prepare ye in the wilderness the way of the Lord; make straight in the desert a highway for our God.' This (way) is the study of the Law (which) He commanded by the hand of Moses so as to act according to all that was revealed time after time, and according to what the Prophets have revealed by His Holy Spirit (viii. 12-16).
>
> There shall be no argument or dispute with the men of perdition, but the counsel of the Law shall be concealed from men of iniquity and the True Knowledge and just judgment imparted to those who have chosen the way . . . and thus to initiate them in the wonderful and true mystery among the men of the Party, to behave perfectly each with his neighbour in all that is revealed to them. This is the time to prepare the way of the wilderness and to initiate all who shall be found to act at this time (ix. 16-10).

This confirms that about the time the End of the Days was supposed to have begun there was a deliberate withdrawal of the Party into the wilderness, where it isolated itself from the Jewish people in order to carry out the special task and mission of its members. It may be thought that light on this undertaking is thrown by the passage we have several times quoted from the *Assumption of Moses*, where the Lawgiver instructs Joshua to preserve the books that would be delivered to him. 'And thou shall set these in order and anoint them with oil of cedar, and put them away in earthen vessels in the place which God made from the beginning of the creation of the world, that His Name should be called upon until the day of repentance in the visitation wherewith the Lord shall visit them in the Consummation at the End of the Days' (ii. 16-17). This book, which dates from about 15 to 20 A.D., gives a definite instruction for the preservation of the sacred writings in earthen vessels. Perhaps from about the same date, or not much earlier, is Section V of the book of *Enoch*, where it is said: 'I know another mystery, that books will be given to the righteous and the wise to become a cause of joy and uprightness and much wisdom. To them will the books be given, and they will believe in them and rejoice over them, and then will all the righteous be recompensed who have learnt therefrom all the paths of uprightness'(civ. 12-13). I cannot help feeling that these passages have a definite bearing on the movement of the Party to Qumran for the specific purposes of copying, writing and storing the collection of sacred literature, and initiating those who should join them there.

I also cannot help feeling that there is a connexion with what is said of John the Baptist, to whom was applied, or he may have used, the same text from *Isaiah* (xl. 3). Concerning John it is stated: 'He shall go before Him in the spirit and power of Elijah . . . to make ready a people prepared for the Lord' (*Lk.* i. 17); 'And thou child, shalt be called the Prophet of the Most High; for thou shalt go before the Lord to prepare His ways; to give knowledge of salvation unto His people by the remission of their sins' (*Lk*.i. 76-77). We know all too little of the Baptist and his followers from other than Christian sources, but he seems to have begun his preaching in the Wilderness of Judea near Jericho in the reign of Archelaus (*Matthew* and the *Slavonic Josephus*), and thus between 3 B.C. and 6 A.D. It was 'almost in the time of John' that the Sadducees (Zadokites) are said to have arisen. The call of the Baptist may not have been unconnected with this development.

All the foregoing considerations point to a rather limited occupation of the Khirbet Qumran area by the New Covenant Party, from late in the first century B.C. until the end of Jewish resistance to the Romans in 73 A.D. The archaeological evidence could support this. Let us assume as correct that there had been an Essene settlement at Qumran from about 100 B.C. as declared by Father de Vaux. It does not follow that this was the only or main settlement in the area. The ancient authorities[1] indicate that there were several Essene settlements in the region of Jericho and the Dead Sea and elsewhere. One of the results of the excavations at Qumran has been to establish that the original buildings suffered very heavily in an earthquake, and that afterwards there were substantial restorations, additions made to the buildings and a new bathing-pool dug. Dupont-Sommer has pointed out that earthquakes occurred in Palestine in 64 and 31 B.C., and in 19, 30, and 37 A.D. It could have happened, though we cannot prove it, that the New Covenant Party, either with the consent of the Essenes or because the settlement had been abandoned,

[1] Pliny, Philo and Josephus.

took over the site, repaired the buildings and set up their own establishment—perhaps somewhere about 25-20 B.C.—following Essene practice closely in their organization, and acquiring and being assisted by the literature in the possession of the Essenes. It is certainly of note that the coins found on the site provide clear evidence of a period of intensive occupation between approximately 7 to 67 A.D.

All accounts of the Essenes in general describe them as celibate. This it would appear the Qumran people were not, since out of 19 graves opened in the course of the excavations in 1949, '51 and '53 several contained the skeletons of women. Further, the *Damascus Document* (ix. 1) tells of the members of the Party taking wives and begetting children. The Qumran Community would thus accurately correspond to those whom Josephus calls 'another order of Essenes, which, while at one with the rest in its mode of life, customs, and regulations, differs from them in its views on marriage.'[1] Josephus gained some personal knowledge of the Essenes when he was about sixteen or seventeen (54-55 A.D.), and afterwards lived with an ascetic called Bannus until he was about nineteen. In his autobiography, where he refers to this, he speaks exaggeratedly of 'a thorough investigation' of the three sects of Pharisees, Sadducees, and Essenes, and of 'passing through the three courses.'[2] But at his age and in the short time he mentions his study must have been fairly elementary. The details he gives of the Essenes could be picked up very easily by anyone coming into contact with them, and the only readily observable difference between the New Covenant Community and the others would be that they permitted marriage. If the statement by Josephus at the close of his account about 'yet another order of Essenes' in fact refers to the Qumran Community we have at least one external testimony to its existence and character at a definite date. This would confirm that it was Essenite, but not that the Essenes and the New Covenanters were one and the same.

Thus I am led to take the view that the New Covenant Party was probably a distinct and rather specialised sect associated in the last phase of its existence with the Essenes and to an extent not yet fully clarified with the Judaeo-Christians, but identical with neither. I also hold that the books peculiar to this sect were written almost entirely in the first century A.D., and probably at Qumran, and that these people built up and stored their library because they regarded it as an essential part of their mission to preserve the books for those who should afterwards need them. It was a labour of love and of divine prompting. They 'contracted out' of the Community of Israel deliberately and severed themselves from the sinners, that in the quietness of their wilderness

[1] *Wars*, II. viii. 13.
[2] *Life*, 2.

retreat they could the better carry out their mandate and make their election sure. In this respect all that I have said in Chapter xiv about the Cosmic Drama is of consequence. These people believed themselves to be pressed into the service of God and were keenly aware of their calling. All that transpired in Palestine during the fifty years from 20 to 70 A.D. only confirmed them in their reading of the Signs of the Times.

CHAPTER SEVENTEEN

Conclusions: Early Period

At the time when the New Covenant Party was based at Qumran, which I have regarded as at least certain for nearly a century before the fall of Jerusalem, its members were in possession of many of the older pseudepigraphic books. Not only is there reference to and dependence on *Enoch*, *Jubilees* and the *Testament of Levi*, but fragments recovered from the caves in the area include additionally the *Book of Noah*, *Apocalypse of Lamech* and one which has been called *Words of Moses*, possibly the original Hebrew *Testament of Moses*. This literature belongs to the second century B.C. onwards, and exhibits no trace of the distinctive New Covenant Party kind of composition. There is ample evidence of the influence of the pseudepigraphic literature on the writings of the New Covenant Party at its Qumran stage, but none, so far as I can see, of the reverse. Either, then, the New Covenant Party had acquired these books in the course of its previous history, or obtained them while at Qumran from the local Essene communities. The truth may be that to an extent which we cannot judge something of both alternatives happened. But unless there was a substantial difference in the character of the movement before its Qumran days, I do not see how we can credit authorship of the older books to former members, or regard those books as their peculiar literary inheritance. This means, that with possible exceptions and generally speaking, while we may utilize all available material to learn something of the origins of the Party, we are at present virtually limited to the *Damascus Document* for knowledge of its subsequent history down to the first century A.D.

There seems to be no good reason to doubt that the rise of the Chasidic Movement at the beginning of the second century B.C. furnishes us with the *terminus a quo*. What can be learnt of the history of this Movement has been given in Chapter iii. Neither is it in dispute that whatever offshoots there may have been the tradition of the Chasidim was carried on by those who begin to be called the Essenes. Josephus actually mentions them under that name as already existing as the third sect among the Jews in the time of Jonathan (c. 145 B.C.).[1] This may be too early, but not much more than a quarter of a century. The Essenes were evidently held in high esteem and individuals are referred to down to the time of the war with Rome. When Josephus wrote his account of the Essenes as he had known them they were not dwelling only in special camps and communities, as in the region of Jericho and the Dead Sea, but settled 'in large numbers in every town.' In classing them with the Pharisees and Sadducees as a third sect among the Jews Josephus obviously regarded them as an element continually present in the life of the nation from the beginning of these divisions down to his own day. This is not what we gather about the New Covenant Party, which traced its origin to an emigration from Judea. The Penitents of Israel who founded the Party 'went forth out of the land of Judah and sojourned in the land of Damascus.' They 'escaped to the land of the North.' Reference is made to 'their generations, and the period of their office, and the number of their afflictions, and the years of their sojournings, and the statement of their works.' Whenever the migration took place, it is clear that they were sojourning in a strange land for a considerable time, which cannot have been much less than seventy-five years and may well have been longer. It is clear therefore that though they eventually returned, apparently before the close of 'the period of the wickedness', they were not in the country at material times when the Essenes certainly were in it. While both the New Covenanters and the Essenes may thus be said to have stemmed from the same source, the Chasidic Movement, their ways diverged and did not come together again until much later.

A crucial date to determine if possible is that of the emigration, and from this we can move more readily both backwards and forwards. The *Damascus Document* is quite clear that the emigration—'the escape to the land of the North'—took place during the period of visitation resulting from the apostasy of Israel, when the faithless perished at the hands of 'the head of the kings of Javan, who came to execute vengeance upon them' (ix. 4-20). This information has an exact parallel in the *Assumption of Moses*: 'And there will come upon them a second visitation and wrath . . . in which He will stir up against them the king of the kings of the earth' (viii. 1). There can be no question that this refers to the time of Antiochus Epiphanes. The emigration can therefore be dated within a dozen years after 170 B.C. I believe, however, that we can fix the year exactly as 159 B.C., as I have argued from a passage in Josephus.[2] At this time 'not a few . . . deserted their country, and went to the Mace-

[1] *Antiq.* XIII. v. 9.
[2] Above p. 20f.

donians' (i.e. Syria, the land of the North). With this date the real history of the Party begins.

The leader of the migration of the Penitents of Israel was a learned Scribe called 'the Student of the Law' to whom is applied the saying of Isaiah, 'He bringeth forth an instrument for His work.' Further in connexion with this escape into Syria the commentator quotes and expounds *Amos.* v. 26-27: 'And I will cause to go into captivity Siccuth your king and Chiun your images, beyond Damascus.' He tells us that the books of the Law are 'the tabernacle (succath) of the King'. While the King means the congregation, 'Chiun the images' are the books of the Prophets, and the Star (mentioned in the same text from *Amos*) is 'the Student of the Law, who went to Damascus, as it is written, "There shall go forth a star out of Jacob, and a sceptre shall rise out of Israel." The Sceptre is the prince of all the congregation.' He understands the prophecy in *Numbers* not in any Messianic sense, but as meaning that the Teacher would leave the land of Judah, would literally go forth out of Jacob, not spring from Jacob. The exegesis may also be taken to imply that the only books which the emigrants took with them were the Law and the Prophets. This is confirmed by a related passage we have several times quoted, that apart from the Scriptures the only document named as in possession of these people in their wanderings was that which contained the precepts of their lawgiver 'the Student of the Law.' Except for these precepts the New Covenanters would get nothing until the Teacher of Righteousness arose in the End of the Days. Some of the pseudepigraphic literature was written at a time when the New Covenanters may be presumed to have been out of the country, and they would not have read it until after their return.

As regards the 'Book of Precepts', this would naturally be the Party's most venerated possession outside the Bible, the work by which they would be guided, the touchstone by which every decision would be tested. We know that the Party had such a book, so revered that its name was doubly disguised as 'the Book of the Hagu', which by the *Atbash* cipher we detected aptly to mean 'the Book of Testing' or 'Proof Book.'

For the New Covenant Party the emigration to which they looked back as the real beginning of their history was as significant as the Exodus of Israel from Egypt under Moses. Their leader was a new Moses; from him they received new laws and through him they entered into a new covenant in the land of Damascus as binding as the covenant at Sinai.

I do not see how we can fail to identify the lawgiver of the Party with the one called in the *Damascus Document* 'the Unique Teacher' or 'Teacher of the Party'. His death is twice referred to as his 'gathering in'. This suggests that he died a natural death in exile some years after the emigration, though he might still be regarded as a martyr. The second of the two references is difficult. We are told: 'And from the day when there was gathered in the Unique Teacher until all the men of war were consumed who walked with the Man of Untruth about forty years those who repented of transgression (in Jacob) observed the covenant of God' (B. ix. 39-41). Appropriate to the parallel between the emigration and the Exodus we have a reminiscence here of *Deut.* ii. 14: 'Until all the generation of the men of war were wasted out from among the host' (during the forty years wandering in the wilderness).

The passage can mean that the New Covenanters remained faithful for as long as it took after the death of the Teacher for the generation involved in the Great Apostasy to die out. If we follow the books of *Maccabees* the Great Apostasy began almost immediately after the accession of Antiochus Epiphanes, and its chief instigator, who may be the Man of Untruth, Scoffer, Prophesier of Lies, of that period, was the usurping High Priest Jason. If we take the figure of about forty years as roughly correct this would bring us to c. 134 B.C., the year of the murder of Simon, last surviving son of Mattathias who had participated in the revolt against the Seleucids, and the accession of John Hyrcanus I. This certainly makes some sense. We have dated the emigration in 159 B.C., and the intervening quarter of a century would reasonably allow for the death of the Righteous Teacher. We do not know what was the age of the Teacher when his ministry began about 176 B.C.—the date given in the *Damascus Document*—but let it be assumed that he was about forty. This would make him about fifty-seven at the time of the emigration. His death could well have occurred within ten or fifteen years of that event.

We cannot get much nearer than this because the *Damascus Document* really tells us very little about the original Teacher and the early history of the Party. The first date given us is c. 196 B.C., which according to Travers Herford coincides with the founding of the Jewish senate as mentioned by Josephus (*Antiq.*XII.iii.3). At this time a number of priests and laymen began to consider their ways, and groped for the right way for some twenty years, when God raised up for them a Teacher of Righteousnees. We may well believe that this development had to do with the Chasidim, the Pietists, though we are unable to prove it. The *Damascus Document* itself does not assist us in identifying the Teacher, who otherwise may be unknown to history. But if the New Covenant Party, and the main divisions of Pharisees, Sadducees and Essenes, had the same common origin in the Chasidim, it is proper to look at their legends and traditions for any further knowledge they can give us. This we have endeavoured to do in Chapters ix-xi. It should be said here, however, that the testamentary work contained in the *Damascus Document* may not be a product of the New Covenant Party, since it is both interpolated and commented upon by a later writer or writers belonging to the Party. It may therefore be an external witness to the existence of the Righteous Teacher, though it would be unwise to stress this. It is to be noted, for what this is worth, that *Testament Damascus* speaks very barely of 'a teacher of righteousness' who appeared at a time when 'there arose a scoffer, who distilled for Israel deceptive waters'. It does not magnify these figures as they are magnified by the later commentator. All the references to the Unique Teacher, the Prophesier of Lies, the Man of Untruth, are in the later work and in the less reliable B. text. The writer could be using terms applied to the protagonists in his own days, as found in the *Habakkuk* and the other Commentaries.

This raises again the problem of the *Habakkuk Commentary*, and we have to face it. I regard the evidence as very strong, if not conclusive, that the book was written in the first century A.D. and that the explanations take their cue from events of that period. But how much has been coloured by stories handed down of the experiences of the original Teacher of Righteousness? Is there even a case for regarding the whole *Commentary* as a dramatisation in the historic present, with a topical twist, of events that had happened long before?

It would by no means be out of keeping with what we know and have pointed out that comparisons should be seen between the life and character of the Unique Teacher of old and that of the Teacher at the End of the Days. Indeed, such similarities would serve as signs which would confirm that the Last Teacher really was the one expected.[1] But some scholars, who think in terms of only one Teacher as the hero of this literature, argue that all that is said in the *Habakkuk Commentary* regarding the Kittim, the Teacher of Righteousness, and the Wicked Priest or Man of Untruth, refers entirely to the time of the Maccabees. It must in fairness and honesty be admitted that the *Commentary* may be interpreted in this way. All that is said of the Kittim can be applied to the Macedonians (the Seleucids) instead of the Romans, and they are called the Kittim in *I Macc.* i. 1; viii. 5. The dramatic *War of the Sons of Light* distinguishes between the Seleucids and Ptolemies simply as the Kittim of Assur (Syria) and the Kittim in Egypt, both dynasties having a common Macedonian origin. Even the vexed passage in the *Commentary* which describes the Kittim as sacrificing to their standards (vi. 2-5) might conceivably relate to the forces of Antiochus; and in view of our discovery of the name Asaph in the *Assumption of Moses* with all its fertile connexions[2] it is significant that the Asaphite Psalm

[1] Above p. 61.

[2] See pp. 86-91.

lxxiv. 4 says: 'Thine enemies roar in the midst of Thy congregation; they set up their ensigns for standards.' This psalm is regarded as of the Maccabean period.

Then what about 'the last priests of Jerusalem' of the *Habakkuk Commentary* (ii. 8a)? Could this not mean the Hellenizing and apostate Zadokite high-priesthood? In *Test. Levi.* xviii. 1-3 it is said: 'And after their punishment shall have come from the Lord, the priesthood shall fail. Then shall the Lord raise up a new priest. And to him all the words of the Lord shall be revealed; and he shall execute a righteous judgment upon the earth for a multitude of days. And his star shall arise in heaven as of a king.' Is not this 'new priest' the same as the priest of the *Commentary* 'whom God placed in the house of Judah to explain all the words of His servants the Prophets' (i. 5.), who is also 'the Righteous Teacher to whom God made known all the secrets of the words of His servants the Prophets' (ii. 1-3)? In *Test. Jud.* xxiv. 1 we are told in the A. text: 'And after these things (the persecution by Antiochus Epiphanes) shall arise the Star of peace, and he shall walk with men in meekness and righteousness.' Should we not identify him with the Unique Teacher, who is also possibly the 'man who reneweth the law in the power of the Most High' of *Test. Levi.* xvi. 3?

The Wicked Priest, or Man of Untruth, of the *Commentary* also qualifies for identification with the High Priest Jason, and his successors Menelaus and Alcimus. Jason was certainly a 'priest who rebelled' who 'when he ruled Israel . . . forsook God, and betrayed the statutes because of riches . . . and followed abominable ways in every kind of foul impurity' (ii. 5-6). Much the same might be said of the other two. All this we find in the books of *Maccabees*. The *Commentary* tells us of the miserable end of the priest who rebelled. And we have this account of the death of Jason in *II Macc.* v. 8-10: 'Fleeing from city to city, pursued of all men, hated as an apostate from the laws, and held in abomination as the butcher of his country and his fellow-citizens, he was cast forth into Egypt; and he that had driven many from their country into strange lands[1] perished himself in a strange land . . . and he that had cast out a multitude unburied had none to mourn him, nor had he any funeral at all, or place in the sepulchre of his fathers.' The High Priest Alcimus also died in great torment (*I Macc.* viii. 55), and Menelaus was executed in Beroea on the orders of Antiochus Eupator (*II Macc.* xiii).

The next thing is the treatment of the Teacher of Righteousness by the Wicked Priest and his associates. The Teacher was convicted or punished by the Man of Untruth. This could mean that the Teacher was illegally executed,

[1] Cp. the reference in Josephus to those forced to desert their country.

and it probably does. But the punishment might have been something less than death. The other reference in the *Commentary* to an attack on the Teacher by the Wicked Priest describes an attempt by the Priest to destroy the Teacher in his place of exile. It is not absolutely clear whether the attempt succeeded or was only thought to have succeeded. And which came first, the attempt on the life of the Teacher in exile, or his illegal punishment, or do these things relate to the same event? When the Lawgiver and his followers were in the land of Damascus emissaries of the Wicked High Priest Alcimus could have been sent to murder him. Both in the *Thanksgiving Psalms* and the *Odes of Solomon* there are references in the first person to the experiences of the hero of these poems,[1] including persecution, exile, and a plot against his life. In *II Macc.* iv. 33-4 we are told how Onias III was murdered after he had withdrawn to Daphne near Antioch (the land of the North) at the instigation of the usurping High Priest Menelaus.

So it is entirely possible to make out a convincing case for the application of the *Habakkuk Commentary* to the life and times of the original Teacher in the Maccabean period of the second century B.C.

I may seem to have dismissed rather summarily the Dupont-Sommer school of interpretation, which dates the Teacher of Righteousness in the first half of the first century B.C. But there seems to me to be too strong a line leading back to the previous century. The explanations given by this school of the meaning of the *Habakkuk Commentary* appear very forced as they are applied to the principal personalities.

But when we have assembled all the information furnished by the Commentaries it turns out that we are really given very little of an overwhelmingly evidential character. The story we can build up from the references is extremely thin, and has more dramatic power than historical qualities. If the explanations relate solely to the original Teacher and his opponent they do not give the impression of having been written with a burning desire to place the facts on record by someone living close to the events who knew all that had happened. What is offered seems to be by way of illustration, as significant signs culled from tradition which had lately received endorsement in contemporary characters and circumstances, in the opposing forces of the End of the Days. For such a purpose only what could be compared as history repeating itself was of consequence. Either this, or the contemporaneous atmosphere is a purely dramatic device to give present emphasis to what had taken place long ago. I, myself, incline to the former opinion. I believe that on the basis of the Party's traditions and of intimations found in the pseudepigraphic literature

[1] Above p. 103f.

there developed an idealised representation of the Suffering Just One and those expectations of a corresponding Messianic figure in the Last Days. As we have seen in Chapters ix-x, both legends about such an individual taking their origin at the time of the Maccabean revolt, and prophecies to which those legends gave rise, are met with in the literature of the Pharisees, Sadducees, Essenes and Samaritans, as well as the New Covenanters and the Christians. Variously presented to us as the Unique Teacher of Righteousness, the Just One, Asaph, the Son of Berechiah, Joseph the Just, Joseph ben Joezer, his actual identity remains shrouded in mystery. So much so, that he appears to us as a composite figure with features borrowed from more than one suffering saint, priest, prophet and judge. In the same way his bitter opponent seems to be compounded of more than one Wicked High Priest of his day, Jason, Alcimus, etc.

So very much smoke without any fire is unthinkable. All the lines we have followed do seem to radiate from a definite point in time, and that time is the first half of the second century B.C. What transpired in the dawn of the New Covenant Party's existence we are only permitted to see in brief outline. We follow the Teacher and the Penitents of Israel into the land of the North, and there we lose both him and them. His end came, but his work went on. The New Covenant had been solemnly affirmed in the land of Damascus, and thereafter there were wanderings and vicissitudes for an unspecified period. Generations passed, of which only the register of the Party preserved the details. Many gave up and deserted the Party. Others remained faithful, true to the precepts of their Lawgiver. We are to infer an eventual return to the land of Judah, but a careful segregation from the corruption in high places during 'the full period of the wickedness' when Israel was caught in the net of Belial. The Time of the End of the Days approached bringing eager expectation of the coming of the Teacher of the Last Days. A call went forth to take to the wilderness to prepare the way of the Lord. We may conjecture that this is what brought the Party to Khirbet Qumran towards the end of the first century B.C. We have suggested that a primary function of the Community in preparing the way of the Lord was to assemble and compose the books which the Elect would need when God again visited His people in mercy on the faithful, and in vengeance on the wicked and apostate. So they copied and wrote, and so they stored away, urged on by the accumulating signs that the Last Hour was at hand.

CHAPTER EIGHTEEN

Conclusions : Late Period

THE DIFFICULTIES in the way of reaching satisfactory conclusions about the New Covenant Party in the first century A.D. are far greater than for the earlier period. For the past we have at least had the benefit of a rough outline of the course of events, though reliable information about the founding figure is absent. We have had to see him and his work through a haze of legend and tradition, which progressively built up prophetic anticipations of his ultimate successor, the Teacher of Righteousness of the End of the Days. We now enter into the strange period of the End Time itself, with the nerve centre of the Party located at Qumran, and only such guidance as to actual happenings as the Commentaries afford. The *Habakkuk Commentary*, as we have seen, is capable of interpretation to make many of its explanations apply to the origins of the Party. I think we may say, however, that while the document is impregnated with these ancient influences it is too graphic to be intended to relate to the life and times of the first Teacher—that is, unless we are to hold that the book is much older than seems probable on all the evidence. We have established that the author is living in the End of the Days, and he writes with such intensity of feeling as to convince us that he has immediate knowledge of a great deal that he describes, and was personally affected by some of these circumstances.

Everything points to the period, approximately between 25 B.C. and 75 A.D., as being that of the most lively activity at Qumran, the archaeological discoveries, the numismatic finds, the scientific tests of materials, the calculation of the End of the Days, the apparent possession by the sect of the works of Philo, and so on. This was the period of the Baptist movement and of the founding of Christianity, the period of intense Messianic expectation. The New Testament, or Covenant, is a major external witness to some of the ideas and even the language of the Scrolls. The explanation of the Prophetic books in terms of the life of Jesus as given in the Gospels comes very close to what we have in the Qumran Commentaries, and Pauline teaching has much in common with the Dead Sea Scrolls and the *Damascus Document*. We have expressions like 'the Sons of Light,' 'the Mystery of Iniquity,' 'the Time of Testing,' and the significant title 'the Just One' applied to Jesus. The differences between Christianity and the teaching of the Qumran sect must not be minimised; but it cannot be doubted that the New Testament stands under the influence of the literature of the New Covenanters.[1] How this influence was exerted, whether by direct contact or by some of the Qumran people joining the Church, cannot so far be ascertained with certainty. There are many unknown and unexplained aspects of Judaeo-Christianity.

We cannot at all afford to neglect the possibility that there was a two-way traffic. The New Covenant Party was on the look out for the coming of the Teacher of Righteousness of the End of the Days and of a Messiah from Aaron and Israel. Notable figures like Jesus, who might answer to the expectation, would hardly have gone unobserved, and even if they were rejected their experiences could have helped in framing the portraiture of the Teacher of Righteousness and his conflict with his enemies. We have seen how the Christian *Odes of Solomon* link with the *Thanksgiving Psalms* in this respect, and we have noted how certain parentheses and apparent interpolations in the *Damascus Document* suggest an editorial intention to indicate that the Messiah has come and his name is known. The interpretation of these crucial passages is too uncertain to be relied upon; but they give us the impression of some afterthoughts and some attempt to change the text to make it relate to later times and bring it into line with the position of the *Habakkuk Commentary*. We know that this kind of thing was going on in order to make the prophecies more exact and more applicable to later situations. We have the Jewish and Christian interpolations in the *Testaments of the XII Patriarchs* and other pseudepigrapha. We have the transposition of certain chapters in the *Assumption of Moses*. The Prophets could not lie, and must therefore have foretold what had now been fulfilled or was on the eve of fulfilment.

There was ample scope for fresh interpretation of the old books and traditions because of the medley of messianic figures of which they seemed to speak. We have illustrated this in our studies; but perhaps we may add here the curious figure of Melchizedek, seen as the archetype of the priestly king in the *Epistle to the Hebrews*. For Philo he is priest, 'even Logos, having as his portion Him who is' (*Allegorical Interpretations*, III. xxvi). The Samaritans

---

[1] See Brownlee, *Manual of Discipline*; Grossouw, *The Dead Sea Scrolls and the New Testament* in *Studia Catholica*, Dec. 1951.

identified him with Shem, and said that the Jews stated he was a righteous man and a priest. In the Ethiopic *Book of Adam and Eve* a special mystery attaches to him as 'the first created of God', a secret known to Shem. After officiating at the burial of Adam, Melchizedek was not seen again until Abraham met him. In the Talmud (*Suk.* 52b) he is placed in the same category as Elijah, Messiah ben David and Messiah ben Joseph.[1] He thus anticipates in many ways the priestly Teacher of Righteousness, and affords another link between the Qumran sect and the early Christians in their reading of the ancient intimations. He is among those who appear and disappear again, as was held would be the case with the Messiah.

In the fevered atmosphere of the first century A.D. the old words nourished and expanded became flesh in a John the Baptist, in Jesus, and in James the Just, and who can tell with what effect on the dwellers at Qumran?

The fact that the organization of the early Christian community exhibits many points of resemblance to that of the Essenes, and that while there is frequent reference to the Pharisees and Sadducees there is no mention in the New Testament of the Essenes, lends colour to the view that they were reckoned as being at least on the fringe of Christianity[2] and numbered among the Saints, the Elect, and the Poor inheritors of the Kingdom. Especially in this context do we have the extraordinary personality of James the Just, who stands in the partly legendary accounts of him with a foot in each camp. In some ways the references to the Teacher of Righteousness in the *Habakkuk Commentary* seem to have more relevance to James than they do to Jesus, as came out in our study of the book in Chapters xii–xiii.

Let us look again at this man distinctively called the Righteous and Bulwark of the People, this other Ben Joseph.

From two lost works, the *Hypotyposis* of Clement and the *Hypomnemata* of Hegesippus, both Eusebius the Church Historian and Epiphanius obtained surprising information about James. James was both a Teacher of Righteousness and a Priest. According to Epiphanius, he wore the high-priestly frontlet and had the right to enter the Holy of Holies 'because he was a Nazorean (?Nazirite) and connected with the priesthood' (*Haeres.* xxix. 4). Elsewhere he says that James 'was of the lineage of David . . . and moreover we have found that he officiated after the manner of the ancient priesthood.[3] Wherefore also he was permitted once a year to enter the Holy of Holies (i.e. on the Day

[1] See J E art. *Melchizedek*.

[2] Eusebius regarded Philo's Therapeutae as the first Egyptian Christians (*Eccl. Hist.* II. xvi–xvii) and other Church Fathers think of the Essenes as a Christian sect.

[3] He thus fulfilled the expectation of a Messiah from Levi and Judah, Aaron and Israel.

of Atonement), as the Law commanded the High Priests, according to that which is written; for so many before us have told of him, both Eusebius and Clement and others. Furthermore, he was entitled to wear on his head the high-priestly diadem, as the aforementioned trustworthy men have attested in their memoirs' (*Haeres.* lxxviii).

Hegesippus, as quoted by Eusebius (*Eccl. Hist.* Bk. II. xxiii), says that James, called the Just by all,

> was consecrated from his mother's womb. He drank neither wine nor fermented liquors, and abstained from animal food. A razor never came upon his head, he never anointed with oil, and never used a bath (i.e. a public bathing establishment). He alone was allowed to enter the Sanctuary. He never wore woollen, only linen garments. He was in the habit of entering the Temple alone, and was often found upon his knees, and interceding for the forgiveness of the people; so that his knees became as hard as a camel's, in consequence of his habitual supplication and kneeling before God. And indeed, on account of his exceeding piety, he was called *Zaddik* and *Oblias*, which signifies Justice and Protection of the People; *as the Prophets declare concerning him.*[1]
>
> Some of the seven sects, therefore of the people, mentioned by me above in my Commentaries,[2] asked him what was the door to Jesus? He answered that he was the Saviour. From which, some believed that Jesus is the Messiah . . . As there were many therefore of the rulers that believed, there arose a tumult among the Jews (Scribes and Pharisees), saying that there was danger, that the people would now expect Jesus as the Messiah. They came therefore together, and said to James, 'We entreat thee, restrain the people, who are led astray after Jesus, as if he were the Messiah. We entreat thee to persuade all that are coming to the feast of the Passover rightly concerning Jesus; for we all have confidence in thee. For we and all the people bear thee testimony that thou art just, and no respecter of persons. Persuade therefore the people not to be led astray by Jesus, for we and all the people have confidence in thee. Stand therefore upon a wing of the Temple, that thou mayest be conspicuous on high, and thy words may easily be heard by all the people . . .
>
> The aforesaid Scribes and Pharisees, therefore, placed James upon a wing of the Temple, and cried out to him, 'O thou Just One, whom we ought all to believe, since the people are led astray after Jesus that was crucified, declare to us what is the door to Jesus . . . ' And he answered with a loud voice, 'Why do you ask me respecting the Son of Man? He is now seated in the heavens, at the right hand of great Power, and is about to

---

[1] With reference to *Isa.* iii. 10 (LXX), and perhaps 'Jacob (James) my servant' of *Isa.* xliff. But the words may also relate to the interpretations of the Prophets by the Qumran sect.

[2] Hegesippus lists them as 'the Essenes, Galileans, Daily-Baptists, Masbutheans, Samaritans, Sadducees and Pharisees.'

come on the clouds of heaven.' And as many were confirmed, and gloried in this testimony of Jesus, and said, 'Hosanna to the Son of David,' these same Priests and Pharisees said to one another, 'We have done badly in affording such testimony to Jesus, but let us go up and cast him down, that they may dread to believe in him.' And they cried out, 'Oh, oh, the Just One himself is deceived,' and they fulfilled that which is written in Isaiah, 'Let us take away the Just, because he is offensive to us; wherefore they shall eat the fruit of their doings.' Going up therefore, they cast down the Just One, saying to one another, 'Let us stone James the Just.' And they began to stone him, as he did not die immediately when cast down; but turning round, he knelt down, saying, 'I entreat Thee, O Lord God and Father, forgive them, for they know not what they do.'[1] Thus they were stoning him, when one of the priests of the sons of Rechab, a son of the Rechabites spoken of by Jeremiah the Prophet,[2] cried out saying, 'Cease, what are you doing? The Just One is praying for you.' But one of them, a fuller, beat out the brains of the Just One with the club that he used to beat out clothes. Thus he suffered martyrdom, and they buried him on the spot where his tombstone is still remaining,[3] by the Temple . . . Immediately after this, Vespasian invaded and took Judea.

What the source is of this account we do not know. It appears to have undergone some alteration in transmission. Hegesippus wrote about 180 A.D. and had access to Judaeo-Christian material. The closing words of the passage link up with a statement in the *Chronicon Paschale* (i. 463) to the effect that, 'Josephus relates in the fifth book of the *Halosis* that the captivity of the Jews occurred in the third year of Vespasian, that is, forty years after their daring against Jesus. In that time, he also says, James the brother of the Lord, and bishop of Jerusalem, was precipitated from the height and stoned to death by them.' Has the author got his reference wrong, and should it have read as in Eusebius, 'Hegesippus in the fifth book of his *Hypomnemata*'? It would appear that something of this story did get into the text of Josephus's *Jewish War*, perhaps in the fifth book, where it was found by Origen, who tells us: 'Although not believing in Jesus as the Christ, Josephus, when searching for the true cause of the fall of Jerusalem, ought to have said that the persecution of Jesus was the cause of its ruin, because the people had killed the prophesied Messiah; yet as if against his will and not far from the truth he says that this befell the Jews in revenge for James the Just, who was the brother of Jesus the so-called Christ, because they killed him, although he was a perfectly just man' (*C. Cels.*

---

[1] This prayer has been attributed to Jesus by insertion in Luke's Gospel (*Lk.* xxiii. 34).

[2] On the significance of Jeremiah see above Chapter ii.

[3] Regarding this commemorative stone Eisler draws attention to a statement in the Slavonic Josephus, which says that an inscription was placed on the barrier of the Temple announcing 'that Jesus (the) king did not reign, (but was) crucified, because he prophesied the destruction of the city and the devastation of the Temple.' He thinks that James was also mentioned (*The Messiah Jesus*, p. 520).

i. 47). The version of the death of James in the *Antiquities* (XX. ix. 1) agrees that James the Just was stoned, but says that this followed an illegal trial initiated by the insolent and highhanded High Priest Ananus. This is close to what is said in the *Habakkuk Commentary* about the fate of the Teacher of Righteousness.

We have to recall here the Ben Berechiah legend of the death of the last great Just One, 'Priest, Prophet and Judge', which Christian records have applied to the father of the Baptist. The closing words seem not unrelated to the death of James in their general character: 'They killed him inside the Temple, and the priests shrouded his body and placed it . . . in a hidden cemetery, from fear of the wicked; and his blood boiled on the earth for fifty years, until Titus son of Vespasian, the Emperor of the Romans, came and destroyed Jerusalem and killed the Jewish priests.'[1]

The material about James the Just comes very close to the Righteous Teacher of the *Commentary*, and we have also seen a likeness between the *Commentary* and the New Testament *Epistle of James*. The honorific title of the 'Just One' applied to both Jesus and James his brother is surely significant, as is the fact that both are made out to have been of the line of David and high priests. We may even think that the title of *zaddik* is connected with 'the Sons of Zadok who are the Elect of Israel in the End of the Days' of the *Damascus Document*'s interpolated lines, and that this illumines the curious statement about the Messiah, that 'in the explanation of his name are their names.' To intensify the mystery there is an extraordinary assertion in Pseudo-Ignatius, *Epistle to John*, that Jesus and James were identical twins.[2]

In dealing with the subject of the Priestly Messiah in Chapter IX we drew attention to the growth of a Ben Joseph legend of a martyred Just One, found in the *XII Patriarchs* in the words applied to Joseph, 'In thee shall be fulfilled the prophecy of heaven, which says that the blameless one shall be defiled for lawless men, and the sinless one shall die for godless men.' We also noticed the expectation of Messiah ben Joseph who would be killed, and other allusions to Joseph the Just. We should now add a reference in the Hebrew *Josippon* which reads: 'In those days (i.e. of the Emperor Gaius Caligula) there were wars and quarrels in Judaea between the Pharisees and the brigands of our people who followed the Son of Joseph.'[3] There is no doubt that Jesus is meant; but it is interesting that at this period that Essene-Nazirite figure James the Just became leader of the Judaeo-Christians in place of Peter, a change which the *Acts of the Apostles* does not at all explain. Neither is it without importance that the chief persecutors of Judaeo-Christians were the Sadducean hierarchy, and that two

[1] Above p. 79.
[2] Rendel Harris, *The Twelve Apostles*, p. 57.
[3] Eisler, *The Messiah Jesus*, p. 79ff.

of these 'Wicked' High Priests, Ananias son of Nedebaeus and Ananus son of Ananus, were slaughtered by the Zealots during the war with Rome.

In all this we approach very near to what is described in the *Habakkuk Commentary*. But it must be no less obvious that the similarities we can detect in the story of James the Just do not sufficiently correspond with what is related in the Qumran Commentaries of the (Good) Priest and the Teacher of Righteousness, any more than they do with the opposing figures of the Man of Untruth, Prophesier of Untruth, and the Wicked Priest. The serious divergences may partly be accounted for by allowing for combination with traditions going back to the experiences of the founding Teacher. Let that be so, there is still the fact that the Commentators in many things are speaking in terms of future events, and no historical circumstances that we know will fit all the explanations. We cannot, therefore, propose that James the Just, or Jesus, or John the Baptist was the Teacher of Righteousness at the End of the Days as understood by the writers of the Dead Sea Scrolls. Neither do I think that we can assert this of someone called Zadok, or another Teacher who is unknown to us.

We have to consider why the opposing personalities are not named. We are familiar with them only from the description of the part they play. This could be because they serve as symbols of primeval forces and are not real people at all. We have taken account of the Cosmic Drama. But if these End Time figures are to be understood of individuals who have walked the earth and behaved as related it is difficult to see why their identity, known to their contemporaries, should require to be disguised. Is it not preferable to suppose that these persons cannot be named because they have not yet appeared? These people have a certain kinship with such apocalyptic figures as the Lamb, the Beast of the Land and the Beast of the Sea, and the False Prophet. The principal difference is that in the Qumran literature the experiences of the protagonists are related with a wealth of circumstantial detail which is quasi-historical.

It does not at all commend itself to me that the Qumran Commentaries are propounding riddles for the Elect, or exhibiting the fulfilment of prophecy in wilfully obscure hints and allusions. It is true that in the pseudepigraphic literature leading personalities are frequently not named; but for the most part the things said about them make them readily identifiable. We have to leave room for this attitude of 'no names, no pack drill.' But when we have done so, and traced out everything that approximates to the descriptions given, nothing comes out just right. Some things stand: others we are forced to discard. We cannot obtain a coherent story that tallies in every particular with any known historical situation.

Some scholars have therefore concluded that the Qumran commentators jump about, sometimes referring to one period and sometimes to another, and additionally to the future, often within a few lines. This is a reasonable hypothesis, and may conceivably be correct. But I am not altogether happy about it.

There are some references to the past in the explanations furnished, but so far as our knowledge goes at present these are stated clearly as in the fragment of a *Nahum Commentary*. And so my own judgment inclines towards an alternative solution of the Secrets of the Dead Sea Scrolls, which it seems to me will meet all the requirements.

After carefully weighing all the evidence I conclude that the Qumran Commentaries, influenced by legend and tradition, and by recent external events, are actually telling us about the future, and by no means a remote future. They are offering us interpretations which are dramatic and prophetic portrayals of what is yet to come, while recognising that the 'mystery of iniquity' is already at work. They are writing history in advance for the guidance of those Elect, faithful to the Law, who will be living in the 'Time of Testing.'

We are not then to seek for the Teacher of Righteousness of the End of the Days, and those opposed to him, in any individuals who have yet appeared,[1] though some historical characters have helped to shape their likenesses, and partial fulfilments have taken place. Such prognostications could well carry conviction to Judaeo-Christians and others that the lives of their own Teachers and Messiahs were the subject of the prophecies.

This view does no violence to the evidence that parts of the exegetical story apply to events and situations in the remote and recent past. The story does not begin in the future: it only culminates in the future; for the End Time, though prolonged, has begun, the Elect are suffering persecution, and evil has manifested itself in high places. The accounts are too vivid and circumstantial to be treated as fiction. The writers, basing their explanations of the Prophets on real experiences, sincerely believe that what they relate will come to pass. They are reading in some detail the Signs of the Times. Josephus tells us that the Essenes were famed for their prophetic powers, and that seldom did their prophecies fail.

[1] The Karaites, who knew the scrolls found in the ninth century, seem to have understood this, for they offered a prayer for his coming. See above p. 64

When we look at some of the Scrolls, the *War of the Sons of Light*, the too ample account of the form of government in the *Manual of Discipline*, the fragments describing the position of the Messianic High Priest and the Messiah of Israel, the ordering of the Elect in Council, when we hear of vast treasure buried, presumably to be recovered to finance the messianic campaigns, of the fate of the good and evil protagonists in the Commentaries, then, it seems to me, we are passing away from what Was and Is and moving into the realm of what Is to Be. See *Rev.* i.19.

All these considerations, and many more, when we go over the records, tell in my opinion of a gigantic effort, of the most careful planning and preparation, so that the Elect of the period of the Consummation would be primed with everything they would need. Everything would be in the books, nothing neglected, and all the books safely stored for their predestined purpose.

This view accounts for much that otherwise would be obscure. It explains why we do not find any exact parallels to the specifically Qumran type of literature in the apocalyptic and pseudepigraphic writings which were in circulation. We are told plainly enough in *Enoch*, the *Assumption of Moses*, and the *Apocalypse of Ezra*, that books were being hidden away for the service of the Righteous in the Last Days. And *Ezra* bears witness to two categories of prophetic books, those which could be made public and a larger number which were on the secret list. He also speaks of the intense scribal activity to complete the manuscripts. This view also explains the ciphers and the symbols attached to some of the scrolls. It would appear that in the caves of the Khirbet Qumran area we have stumbled upon books designed for the faithful in the last great struggle with evil, books for the skilled to understand and not meant to be accessible before the time,[1] as well as other books permitted to be circulated among the uninitiated. Once the period of the End of the Days had dawned towards the close of the first century B.C., as established by the prophecy of Daniel, that was the signal 'to take to the wilderness to prepare the way of the Lord.'

Whether the people who carried out this work with enormous diligenec were or were not the Essenes is a secondary matter, and does not affect the conclusions reached. What is outstanding and surely unique is the nature of

[1] This may be what is meant by the comment in the *Damascus Document* that except for the precepts of the earlier Lawgiver the faithful would get nothing additional until the coming of the Teacher at the End of the Days. Like the Samaritan Taheb he would reveal the whereabouts of the hidden books. We may also think of the words of Jesus that the Law and the Prophets prophesied up to John, but from that time the Kingdom of Heaven is proclaimed. There were things that could only be told to 'those outside' in parables, but 'those inside' would know the Secrets of the Kingdom.

the task they set themselves. To have informed their successors so comprehensively and on such a lavish scale of what was in store and how their affairs should be conducted was indeed a feat both of faith and imagination, and it has to no small extent deceived us, who now read these writings, into seeking completely to historicise their anticipations.

It may well be that the settlements at Qumran were overwhelmed during the war with Rome, perhaps, as I have suggested, in Silva's attack on Masada in 73 A.D. It would be natural during the terrible conflict for the New Covenanters to take emergency measures to speed up concealment of their treasures and bury directions for their recovery. A number of indications have been found of such last minute activities. But the assembling, writing and copying of the scrolls forming the Library of the Last Days, and storing them away in jars in a series of pits and caves, I regard as an industry carried on intensively for a good many years and up to the last possible moment, to include, so to speak, Stop Press News. It was a major function of the Community. We know now that hundreds of scrolls were involved, and originally there may have been a thousand or more, occupying teams of trained scribes for a very considerable period. The cost would also be great, and was no doubt met by those who joined the Community and made over to it all their worldly possessions. Here, truly, was the patience and faith of the Saints.

The People of the Scrolls did not quietly die out. Perhaps the New Testament *Book of Revelation*, held by some to have been a Jewish work taken over and added to by Christian hands, has something to say to us on the subject. A remnant would have escaped the wrath of the Dragon and the forces of the Roman-Kittim. We cannot say with assurance whether the latest of the Qumran documents were written before or not long after 70 A.D. Mystery still shrouds the end of the settlement at Qumran. But we do know that not all the teachings of the sect were confined in caves until chance should reveal their hiding place. Much remained outside to be utilised by Judaeo-Christian and other groups, and more than one trace can be found of the persistence of the living tradition among those of differing names and associations, who continued to await the Consolation of Israel.

Index